CHANGING THE STATUS QUO

ALLAN STRAIN

◆ FriesenPress

One Printers Way
Altona, MB R0G 0B0
Canada

www.friesenpress.com

Copyright © 2022 by Allan Strain
First Edition — 2022

All rights reserved.

No part of this publication may be reproduced in any form, or by any means, electronic or mechanical, including photocopying, recording, or any information browsing, storage, or retrieval system, without permission in writing from FriesenPress.

ISBN
978-1-03-914324-1 (Hardcover)
978-1-03-914323-4 (Paperback)
978-1-03-914325-8 (eBook)

1. BIOGRAPHY & AUTOBIOGRAPHY, PERSONAL MEMOIRS

Distributed to the trade by The Ingram Book Company

CHANGING THE STATUS QUO

CHAPTER ONE

I GREW UP IN NORTH VANCOUVER, British Columbia, in the great country of Canada. It was myself and my brother Carl, my mom, Sara, and my father, Bill. My brother was eight years older than I, and my parents were quite old. As a matter of fact, in my younger years, my parents were often mistaken for my grandparents. My mom was English and still had the accent to prove it. My dad was Canadian, with a Dutch background.

My childhood was pretty normal, for the most part. Being raised in North Vancouver had its advantages. I was quite sheltered from the "city life," as North Vancouver is a suburb of Vancouver. Most of my friends came from middle to lower-middle class families.

We had lots of things that we did for fun, and we never really got into much trouble in my younger years. My friends and I would ride bikes, build forts in the forest, and play hide and seek around the neighbourhood. Our parents never worried back then about letting us go out on our own. I can remember playing with friends in the neighbourhood from as young as about seven years old. Of course, there were no cell phones in those days. I knew it was time to go home when I heard, "ALLAN!!! AAAAA-LLAAAN!!!

As I mentioned, one thing we loved to do was build forts in the forest. We spent hours upon hours going through the alleys in the industrial area checking dumpsters for discarded wood we could use for our forts. We would bring shopping carts and load them up with wood.

We called this area of North Vancouver, "The Wood Place." In the forest, we carted in wood, nails, tools, and rope. We went deep into the woods and built our forts. This was our own little sanctuary. We felt a bit of independence, building our home away from home. Here the rules were what we said they were. We were afraid of intruders, so we built traps. The traps were holes about four feet deep by four feet wide, covered up with branches and scattered with fallen leaves to look like the ground. More than once we fell into our own traps.

My brother was the typical older brother, usually harassing me in some way and making my life miserable in the most loving way possible. Carl would do things like make me get up and change the channel on the TV. I was raised in the 80s and back then, it was pretty common for the youngest one to be the "remote control," getting up and turning the big knob on the tube television and occasionally adjusting the "rabbit ears."

Although we grew up quite poor, I never knew I was poor, nor did I feel like I was. My parents did a very good job of ensuring that we kids had everything we needed. Maybe not every single thing we wanted, but definitely everything we needed.

Specifically, I remember that Christmas and my birthdays were very exciting days indeed. Our stockings were always overflowing with goodies, and when we woke up on Christmas morning, you can bet there would be an abundance of gifts under the tree. Little did I know that Mom had looked for and purchased gifts, one at a time, throughout the entire year to make this happen.

One Christmas that truly stands out in my mind was when I was about five years old. I woke up Christmas morning and after rummaging through my stocking, I went downstairs. I saw so many gifts under the tree. When my parents woke up, I was allowed to start opening presents. I noticed in front of the tree there sat a beautiful teddy bear. I seem to recall there was a tag on the paw that said, "Dearest Allan, Love Santa."

My parents asked what I would name him. I quickly replied, "Mr. Bear." I opened another gift labelled, "Dearest Allan, Love Mrs. Clause." It was a yellow knitted sweater, and a yellow knitted hat, both Mr. Bear-sized. Mr. Bear quickly became my best friend. He accompanied me everywhere and slept with me every night.

I have a few memories of a man I called "Uncle Lionel." I wasn't sure exactly how he was my uncle, but I never asked, either. I was too young to consider these things. I would say I was about four or five the last time I saw him. I remember him coming to pick me up in an old van that had one of those round windows at the back corner.

Uncle Lionel would take me to his place and we would spend the weekend together occasionally. I don't have a lot of memories of Uncle Lionel because I was so young. I do recall baking some kind of ceramic teddy bears and we let them cool and then we painted them. And I remember he gave me toys. He gave me a toy van that looked exactly like his.

My fondest memories of my mom are when she took us on adventure walks. This usually consisted of a walk along 2nd Street to St. David's, then up the hill to 3rd Street, where we turned right, then all the way to Ridgeway, where we would turn left, then further up the hill to Ridgeway Annex, the elementary school. There we would play on the playground, maybe stop playtime just long enough to have a snack, and then we would walk all the way back.

Mom brought the little wagon in case I got too tired on the way home. Of course, Mr. Bear came along every time, and I always made sure he was wearing his hat and his sweater so that he would be warm enough. One day, after our long adventure to the playground and all the way back, we got into the house. I took off my rubber boots and jacket and suddenly realized I did not have Mr. Bear.

This was tragic! Where could he be? He must have fallen out of the wagon on the way home. How could I be so careless? Would I ever see him again? I cried and cried for Mr. Bear. So, the rubber boots went back on, the jacket went back on, and out the door we went, painstakingly retracing each and every step we had taken. I thought I would never ever find Mr. Bear, but then a miracle happened. There, on the side of the road, leaning up against the curb, one foot in the mud, was Mr. Bear. He was a little dirty, but otherwise unharmed.

I loved both my parents very much, and I felt incredibly loved by them both. Mom was the disciplinarian, and Dad was the soft one. An example of this was when I woke up early one morning before anyone else. I discovered my paints.

The thought occurred to me that I could "surprise" Mom and Dad. I proceeded to paint my dresser drawers. I carefully painted one line at a time, each a different colour. When I was finished, the drawers were all rainbow coloured. My mom came into my room took one look and yelled "Allan!" But my dad just looked at her and smiled, and then they both started to giggle.

As with my mom, I have very fond memories of my dad. I remember going on vacation to Salt Spring Island, and waking up super early in the morning to go fishing with my dad and brother. At the bait and tackle shop, they had a sign telling fisherman about a 400 pound halibut that had yet to be caught.

At some point during the day, my brother's fishing rod bent way down and he began reeling in "The Big One." He tried and tried for a long time to tire out the enormous fish on the end of his line. Suddenly, the fish pulled super-fast and the fishing line sliced my brothers fingers open, blood pouring down. The line was all used up and it snapped off.

To this day, my brother swears he had the 400 pounder on his hook. I guess we'll never know. My childhood photo album has a photo of me lying on the bench of the boat, wearing a life jacket, with a hat dropped across my face. Later that day, my brother caught another fish and landed it this time. It was a 16 pound salmon. My brother's childhood photo album has a photo of him holding up his big catch. We were young and carefree. Life was good.

Life continued this way for some time, and really, attending school was the biggest chore we had. When I was a little bit older, around eight or nine years old, I got my first "job." It was a paper route, which I shared with my friend who lived on the opposite side of our duplex. It was our job to "stuff" the papers prior to delivering them.

This consisted of making piles of each different flyer, taking one of each, and putting the selected flyers into the centre of the newspaper, setting that one aside, and repeating until every paper was "stuffed." We delivered to every house on our route on Wednesday, Friday, and Sunday.

I remember when I got my first cheque and cashed it at the bank with my mom. After two or three cheques, I had an envelope in our kitchen drawer with $116 in it! I felt rich! I truly feel that these early lessons of earning money contributed to the great work ethic I ended up with as an adult. The lesson was simple: complete a task, you get money, complete more tasks, you get more money. I loved knowing that I could just do tasks and get cold hard cash in my hand, and that if I worked a bit harder, I would have a bit more money.

I met a lot of great people doing my paper route, mostly older people who loved to invite me in for tea and biscuits. One elderly couple always invited me into their home. It was a medium-sized house with a nice backyard. From the stories they told me, I learned that particular house had been around longer than they had.

I could feel the age of the home as I sat at the small round kitchen table. On the countertop there was a ceramic bunny. I knew from experience that this bunny's head lifted off to reveal homemade sugar cookies. In front of me was a window that looked out onto the lawn, which was surrounded by a white picket fence. A screen door creaked as it gently swayed back and forth with the summer breeze.

At the edge of the picket fence was a lane, and occasionally a car would drive by, kicking up dust as it passed. I loved the feeling in this house. So homey. So quaint. Come Christmastime at this house there would be a box of chocolates and a $10 bill tucked inside a Christmas card. The envelope was labelled "For the paper boy."

Some other pleasant memories I have from my early years is the fact that I had interactions with lots of children. This was because my mom ran a daycare out of our home. Some of the children that came to our home became lifelong friends; they came to our home as babies and my mom watched them for many years up until the age of 10 or 11 years old.

My mom also had a friend that came over for coffee and cookies, a native lady named Lillian. Lillian had three girls that were all a few years younger than I was. I loved it when Lillian and her girls came over for visits. Her daughters and I would play for hours. We played hide and seek, sometimes hiding in pairs under the kitchen table, giggling the whole time.

I also loved having kids in our home that were younger than me. I loved to be part of teaching them new things, and since they came to our home for years, I got to see them change as they grew up. I helped teach them the rules of the house and made sure the rules were followed.

I would say the biggest rule we had was to clean up the toys we were playing with before taking out new toys, and cleaning up all the toys when it was lunchtime or nap time. We had a little wooden wagon that was full of wooden blocks. In order for the blocks to fit back into the wagon properly, each one needed to go back into its original spot; they were all shaped differently, and you had to arrange them the same way each time like a puzzle.

I had made some good friends around the neighbourhood. I had one friend whose house I really enjoyed visiting. He was an aboriginal kid named Alex. Alex lived on the reserve not far from my house. I would go there sometimes; I went for his birthday a couple of times, and sometimes just to hang out. We played soccer in the backyard and we played games around the house. I remember watching his family carve native artwork in the living room. The whole family was involved. The adults taught the children to sand, and how to paint the carvings.

I loved this way of life. I was fascinated by it all and mesmerized by the smell of cedar dust in the air. I watched eagerly as the wood chips were sliced off each piece of wood, gently falling to the ground. I very specifically remember thinking, "I wish I was native." Alex's mom used to say to me when I visited, "There's our little Indian boy!" I would explain to her that I was not native. I was English and Dutch. She said to me "Nah, you're our little Indian boy. It's ok, we see each other. We know." "How strange," I thought to myself.

When I was about eight years old, we got a dog. My dad was mostly responsible for choosing which dog would be ours. I remember a man came to our house with a three-year-old German Shepherd. I fell in love. My dad was in negotiation with the owner of the dog.

I remember Dad pulling a package of Players Light Regular out of the breast pocket of his shirt and reaching into his other pocket for his pen. He held his cigarettes, pushed on the bottom of the package with his thumb, sliding up the inner sleeve. Then he flipped open the top of the package, and used it for a place to write.

He asked for the man's phone number. He said, he was quite interested and would give him a call soon. The man drove away, and I got so excited. I asked when we would buy this dog. Dad said, "We're not buying that dog!"

I asked what he meant. He said, "Allan, we are not buying a dog that is three years old. We want a puppy."

So, the search continued. Eventually my brother, myself, and my dad went to see a dog breeder. These people had a litter of purebred German Shepherd puppies. They all jumped around us barking and licking, tails wagging. One in particular stood out from the rest. He was all black and seemed to be drawn to us.

We knew pretty quickly that this was the one. After my dad paid the people, we took him into our car and proceeded to drive home. The next step was to choose a name. My mom was the one who ultimately chose the name that we went with... Caesar.

My brother Carl got to work right away, building a giant pen for Caesar downstairs in our basement. He lined the inside of the pen with newspapers for house training and he made a big sign from cardboard and a Jiffy Marker, which he placed on the back wall. The sign read "Caesar's Palace."

Caesar was such a cute puppy and he quickly grew into a full-sized German Shepherd. He was very protective of me when I took him for walks. I remember walking him one day and a drunk couple approached us. The lady was quite intoxicated, and she started saying, "Oh what a cute puppy!" She stumbled slightly and gently bumped into me, and without hesitation, Caesar leaped forward and bit her right in the boob! He "nipped her nipple," so to speak! He was not vicious; he was only protecting me from a potential threat.

We had neighbours to the west of us who owned a Chihuahua. The family was of East Indian descent and the dog's name was Ragu. When Caesar was a puppy, Ragu got off his leash, ran into our yard and bit Caesar in the back. After that, for several years, Ragu would stand behind the fence and yap at him every chance he got. One day, Caesar had enough. He saw the front door was open; he took his opportunity and ran down the steps into the front yard, jumped the fence and grabbed that little Chihuahua by the back, and swung him around like a rag doll.

Ragu required a visit to the vet and ended up getting a whole lot of stitches. The bill was $700! The neighbours submitted a complaint about Caesar, saying he was vicious and should be put down. About a week passed and a man from the SPCA stopped by to see Caesar for himself. Caesar barked uncontrollably. It was not a good visit.

We wanted a second opinion. A few days later, a police officer called to say he was on his way to visit with Caesar. I remember holding Caesar's face, looking him in the eyes and saying to him, "You have to be good or they will kill you!" A few minutes later, the officer arrived at our door.

We brought Caesar. To my surprise, Caesar sat down and looked very submissive. The officer held out his hand and Caesar gave it a little lick. The officer said, "This dog is nowhere near vicious." And that was that. Caesar was safe once again.

At this point I must mention one of my favourite getaway spots, a lakefront property that belonged to my Uncle Mike and Auntie Darlene. Mike was really our cousin, but I didn't discover this until I was older. As it turns out, my dad had a sister, Joan, who I knew quite well in my younger years. Joan and her husband Mike Senior had four children, Mike, Linda, Betty, and Debbie. Mike and Darlene were much, much older than my brother and I, so I grew up calling them Uncle Mike and Auntie Dar.

Their lake on the Sunshine Coast was such an amazing spot to go. They had a bunk house and a camper tucked away in the forest, with stairs built from logs that led down to the dock. I heard that my brother had helped Uncle Mike build the stairs several years before I was old enough to really remember.

As kids, we came here in the summers for a week at a time, usually. There, we would play all day in the water, always wearing a life jacket, as per the rules. This is where I learned to dive. Auntie Dar stood an inner tube on its side and had me stand in front of it. Then she rolled it off the edge of the dock with me on it. She said, this was the correct posture to have when diving.

My favourite part of going to the lake, though, was waterskiing. I learned to ski on two skis first. The next year, I learned to get out of the water on two skis, and drop one. The following year, I learned to get out of the water on one ski.

I'll always remember uncle Mike trying to teach me the correct posture when water skiing. He said, to push my hips forward. When I wasn't getting it, he said, "Pretend you got a quarter between your butt cheeks and you're trying not to drop it!" An interesting training technique, but it worked! I figured it out after this.

I think the reason I loved this so much was that my brother Carl could not get the hang of this, for the life of him. Carl was perfect at everything. I could never compete with him because he seemed perfect. For the first time in my entire life, I was better at something than my big brother.

So now I was around nine years old. I attended school, I had great friends. I owned a bicycle, a skateboard, and a pogo stick, many toys, and a dog that loved me no matter what.

In the summer, we played outside all day long, and our curfew was when the street lights turned on. There were summer trips to the lake where we made the best of memories. I was still young. I was still carefree. But life was about to take a turn for the worse.

CHAPTER TWO

DAD WAS QUITE RELIGIOUS. He taught me all about God. He sent me to Sunday School. He bought me a Children's Bible for my birthday one year. He taught me about prayer. Dad told me that praying is how we talk to God. He said, we can speak to God any time we want, and we patiently wait for answers from him. "God has all the answers and he will tell you," he said.

One day, I was in my bedroom by myself. I decided to pray to God. I don't remember what I said, to God, I just remember waiting and waiting for him to answer and listening really hard, and I could not hear anything.

I descended from my bedroom to the kitchen in tears. My dad asked me what was wrong. I told him that I was praying to God and waiting for an answer, just like he told me, and I couldn't hear anything at all. Dad chuckled a bit, and then put his hand on my shoulder. He said, "Oh, Allan. We can't hear God with our ears. He speaks to us in our hearts. We listen with our hearts. Does that make sense?" And it did. I felt much better.

When I was 10 years old, my dad became quite ill. He was ill for some time. At least once, I remember staying home from school so that I could run up and down the stairs from the main floor to my dad in bed, bringing him heart pills, water, and anything else he needed.

Dad was fragile, it seemed. Sometimes he came with me to walk Caesar. He would stop every 20 steps or so, to catch his breath. At some points during the year it seemed Dad was getting better. But these moments were brief.

I just wanted Dad to be well. I lay in my bed at night praying to God as hard as I could to make Dad better. My prayers were usually interrupted by the sound of Dad's relentless coughing. At some point during winter, Dad was so ill that he went into the hospital. I knew this was bad because Dad refused to go to the hospital. He was very fearful of hospitals, something he got from his own mother.

One grim morning, about two weeks before Christmas, I woke up and had to use the washroom. I was sitting on the toilet when Mom knocked and asked if she could come in. To this day, I wonder why she approached me when I was doing my business. Anyway, she came in, and kneeled beside me. It was quite awkward, to say the least.

She said, "Allan dear, I have something to tell you. Daddy died last night." I was silent for a moment, then I just looked at her and said, "Ok." And she looked back at me, and said, "Ok then." She left the bathroom, much to my relief.

When I finished in the bathroom I went downstairs. I said to Mom, "I'm going to go ride my bike." My mom replied, "Ok, love." I rode my bike down the block. I was dazed. Stunned. Confused. I wasn't sure how I felt. It didn't seem real. I was at the very beginning stages of my grief. So many thoughts. I would never, ever see my dad again. Not ever.

Dad's passing changed my entire life. There were so many sad moments surrounding Dad's death. One specific moment stuck with me. I was in school. Our Grade 5 teacher was handing us back the Christmas cards we had made for our parents. It's hard to explain, but even things that should have been very sad, were not, at least at this point. I think my mind was blocking the emotions to protect me.

When my teacher gave me back the card I had made, I placed it down on my desk in front of me. This is when I realized I needed to "fix" it. It read "Merry Christmas, Mom and Dad." My thought was that I better fix this, or my mom will be sad because it will remind her that Dad was dead. I myself did not have sadness at this moment. What I had was concern for my mom.

As I sat there using a black felt pen to carefully scratch out the word "Dad," I suddenly felt a hand on my shoulder. My teacher had been standing behind me, watching with great sadness. It wasn't until this moment that I realized what I was doing, and how incredibly sad it was.

I brought the card home to my mom. Again, it wasn't until I saw sadness in her, that I felt emotional about it. I gave it to her, and she started to read it. I read it, too. I realized I had not done the best job of "editing" it. It read, "Merry Christmas Mom and."

I said, "Yeah, I just made a little mistake on this part." Tears poured down her face as she held me. She said, "That's ok, love, it's alright." It was at that moment that I felt sad. At no point before this did I feel anything at all. Again, looking back I think my brain must have been numbing out the harsh emotions, in order to protect me. I don't know how else to explain it. As time went on, I had many days that I cried over the loss of Dad. Always by myself, never in front of anyone. I kept these feelings to myself.

Things began to get very tough in our home. My mom had a very difficult time with being a widow. Somehow through all of this, Mom had to raise two boys, one eighteen, one ten. If I didn't feel like I was poor before, I started to feel it now. I always heard how Mom was trying to make ends meet. We still always had our Christmas, but it was impossible to ignore the fact that Dad wasn't there.

I would be lying if I said, I wasn't a bit lost. I began to wonder if God was even real. What kind of a God would do this? I tried to talk to my dad through prayer. I told him I loved him, and I missed him. I still said my prayers at night, too. "Our Father" and "Hail Mary." It brought me comfort.

While praying "Our Father," I imagined at times that I was speaking not of God, but of MY father. It seemed fitting. "Our Father, who art in Heaven…" Our father was indeed in Heaven.

Later the prayer goes on to say, "Thy kingdom come, thy will be done, on earth as it is in Heaven…" and I was at this time speaking to my dad, telling him I would always do what I knew he would want me to do. I would always be a good boy and make him proud.

Over the next couple of years, I felt a bit better. I was still dealing with grief, of course, but I was coping well. Dad and I spoke often and he was always right by my side. Strangely, though, adults in my life, mainly teachers and my mom felt I was acting out and having a hard time coping with the loss of my dad. I wasn't. I was over it. I couldn't understand why everyone thought I was sad. Was I supposed to be sadder than I was? I wondered if there was something wrong with me. How do I know if I'm the right amount of sad? Is it ok if I'm not sad at all? Or did that make me emotionless and cold? And why did everyone want to get in my head and know how I felt inside?

Man, people were starting to act strange. Me, though, I was alright. I had some good friends at school, and I had a couple of friends in the neighbourhood that I hung out with. I was not wallowing in sadness. No need to. Move on. Life goes on, right? I'm good. Still young, still carefree. Life was still good... pretty good. But life was about to throw me another curve ball.

The next couple of years were challenging. There was noticeable tension at home, and I was dealing with the emotions of losing my dad. Every time we made something for our parents at school, I was reminded that I only had one parent. Kids at school would be talking about what they did for their dad for Father's Day.

Occasionally I would meet someone I didn't know, and they would inevitably ask something like, "What does your dad do for work?" These moments were always awkward because I didn't want people to feel sorry for me, and I knew they would when I told them my dad wasn't alive anymore.

By 13 years old, I was beginning to cope with the loss of my dad, and life was starting to look somewhat normal again. And then I got some news that would complicate things considerably. I was in grade 7. The last grade before going to high school.

I was in class one afternoon and my teacher was talking to us about families. She explained that no two families were the same, and she was talking about some of the things that made families unique. She said, "Some families are small, with only one child. Some families are much larger, with many children. In some families, the parents are divorced, and the children know two homes, Mom's house and Dad's house."

It all made sense so far. I was thinking that perhaps she wanted to make sure kids from broken homes didn't feel different, or something to that

effect. But then she continued, "And then there are situations like Allan's…"
"Ok, I'm listening." I thought. "What could she possibly say next?" There was no way I could have prepared myself for what she said.

"Allan is super lucky, because he has TWO families!" Not exactly sure what she meant, I asked "Oh, like I have such good friends, they are like a second family... or something?" The teacher replied, "No Allan, I mean your actual TWO families."

I was confused. She continued. "You see Allan is so lucky because he has two families. He has the family that raised him, and also his biological family. You see class, Allan is adopted!!!" A chuckle escaped from my mouth. "No, you're thinking of somebody else. I'm not adopted." The teacher was persistent. "Yes Allan. Yes, you are."

She continued "It's ok. This is what I'm saying, all families are unique." I laughed out loud. "I'm sorry, you're thinking of some other kid or something. I'm definitely not adopted. I promise." Suddenly a look of horror crossed her face as she said, "Oh no. Oh. You don't know?" At this point I'm thinking, "Man, she really needs to let it go because she's going to be so embarrassed when she realizes it's not me she was thinking of, but some other kid."

Then she asked if I would step outside into the hallway for a little chat. As I stood up from my desk, my chair slid on the floor and broke the silence. This is when I realized that all eyes were on me. Everyone was in shock. I exited the class with my teacher.

I stood beside her in the hallway, and she began to speak. "Allan, I'm so sorry" she said. "I had no idea that you didn't know. Sara is not your real mom." I didn't know what to think. She continued, "Allan, this is my mistake, and it's my job to fix it."

She told me not to say anything to my mom that night because she needed time to speak with her. So, I went home that night and said nothing. And I went home the next night and said nothing. As time passed, I was getting resentful, because I now knew that my mom had hidden this from me and she was ignoring the problem.

After about a month, my mom and I weren't getting along the greatest, but I didn't equate it to the situation from school, I just thought she was a bitch and she was mad about everything. One day she took me to what looked like a Dr.'s office. "We have an appointment," she said. I asked what it was about. She told me that we were just going to go and talk with this lady.

I read the little placard on her door, "Rosemary Lim –Psychologist." I said, "You think I'm crazy?" She said, "No, of course not. why would you think that?" I said, "Because you're taking me to a psychiatrist!" She laughed and said, "Read it again." I read it carefully. "Psycho...logist?" "Yes," she said.

I asked what the difference is. After all, this one has "Psycho" right in the name. She laughed again. She explained that a psychologist is just a person who you can talk to, and she may ask you some questions, you can answer them, or not; it doesn't matter. "She's just a person that you talk with, that's it."

I was cool with that. I love talking to people. So, we went in and we spoke to her together that day. She seemed nice. Dr. Lim was an Asian lady, about 50 years old, with black hair. I noticed that hanging over her silk blouse was a beautiful pearl necklace.

I sat on the couch across from her, my mom sitting just beside me. Dr. Lim was holding some papers and she adjusted her glasses as she read them.

She began asking me a few questions. I felt super chill when she spoke. I felt like she could be trusted. She asked if I would come to speak to her the following week, by myself. I agreed.

The following week, my mom and I took the bus there again. My mom said she would go and get her hair done next door while she was waiting for me. I went and sat with Dr. Lim and we had a good talk. I recall that she asked if any big events happened in my life. I said, "No, not that I can remember." She said, "Well your mom tells me that you lost your father. Is that correct?" I said, "Well, yeah, a couple of years ago."

She asked me about that and how I felt, how I was coping. I told her it was hard at first, but I'm much better now. She asked if I had any moments of great sadness around that or anything else. I said, "No, not really." And she replied "Well this is great, it seems you are a very happy young man." I agreed that I was. She asked if I would come back the following week. I agreed, and starting the following week, I began to take the bus to Dr. Lim by myself.

The visits continued for three or four sessions, and each week Dr. Lim would eventually ask again if there were any big events in my life that may have upset me. I kept assuring her that there was nothing of the sort.

One day I inquired why she kept asking me this. She told me that my mom felt that there was a change in my demeanour lately, and she was concerned that maybe something had happened to me, and perhaps I needed to talk about it. She said that my mom just loves me and wants to make sure I'm ok.

I thought about it silently for a moment. I looked at the floor as I adjusted my position in my chair, and cleared my throat. Then I looked up at her, and I said, "Yeah, well there was this one thing, I guess. My teacher at school said Sara is not my real mom because I'm adopted, but other than that, no there's nothing really that I can think of."

Dr. Lim looked shocked. She paused a moment, and then said, "Ok. Well, I think that's pretty significant." And of course, she asked why I had not told my mom. I said, I was waiting for the teacher to tell her because she knows it was her mistake, and she needs some time to tell her. You can imagine her surprise. She couldn't believe I had kept this to myself for the past two months. She said that although our sessions are confidential, this is one of those things that she will need to tell my mom, and she asked me if I was ok with that. I told her I was.

When I arrived home, Mom was waiting for me. She asked me to sit down on the couch so we could talk. She told me that Dr. Lim had told her what I said. I asked, "Well... is it true?" She confirmed that what my teacher had told me was true. She apologized profusely for not telling me sooner. She said, "Your father and I had many talks about when we should tell you."

"When you were five years old, we agreed you were too young to fully understand. Then the years passed, and you were getting older and we wondered if too much time had passed. Then Daddy died, and I wasn't going to tell you then because you had enough on your plate."

I understood why they didn't tell me. Of course, I wanted to know if they knew who my birth family was. She confirmed that she did know my birth mother. She asked me if I remembered Lillian who used to visit with her three girls. I said, "Yes, but what does she have to do with this?" She said, "Well... she's your birth mom."

At this point, speaking of my two moms may get confusing, and perhaps difficult to understand which mom I am referring to, so I will simply refer to them by their names, "Sara" for my adoptive mom, and "Lillian" for my birth mom.

Wow. Ok. After thinking a moment, I replied "Ok so if she's my mom, then her girls..." "Yes," replied Sara. "They're your sisters." It took a while for all of this to sink in. I had three sisters. Then another thought occurred to me. I asked Sara, "So does this mean I also have another dad?" The look on her face told me that she was expecting that question, and really didn't want to answer it.

"What?" I asked. Sara replied, "I don't know your father. I'm sorry to tell you, but he's not a good person. It's really not my place to discuss him… The only things I know about your father are what your mother told me and what I read in the newspapers."

I replied, "Ok, but do you have any idea where he is? Is he alive?" Sara answered, "He is alive. He went to prison when you were three years old and he won't get out of prison before your 16th birthday." I said, "Well he must have killed somebody." Sara replied, "It's not my place to say."

She did have some other information for me though. She said, "I don't know your father, but do you happen to remember Uncle Lionel who used to take you for weekends sometimes?" I said, "Yes I do. Is that my real uncle?" "No," she replied, "Uncle Lionel is your father's father. He's your biological grandfather." She said that she eventually stopped the visits because when he came to pick me up, he was often quite drunk.

Sara then pulled out a big paper bag. She said that I could open it up. Inside were birthday cards. A card for my birthday, one for each year, from Lillian. Sara said she had saved each of them for me. I asked if she still knew Lillian. "Yes, she lives in Vancouver." She replied. She also said that we could arrange a meeting.

Sara explained that Lillian was just very young when she had me, and really not in a place to have a child. She told me that I was an infant in Sara's daycare. Apparently, Lillian and Sara became very close. She said that Lillian told her she was like a mom to her. At least, she was the only mom she had ever known.

Lillian approached Sara one day and said that she could no longer take care of me. She said the Ministry of Child and Family Development was going to take me, and if they were going to do that, she wanted me to at least be with someone she knew would take good care of me. Sara discussed it with Bill, and they agreed to take me.

So much to think about. I was still young, still happy, but a bit confused at this point. Not quite as carefree anymore. I wasn't resentful towards anyone. Not at all. I wondered what would happen when I met my mom. I was about to find out.

CHAPTER THREE

ABOUT A WEEK AFTER THE TALK WITH SARA, I had the meeting with my birth mom, Lillian. A social worker arrived at my school with Lillian and brought us to a coffee shop where we sat and talked. Lillian asked me if I had any questions. I said, "Well, yeah a few."

I looked closely at her, and then said, "You're native!" She said, "Uh, yeah hello, so are you!" Hmmm. I guess my friend's mom was right all along. How did she know? My skin is white. I don't look native. As a matter of fact, although Lillian has darker skin and is unmistakably native, she is only half native, and my dad is non-native, making me only a quarter. I guess it's like she said, "We see each other... We know."

The next thing I wanted to know was about my father. So I asked about him. When I did, Lillian got super quiet. She looked at the ground. She said, with a very soft voice, "Umm... I don't want to talk about that much with a social worker sitting with us." She turned to the social worker, and said, "Yeah, sorry, I really don't like social workers. No offence." The social worker cleared her throat, and replied, "None taken."

Lillian continued, "I can tell you a bit about him, though. He is very very tall, and he's a strong man. He has a great sense of humour." I'm thinking, "Awesome, I feel like I know him already." And obviously my thoughts were filled with sarcasm. Lillian pulled out a bag. She said, "This was really your sister's, but I don't think she wants it, so I brought it for you."

The plastic bag was filled with coins and old bills from around the world. She said, "I don't know how much it's all worth because it's not Canadian money, but I think it's pretty cool." I thanked her very much. I agreed that it was very cool indeed. We agreed that I should meet my sisters soon. We arranged a visit that would take place in the next few weeks.

A few weeks later, I arranged to meet Lillian and my sisters. The first visit took place in our home. It was so strange to meet all three girls again, knowing this time that they were my sisters. I sat and talked with each of them.

Tracy was the oldest. She was three years younger than me. I was 13 and she was 10 at the time. Tracy had brown hair and brown freckles on her face. Tracy said, "Wow, so we have a brother!"

Next, I turned to Leslie. Leslie was the next oldest, and she was two years younger than Tracy. Leslie had noticeable green eyes, and blonde hair that reached just past her shoulders. Leslie seemed super excited to meet me. She gave me a huge hug and didn't let go for at least a whole minute.

Next, I turned to my youngest sister, Krystal. Krystal was only 10 months younger than Leslie. Krystal looked more like Leslie than Tracy did. She, too, had green eyes and medium length blonde hair. It was clear that Krystal was the baby of the family. She seemed to absolutely adore me. She, too, gave me a long hug and said, "brother!"

After the initial visit, there were several other visits. We often went to Stanley Park for walks and picnics. It was really nice to start building a relationship with family I never knew I had.

I used to take the bus downtown and meet Lillian at the corner of Granville and Georgia Street. There were a couple of disappointing days when she would either be over an hour late or just didn't show up. When she did show up, though, we had fun. One time we walked down Granville Street looking at things vendors were selling. She found one vendor that was selling rings. She asked me if I wanted to choose one. I looked for a while and then chose one that had a Yin Yang symbol on it. Then Lillian looked in her wallet. She pulled out a $50 bill and put it in my hand. She said, "You should take this."

One other very memorable visit happened shortly after I met Lillian. I took the bus downtown, and she met me at Granville and Georgia with my sisters. She took us to Stanley Park. You could take the train around the park to view the animals. Lillian said that we didn't need to waste money on the train. She told us we could just walk where the train went.

So, we walked around the park, looking in the cages at all the animals. When we got to the wolves, we stopped to take a closer look. My sister Tracy walked up to the fence. Lillian didn't want her to go that close. Tracy said it was ok. Suddenly Lillian yelled, "No! Look out! That wolf is out of the cage! My sister ran through the woods towards us, hopping over roots. She caught her foot in a hole and twisted her ankle. When she got to us, Lillian started laughing! She said, "Oh my God that was so funny!" Laughing more she said, "You actually believed me!" The wolf was nowhere near Tracy. Lillian just thought it would be funny to scare her.

As we were leaving, Lillian started talking about how much Sara loved to garden. She was correct. Sara loved her garden and took incredible care of it. Lillian said, "We should bring something home for her." There were gazebos around the park, and there were some huge, beautiful hanging baskets.

Lillian is short. She looked up at one of the hanging baskets. She said, "Allan, I can't reach that. Do me a favour and get that down for me ok?" I reached up and unhooked it. Lillian said, "Ok you need to carry it. Let's go." As I walked, I was trying to tell her that these hanging baskets belonged to the park. She said, "Shut up! Don't talk about it!"

I kept walking. We got close to the edge of the park. Lillian yelled at me again "Hurry the fuck up! Go! There is a guy behind us! Holy shit, keep going!" I walked as fast as I could. We saw that there was a bus coming. Lillian yelled "Shit! That's our bus! Get on that fricken bus!" We all ran towards the bus.

There were some people boarding the bus. We ran and caught the bus before it left. We got on and sat down. We kids were full of adrenaline. We were all talking about how we almost got caught. Lillian whispered loudly, "Shut the fuck up! Are you guys stupid! Don't talk about it!"

We arrived at my house. Sara was shocked to see such a giant, gorgeous hanging basket. She got mad at Lillian saying, "You really shouldn't have!

I know you don't have much money and I know how much this must have cost. You can't afford this, Lillian!" Lillian replied "Oh it's ok. I knew you would like it." I started laughing so hard!

Lillian and my sisters left. When they were gone, I told Sara what had happened. She said, "You STOLE it?!!" I said, "Well, we took it... without permission." I asked if I should bring it back to the park. Sara replied, "Well I don't condone this, but it is very beautiful and what's done is done." So, we kept it. And Sara took great care of it.

At this point life was ever-changing. I was starting to go through puberty, which for a young man is challenging enough. My dad had died three years ago, now I knew I was adopted, but I didn't have another dad because he was in prison. I was happy to know that I had three sisters and that my biological mom, Lillian, lived nearby. I was about to enter high school. And life was about to change a little more.

Dad had worked for the union on the school board when he was alive. He was a janitor at a local school. Life without Dad's income was increasingly difficult. Sara received a small pension after he died, but it wasn't much. I think at this point, Sara was down to only two kids in her daycare. To add insult to injury, our landlord raised our rent by $300/month.

We were looking for a new home. We could not afford to stay here. We went to see a few places before we found one that was affordable. We began packing and I knew that the home I had grown up in was not going to be my home much longer. I was just turning 14 at this point, and I had lived here my whole life.

I remember the night before moving day very well. In my room, I had a door that opened onto a balcony. I had a view of the harbour and Lion's Gate Bridge. I used to sleep with the door open, and I would fall asleep watching the "W" on the Woodward's tower turn around, and the blinking light on top of the SeaBus as it crossed the harbour, bringing passengers to downtown. This night as I lay there with the door to my balcony open, tears poured down my face. I spoke to the house. I said, "I'll miss you house. You're the only house I've ever known. Goodbye old house."

Following the conversation with the house, I spoke to my dad. "Dad, I know you have been with me all this time in this house. We are leaving now, and I would very much like it if you came with us. I will need your help more than ever now because I think life is about to get different." "I'm coming with you." I heard him say.

We moved into a smaller house that was only about five blocks away from my new school. I was about to be a high school student. I was very nervous. I didn't know anyone there. How was I supposed to make friends with people I didn't know? All my friends from my elementary school went on to the Catholic high school a block away from the elementary school. I was entering a public high school. I wasn't sure what to expect.

Most of my fears came true in high school. There wasn't really anything good about the transition. The school work was harder, we had more homework, and I struggled with my studies, especially math. I knew nobody. Kids picked on me. I had started to be overweight which didn't help with my bullies. Kids had all the newest brand-name clothes. I had some Adidas pants and Nike shoes but for the most part I had old clothes, or new clothes that were not "cool." Making friends was tough.

I was placed into "L.A.C." for help with math. It stood for Learning Assistance Centre. I was in there with some pretty slow kids. At least I wasn't in "L.D" next door. That stood for Learning Disabilities. I was already called "Fat" and "Stupid." I didn't need the bullies to add "Retard" to the list of insults.

I met a couple of friends in L.A.C. We were the same in regards to not fitting in with the "Cool Kids." It was nice to know a few people that I could talk to, eat lunch with, and occasionally hang out with. I tried hard to avoid the bullies.

I had heard stories of them "Curb Stomping" a kid. Curb Stomping is when they grab a kid, force him to the ground, make him open his mouth and bite the curb, then as hard as they could, they would stomp on the back of his head. This inevitably ended with the kid having a broken jaw and several missing teeth. I was terrified of this happening to me. I never witnessed this, but the stories I heard were bad enough.

Around this time Sara sent me to a summer camp. I had been there once before and it was a bad experience. I was bullied there as well. I went when my dad was still alive. I told my parents I had a great time because I didn't want them to feel bad for me.

It was a Bible camp. They would sing songs about God and faith, and so on. The second time around went much better. My hormones were going crazy at this point, 14 years old. I met some girls who I liked very much. As it turned out they were from Vancouver. I heard my dad say, "Careful with these ones, Allan… they're a bit wild." And I replied, "Don't worry Dad, I'll be good. I promise." We exchanged phone numbers and I called them when I got home. We started to hang out together in East Vancouver.

These girls introduced me to alcohol. I went to meet them one Friday evening. We walked to an East Van playground and gave some money to a few guys who were much older than us. They went to do a liquor run for us since we weren't of legal age to buy alcohol. About half an hour to an hour later they returned with a forty-ounce bottle of "Black Liquorice Vodka." Sambuca. We all stood in a circle and the older guys cracked the bottle open.

The bottle was passed around the circle from person to person, each person taking a sip and passing it on. It came to me. I took a sip. As the liquor passed my lips to my tongue my taste buds went crazy with delight. As I swallowed the Sambuca, it warmed my belly and my soul.

I felt alive! This stuff was magic! I knew immediately that I needed more. After I swallowed, I tilted the bottle and took several big gulps, before it was wrestled away from me. They all got angry with me and said, "Take a sip and pass it!"

It came back to me and once again, I took several giant gulps. After that, I almost missed my next turn, so I said, "No, no sorry I'll be good, I promise." This sentence was reminiscent of my conversation with my dad. I realized I had already broken the promise I made to him, which was that I would be good. I got another chance and I behaved myself a bit, because I knew if I didn't then I would not be given any more.

Things get a bit blurry after this point. I vaguely remember somebody yelled "Pigs! The pigs are coming!" Everyone was running and I was stumbling, trying to keep up, but I kept falling on my face. The next thing I remember is my face bouncing off a guy's ass, while I puked down the back of his legs.

Don't worry it's not what it sounds like. He had thrown me over his shoulder and was running with me as I couldn't even stand up. We came to a chain link fence. Since there was no way in hell I could climb it in the state I was in, I was tossed over, and once the rest of them climbed over I was picked up again and the journey continued.

We got to one of the girl's houses. We walked in and the first thing I realized was that these girls lived a much different life than what I was used to. The house was old and dirty and smelled like mould. I think every dish they owned was piled in the sink and across the kitchen counter. The paint on the cupboards was peeling off. The house was mostly dark, with only a single lamp illuminating the living room.

As I looked across the kitchen into the dimly lit living room, I saw a native lady sitting on the couch, smoking a hand rolled cigarette, sipping a beer. "Hi Mom," my friend said. The lady looked up and grunted, "Hey... 'sup?" "Nothin' much," replied my friend, "We're going to bed." The lady replied "K, see ya babes."

I woke up in the same bed as one of the girls. I had hickeys all over my neck. Apparently, I had a great night! Too bad I didn't remember it. The girl said, she respected me so much because most guys just wanted her for sex, and I didn't even try. Now I was thinking, "Damn, I could have gotten lucky?" They didn't know this, but I was still a virgin. Later on, the question came up… How many girls have you had sex with?" I was scared to admit I was a virgin. My response was, "Oh, so many I lost track. Probably like 100."

I was happy to have some friends. Every kid needs some friends with similar interests. It's a lonely life when you spend all your days by yourself. I finally got in with a few people. The people I was friends with spent their days skipping school to smoke weed and drink. I had this in common with them. From my first taste of alcohol that day in the East Van park, I knew it was for me. I literally couldn't get enough.

We were still in the house close to my high school. Even though the rent was less than our old house, we really couldn't afford to live there. We were about to move again. And my life was about to see some more interesting changes.

CHAPTER FOUR

SARA HAD APPLIED FOR LOW INCOME HOUSING. We went for some interviews. Somehow Sara had managed to save some money throughout the years and had around twenty thousand dollars in savings. She was very honest about her savings during the interview process. Her honesty ultimately made us not qualify for the subsidized housing.

Sara was upset that we were not being approved for subsidized housing. When we went to the interview the last time, everyone else that was there for interviews as well were driving up in brand new Mercedes, and BMWs. We couldn't even afford a used car. They were approved. Sara heard through the grapevine that they had put all their money into other peoples' names and lied about the amount of savings they had.

Somebody told Sara to take her savings out and put it into an account in England. She had family there that could manage the account for her. She eventually took this advice and we returned to an interview and showed bank accounts that had close to zero balance. We were approved. It was time to move again.

There was one big problem with our move. The subsidized homes did not allow pets. Caesar would need to go to a new home. My brother was very angry about this. Caesar had become his dog over the years. Carl did everything for Caesar. He was the one to walk him, feed him, cut his nails, brush him, etc.

My brother got busy, asking everyone he knew if they could take Caesar so he would at least be somewhere we could visit him. He spoke with a friend of his and we managed to convince his friend's mom to let Caesar live there. I would go to Carl's friend's house with Carl to get Caesar and take him for walks. Caesar was part of the family, and for now at least, disaster was averted.

We soon moved to our new home. They were new homes and quite nice. The nicest part was that it was affordable for our family. It reduced the stress level in Sara. But I would soon give her stress of other kinds.

At this point I was experimenting with weed and drinking alcohol when I could get some. My brother Carl hooked up with the neighbour girl and soon after, he moved in with her. I used to go next door to "visit." They didn't know this, but one of the main reasons for my frequent visits was because they had a well-stocked liquor cabinet. If I went over to hang out with them, they would inevitably both leave the room at some point and I would jump at the opportunity to transfer a little from each liquor bottle into an empty bottle that I would bring with me. This is how I managed to get drunk in the early days of my drinking.

One day I went to visit another neighbour who I had befriended in the complex. He had a Mickey of vodka that he shared with me. Then he showed me a potato gun that he had. Basically, you would plug the metal end into the potato. This would get a chunk of the potato stuck in the end. Then you could squeeze the trigger and air would build up in the barrel of the gun, forcing out the potato chunk.

After we drank and played with the gun, we wandered across the way, back to my house. I brought him to my room to listen to my CDs. Sara started yelling that the music was too loud. I got upset with her. We began arguing and I was a bit intoxicated, so I started laughing at her uncontrollably. I suddenly had the brilliant idea of shooting chunks of potato at Sara.

She was standing at the bottom of the stairs and I was at the top of the stairs. Laughing hard as I descended the staircase, I took one good shot at Sara with the potato gun. The potato chunk nailed her in the cheek. It must have stung a bit, and it pissed her off.

As I got to the bottom of the stairs, Sara took one good swing and slapped me hard across the face. I was shocked. Sara had never hit me before, not ever. I got mad and left. I returned later that day. Being Sunday, I went to school the following day.

I attended school as usual. I gave no thought to the situation that occurred the day before. When the day was nearly done, I was called to the counsellor's office. They wanted to speak with me for some reason.

I went into the office and sat with the counsellor. He asked me if I had an altercation with Sara the day before. I thought my friend must have called social services. I told them that I did have an argument with Sara, but it was no big deal. He asked if she had hit me. I said, "No not really." He said, "Are you sure, Allan?" I asked "Who have you been talking to?"

He told me Sara had called and talked to the social worker and they had called the school. I asked why Sara would call. He told me she felt guilty. I said, "Well she didn't hit me, she slapped me across the face, but only because I shot her with a potato gun." I added that she had never ever hit me before and I kind of deserved it. He said, "Ok, well a social worker is going to meet with you at your house, just to talk."

I got home and there was a social worker there with Sara. She explained that Sara felt horrible about what she did, and she had called them because she felt she was losing control of herself. They said, that I would go with the social worker to a foster home.

To say I was shocked and confused would be an understatement. I could not believe what I was hearing. Ever since I found out Sara was not my birth mom, I had been hearing about how the Ministry was always trying to take me and how she fought to keep me in her home. You see, I was never legally adopted. I was what they called a "Ward of the court." I was a foster kid. But Sara and Bill had no intention of letting me go.

Sara told me that one day a social worker arrived at the house asking for a photo of me. They wanted to put my picture in the paper in the "Sunday's Child" column. Sunday's Child was published every week and it was for children who were in foster care who needed to be adopted.

Sara argued that I didn't need to be adopted and that this was the only home I had ever known. When they were relentless, she would mention how much the media would love to hear about this. Then they backed off.

Sara fought furiously to keep me, saying I was as much her child as Carl was. Now, suddenly, when I needed her the most, she was just going to send me to a foster home?

When it was time for me to leave with the social worker, Sara gave me a big hug and said, "It'll be ok dear." I cried uncontrollably. I really tried to hold it in because I was embarrassed, but it was hopeless. Tears just poured down my face. My knees started to shake. I felt unwanted, abandoned, not good enough. Yes, I had caused some problems for her. Yes, I had sworn at her, and yes I was a little shit at times. But I loved her. So many thoughts. What would happen to me now? Would I return to Sara? What about my brother? Were they still my family or were they just done with me?

If ever I wished I had been a better kid, it was at this moment. "I can change," I thought to myself. "I'll be better." But it was too little, too late; I should've thought about that before. Should've been a better kid. I got in the car with the social worker and tears continued to fall down my cheeks as I silently wept. We were off to meet my new foster parents.

I arrived at the new foster home late in the afternoon. The house was nice. The foster parents seemed nice. They were English, like Sara, but from a different region; I noticed because the accent was slightly different. They were both smokers, like myself and like Sara.

I quickly noticed that there were wine goblets on display in the kitchen, hanging above the marble countertop. Also, I noticed immediately that just past the glass doors that led into a den, there was a liquor cabinet with whiskey glasses and a bottle of whiskey on a tray on top of the cabinet. "This place might be ok," I thought to myself.

They introduced me to their daughter, who was just finishing high school. After that, I was introduced to Ben. Ben was a Great Dane, a beautiful dog with a calm demeanour. He sat in front of me and pushed his head into my thigh. I gave him a little scratch behind his ear, which he seemed to like a lot.

They showed me to my bedroom, downstairs. They said I should always feel free to help myself to anything in the house. "Yes, anything indeed," I thought as I tried hard not to look towards the den. They said that my weekly allowance would be $30, paid each Friday. They both worked every day at a hair salon that they owned.

The first chance I got, I skipped school, rode the bus home, and raided the liquor cabinet. There was a forty ounce bottle of rum I got into. It was about half full when I started. When I stopped, it was about a quarter full. I remember lying on the floor asking Ben why he was so crazy. Then I got up, ready to get into mischief.

I had a good buzz, but I didn't feel completely drunk. After wandering around the kitchen a bit, I found the car keys for the spare car parked in the driveway. The thought occurred to me that it would be ok if I just took it for a little spin. I had never driven before as I wasn't quite 16 yet, and I did not have my driver's licence. But still, it seemed like a good idea at the time.

I got into the car and started it. It was parked beside the house, at the bottom of a very long, very steep driveway. I pulled out, onto our street. I proceeded to the end of the block and stopped at the red light. When the light turned green, I turned right, and merged onto the highway.

I started to think I was in a bit over my head. I got off at the first exit, and ended up down a little road that was a dead end. I had to turn around. I pulled forward and to the right until I reached the bush, then stopped. I cranked the wheel left and started to back up.

A man came running out of a house behind me. He said, "What are you doing? Didn't you see my mailbox?" I looked and saw that I had backed into the mailbox. It was the kind of mailbox that was on a wooden post with a little metal arm that sat in the up or down position depending on whether there was mail in it. I had pushed the wooden post out of place and cracked it a bit.

I said, to the man, "No, it was like that when I got here." He said, "I just watched you back into it!" I said, "You are mistaken, my friend. I need to go now." And with that I drove off. I could see in my mirror that he was yelling and waving his arms. I just kept going.

Somehow, I made it back down the highway and managed to back down the steep driveway without doing any more damage. I thought it would be a good idea to return to school. I took the bus back, and actually just went to the smoke pit, bummed a cigarette, and then school was over. I called the foster parents and told them I would be late, as I was planning to go to a friend's house. They said that was not a problem, and thanked me for letting them know.

I wandered around the city and went back after they were asleep. The next morning was Saturday. When I woke up, my foster parents were there to greet me. They asked if I wanted coffee. I happily accepted. The foster mom asked, "How was school yesterday?" I said, "Oh, as good as it could be, you know, it's school." She said, "But not bad?" I said, "No, not bad at all." She asked if anything else happened, anything exciting, anything… out of the ordinary. "Nope." I replied. The foster dad said, "Are you sure?" I said, "You guys are acting a bit strange; what's going on?"

The foster dad said, "Allan we don't have a lot of rules in this house, but the ones we do have are important." "Ok," I replied. He continued, "One rule we have is that we are always honest, even when we've done something that's maybe not that good. And if nothing huge happened as a result of bad behaviour, we will probably not be too concerned with it. We are very concerned about dishonesty though." "Ok." I said.

He continued "So, now that you know this, was there anything that happened yesterday, perhaps during the time that you should have been in school?" "Ohhhh," I said. "Well… I might have come home for lunch and even missed some classes." "Go on," said the foster mom. "And while I was here, I might have taken the car out, just for a little spin around the block and back because I thought it would be cool… and I'm sorry about that."

They both smiled. The foster dad said, "Thanks for being honest. You did an excellent parking job. It was parked exactly how I left it." "Then how did you know?" I asked. "Because we have neighbours and they saw you." "That makes sense." I said.

I enjoyed that liquor cabinet quite a bit. There were a few Friday evenings that I helped myself to a bottle. I ended up in the drunk tank at least one of those times. I took a bottle of Crown Royal and found a nice log in the forest close to the house. There I sat, enjoying my drinks.

The feeling of superiority that consumed me was in itself, intoxicating. I felt as though I had not a care in the world! I was excited, happy, brave, unstoppable! I could do anything! I yelled that out loud, "I can do anything!" I rose to my feet and then fell on my face! "Anything except walk," I thought to myself.

I tried to get to my feet. "This shouldn't be as hard as it seems," I thought. Eventually I stumbled to my feet. I wanted to leave the forest, but my level of intoxication was making this a challenge. It didn't help that I had to climb over logs and uneven ground.

When I finally managed to exit the forest, I found myself at a gas station. I went in there with the two dollars I had. I told the guy, "Sell me some singles." "What?" he asked. "Singles! Single cigarettes for twenty five cents each!" "We don't do that here." He replied. I looked at him straight in the eye, and said, "You're fucked! You're lucky to be alive, you piece of shit!"

I left the gas station and stood by the bus stop. A short while later—I'm not sure how long, exactly but I think maybe 10 minutes after I left the gas station—a police cruiser pulled up and turned on his lights. He got out of his car and walked towards me.

"Oh, you must be here to sell me a cigarette!" I exclaimed. "Not exactly." Replied the officer. He asked what my name was. "Nic," I said. "Nic what?" he asked. "Nicorette." I said. Then I burst into song "Nicorette! Nicorette! I don't need no Nicorette, 'cause I have a cigarette!"

The officer looked at me and said, "I'm just going to pat you down." I looked at him and said, "That's what they all say! You're fucked!" He then told me to put my hands against the car. I tried to cooperate, but I fell sideways and landed on the ground. "Stop tripping me!" I yelled, "You're fucked!" I ended up in the drunk tank that night.

I attempted to punch my way out of there. My knuckles quickly became cut and swollen. I eventually fell on the floor, curled up beside the metal toilet and began to sob. I cried out loud "Dad! Daaad! I'm sorry, Dad!" He replied to me, "I'm here, Allan. I'm always here. You really made a mess of things this time, didn't you? Sleep now. Get some rest." As I lay there crying, I eventually passed out.

My foster parents came and got me the next morning. I had the worst headache ever! Most of what I did I could not recall, however, the things I did recall embarrassed me a great deal. I was ashamed to have acted this way.

This type of behaviour continued. I got into the habit of skipping school to go and drink. One day I skipped class, took the bus home, raided the liquor cabinet and decided I really should be back in class. After all, the last class of the day was Drama class, which I enjoyed.

I went back to school after helping myself to about half of a forty pounder of vodka. When I arrived, the door to the classroom was closed. I opened it and looked inside. I saw my friend Mike sitting up high on an elevated platform.

"That's strange." I thought. I went up to him, and looking up at the bottom of his sneakers, yelled "Hey! Mike! Get down from there! Why are you way up there?" He started whispering in an angry tone "Allan, go away! Get out of here!" I was confused! I yelled, "What are you doing up there?!!!"

Suddenly I heard a roar of laughter mixed with some quieter giggles. I turned and noticed the entire class was looking at me. I was on stage with Mike. He was in the middle of a play. Then I saw a very angry drama teacher storming towards me. He actually pulled my ear! He started twisting my ear and pulling me towards the classroom door. When we got out of the class, he ordered me to the principal's office. Then he went back into the classroom and closed the door.

Some of my classmates and other students suddenly appeared in the hallway to observe the drunk kid. I was close to a blackout, so it's a bit fuzzy, but I do recall the kids yelling orders like, "Stand on one leg!" Which I happily obeyed. Then one kid yelled, "Cluck like a chicken!" I proceeded to run down the hallway "flapping" my little chicken wings and saying, "Bawk! Bawk! Bawk!" I left school and caught a bus. I got to the main bus loop and an officer arrived. Once again, I found myself in the drunk tank, this time in the middle of the afternoon.

This went on for some time. My life was on a downward spiral, at a very fast rate. Most weekends I was in the drunk tank. I started to steal every chance I got. I was a regular at the pawn shop. I missed more than half of my classes. Eventually the school said they did not want me, and the foster parents said that I needed more help than they could provide. I was about to find myself in a new school and a new home, and life was going to change again... not for the better.

CHAPTER FIVE

I LEFT THE FOSTER HOME BEFORE I left my school because the school year was ending for the summer. The school said I would need to find somewhere else to go after the summer, and the foster home said I needed to leave immediately.

I met with a social worker who told me I would be going to a group home. My understanding was that these were a bunch of kids who weren't wanted at their foster homes. They had staff who did shifts, and they had rules that needed to be followed. If I did my chores, I could earn an allowance. I was thinking it was not too bad.

I would go out on Friday nights to the rec centre for teen skate night. This was a good place to hook up with girls, and I was liked there because I always showed up with booze. I had many secret ways of acquiring alcohol. I knew the schedule of my former foster parents so I would go there and break in through an open window and help myself to a bottle or two occasionally.

I also had a friend who I used to hang out with before I got heavy into drinking. He was still a "kid." He wasn't into anything bad like me. Friday nights consisted of potato chips and pop with a nice movie. Maybe if he had a friend over and they got wild they would turn the music up a bit too loud. But his parents had a wine cellar in the basement. One night when I was at the teen skate, the alcohol ran out, and there were all these girls flocking to me in search of more booze. I told them if they waited for me, I would return with some wine. They agreed.

I caught the bus down to my friend's house. The lights were off, but I could see the glow of the TV through the living room window. I walked around to the side of the house. I tried a basement window which was open. I let myself in. I walked through the basement to the wine cellar. I tucked one bottle in the waistband of my pants. I was grabbing another one as I heard the sound of someone coming down the stairs.

I stood up with my back against the cellar wall. My friend walked into the cellar and turned on the light. He was there for pop. He grabbed a bottle of pop and was leaving. He had not seen me at all. I was already drunk, so I wasn't thinking clearly.

Even though he didn't see me, and would have left without spotting me, I decided to yell out. "Oooga Booga!" Well I've never seen anyone so startled in my entire life! He must have jumped a full two feet off the ground as he let out a terrified scream. As he turned, he yelled, "Allan!!!" Then he yelled "Ahhhhhh!" and ran upstairs.

I grabbed a wine bottle in each hand plus the one in my pants and made my exit out the same window I entered through. As I ran to the street my bus was pulling up to the bus stop. I got on the bus and rode it back to the rec centre, as promised, and boy, did I have girls hanging off me!

As we became more intoxicated, we started to wander away from the rec centre and down the street. As we walked, with girls hanging off me, I saw flashing blue lights. The police stopped us for questioning. I was immediately handcuffed because it was obvious, I was drunk. When the cop asked me my name and address, I did the stupidest thing ever. I blurted out the name of my friend, and when he asked my address, I blurted out his address, too. He said, "That's the house that just reported the break and enter!" Yes, I know. Not too swift of me.

I was charged that night with break and enter and theft under $5000. I saw the justice of the peace the next morning, right in the police department, and they gave me a notice to appear in court. As I waited for my court date, I continuously got myself in trouble. I was constantly in the drunk tank. I was constantly breaking car windows because it was fun. And I began to have a fascination with fire.

I lit several fires before I was caught. I don't know why I ever thought this was a good idea. I just started doing it one day. One day, after going for dinner at Sara's, I got very drunk in a parking lot. I thought I would go and catch the bus back to my group home.

I walked through the parking lot and saw a dumpster. The thought occurred to me that I should light it on fire. So I started a fire in the dumpster and let it burn. Then I walked into the Denny's restaurant that was there. I ordered a coffee. Then I went to use the washroom. While in the washroom, the thought occurred to me that it would be a good idea to light the toilet paper on fire. I did. I exited the bathroom, and someone was coming in, so I ran to a waitress and said, "Someone set a fire in the washroom!" I thought this would remove any suspicion that I was the one who lit the fire.

As I was walking out the door, two guys grabbed me and dragged me back into Denny's. They told me that they were holding me until the police arrived. I asked why. They said they knew I was the one setting the fires and I was going to be held accountable. I denied it. Regardless, I ended up in the drunk tank, and when I woke up in the morning, I was told that they had charged me with arson. They gave me a court date.

I was still living at the group home, still getting into trouble most days. I decided I really didn't want to face the consequences of my actions. The court date came, and I did not show up. I knew that when you don't show up for court, they issue a warrant for your arrest.

On the day of my 16th birthday, I was at the group home having breakfast. There was a knock at the door. A staff member asked if I could get it. I went downstairs to answer the door. There was an officer standing there. He said, "Hello young man. I'm here to speak with an Allan Strain." I turned and looked up the stairs, then turned back towards him.

Looking the officer straight in the eye I said, "Yes, come on in, he's upstairs having breakfast." "Thank you," replied the officer. "No problem." I said. As he started walking up the stairs, I was out the door. I was about to be homeless by choice, and the downward spiral would continue.

This was not exactly how I planned to spend my 16th birthday. I ran and ran down the street, zigzagging through alleys, off the beaten path. After an hour, I reached the bus terminal at Lonsdale Quay Market. I had no money, but I managed to hop onto the SeaBus.

I wasn't too sure what my plan was as I exited the SeaBus on the Vancouver side. I just knew my plan included NOT going to jail. This meant I could not go back to the group home, or to Sara's. I would need to figure out a place to stay. For a few days, I just wandered the streets and didn't sleep much. I would sleep a bit at tables in Burger King during the day, then get up and keep walking around.

I mingled with the street kids on Granville Street. I learned from these kids that I could make money panhandling. I continued to hang out with street kids my age, and they showed me the ropes. I learned that there were several abandoned houses around the downtown area that were referred to as squats. These were places I could go to sleep. There is one in particular that I remember clearly.

I arrived with three street kids. They showed it to me. It was a house right downtown. The front yard was overgrown with grass and bushes. There was no glass in any of the window frames. The white paint looked as though it had been peeling off for years. After we pushed our way through the bushes, we came to a doorway that was at one time a grand entranceway. There was no longer a door. Instead, there were a couple of pieces of plywood propped up in the doorway, held in place by some long planks.

I walked through the entrance way. A cat scurried out of my way, as I stepped on old boards and made my way through the darkness. To my left, there was an archway that led into what I think must have been a living room. We turned right and went through a little hallway. At the end of the hallway was a staircase that led upstairs to the bedrooms.

One of my new friends led the way with the flickering flame of her lighter. I was shown a room that had a king-sized bed and mattress. "This is the master bedroom." The girl said, to me. "You can sleep here tonight. Make yourself at home." She continued with the rules of the house. "You need to share this bed with the three of us. There is no stealing, or you'll be kicked out of here, so don't take anything that doesn't belong to you."

I turned to the bed to investigate where I would be sleeping. The condition of the mattress was almost unspeakable. I'm pretty sure all five cats that lived there had soiled it. To this day when I think of the smell, I gag a bit. There were mouldy stains and urine stains throughout. I leaned over and felt it. Just as I suspected, it was damp to the touch.

In addition to the condition of the mattress itself, I was sharing this bed with a guy and two girls. Homeless people don't shower and all three of them were pretty ripe. I tried my best to get some sleep, but people were in and out all night, so I didn't sleep much.

The next morning, I went with the girl to the SkyTrain. We hopped on, of course without paying, and took the train two stops to Burrard Station. I was told this was the best place to panhandle because it was busy and most of the people who take the train are businessmen and women.

I gave it a shot. I was taught the basic "script." Put on a sad face, and say, "Excuse me sir, can you spare some change for a bite to eat?" I panhandled for 45 minutes and I had $70. We did this every single day. Occasionally someone would ask something like, "Do you not have a home? You're so young, where are your parents?" I would say, "I had to leave home because my dad hits me. It's not safe there." Usually this would invoke enough sympathy and they would hand me a five dollar bill. Yes, I know… horrible. It worked, though.

This new "homeless" life continued throughout most of the summer. I would panhandle every day in the morning for a couple of hours, and I would usually get about $100. Then I would use that money to buy a pack of cigarettes, a Mickey of vodka, two hits of acid, and I would use whatever was left over for weed. Occasionally, I would get a hot dog from the vendor down the street, but eating was the last priority.

I started to stay with one of the girls I had met at camp. I guess you could say she was my girlfriend. She helped me hide out since I had warrants for my arrest. One day, the phone rang. My girlfriend's mom answered the phone and passed it to me. I couldn't understand how the phone would be for me. It wasn't my house and I had only been staying there for a few days at this point.

I grabbed the phone and put it to my ear. "Hello?" On the other end of the phone I heard a man's voice, "Hello Allan. My name is Constable Steeves. Sara is very worried about you." "What? How does she know this place and how does she know I'm here?" "I guess she's done her research," he said. "Perhaps she should have been a detective."

I told the officer that I would call Sara and thanked him for calling. As soon as I hung up the phone my girlfriend said, "You need to get the hell outta here! You're bringing way too much heat around here and we don't need this!" So, with that, I had no place to stay again. It was back to the squats for me.

I eventually did call Sara. I got mad at her for calling the police on me. She said that I really should come home. Of course, I got mad and told her that she didn't even want me and she had sent me off to some foster home, which proved she didn't want me. She told me the door was open if I changed my mind.

Living on the streets gets old pretty quick, especially when you know for a fact that there is a warm house, with a bed that has sheets that are cleaned weekly, and home cooked meals. It wasn't too long before I walked through her door again. It was a bit awkward at first, but things went back to normal pretty quickly.

Sara convinced me to "face the music" and go turn myself in. She called the legal aid lawyer we had been dealing with. He said he would call us back shortly, which he did. He said that he could get me into court the following day and he could meet us there.

The next morning, Sara picked out the nicest clothes she could find in my closet (my bedroom had remained as it was the whole time I was gone). We took the bus up to the courthouse, we met with my lawyer before court, and then we went before the judge.

The judge set a date for me to attend court to deal with the charge of break and enter and theft under $5000. The date was nine days away. The judge continued to speak, saying that he believed I would run again. He ordered that I be sentenced to the juvenile detention centre while I awaited trial.

I got butterflies in my stomach. This meant I was going to jail with kids as old as 18. I had heard about what happened to skinny little 16-year-olds in jail and it wasn't anything I wanted to be a part of. I was terrified. I had no idea what would happen to me there.

They led me through the doors at the back of the court room. From there, I was escorted along a hallway with a cement floor and brick walls to a stairwell. I was led down the stairs to another hallway. This is where the cells were. I was shown to a cell. I stepped in and the heavy metal door slammed behind me. I was told to "Sit tight."

I had time to think while I sat there, alone on a hard metal bed. How had I ended up here? I sure hoped my dad wasn't watching me now. I always wanted Dad to be proud of me, and at this point, I was certainly a disappointment. "I'm sorry, Dad." I said. I listened for him, with my heart, not my ears, as he had taught me all those years ago. "I know, son." He replied.

After about an hour, I heard footsteps walking down the hall. A sheriff arrived at my cell. He unlocked it and walked me down the hall to another cell. There were three other guys in that cell. They were all handcuffed together. The Sheriff opened the cell door and pushed me in. He took my left hand and handcuffed it to the right hand of the last guy in line.

The door slammed shut and the Sheriff disappeared down the hall. Once we were alone, the three guys shoved me into the corner. The guy furthest from me approached me. "Hey!" he said. "Hey!" I replied. "Did I say you could talk?" He asked. I replied with "Uhh, what?" BOOM! He punched me hard in the side of the face. "I said... Did I say you could talk?" "No!" I replied. BOOM! I took another hard hit to the side of the head.

The guy beside me held onto the cuffs right from the chain that linked his half to mine. They all worked together and managed to swing me around in circles, eventually slamming me into the wall. Then the same guy who had been punching me before got right in my face. "What do you have to say for yourself?" He asked.

I couldn't help but think this was a trick question. I knew the moment I answered I would get hit for talking without permission. To my relief the Sheriff arrived at the cell door to transport us to jail. I was thinking "Man, I have nine more days of this shit!" They loaded us into a Sheriff's van and off we went.

I managed to make it through my nine days in "Jeuvy" relatively unharmed. My lawyer met with me and strongly suggested that I tell the judge that I have an addiction to alcohol and that I needed help. He said, in this way, he could get me sent to a treatment centre rather than getting a sentence of up to six months in jail. I really didn't want to go back to jail.

When I went back to court, the judge looked at me, and asked me if I thought I had a problem. "Yes, your honour" was my response. "Do you want help?" He asked. "Yes, I would like that," I answered quite submissively. "Well..." he began. "...I'm not sure you've learned your lesson. I'm looking at your history and you've been arrested numerous times. I was about to suggest four months at the institution you just came from."

My lawyer interjected. "Your Honour, it is obvious that this young man has a problem with alcohol. Sending him to jail, in my opinion, will not fix his issues. I'm suggesting treatment because he may get something useful out of it and he's young, so perhaps it's not too late for him to turn his life around."

The judge looked ahead silently. "Very well." He began. "Mr. Strain, I sentence you to 90 days at Exodus Rehabilitation Centre in Langley, BC, and I sincerely hope you take this help that is being offered to you seriously. You're only young and you have a chance to change. If I see you in my court again, you will see a different fate. Good luck, young man." I looked at him and said sincerely, "Thank you."

I wasn't being sincere when I said I wanted help. But somehow, everything the judge said really hit home with me. He put my life into perspective. Life wasn't over. It was only just beginning. I didn't want to be a bad kid, I really didn't. Maybe I could take this seriously. Maybe I could turn out to be a good man after all. Maybe. What I knew for sure was that anything would be better than going back to jail. I was frustrated that I still had my virginity, but I certainly didn't want to lose it in there! I was at a crossroads in my life. It could go either way.

I was released to Sara's care that night. I went home to my bedroom and thought deeply as I packed. I would be leaving for treatment early in the morning. I was a bit nervous, but happy that I was out of jail and not going back.

I arrived at treatment first thing in the morning of the following day. It felt very institutional to me. As strange as it sounds, I enjoyed the structure and discipline of it. I didn't know it or acknowledge it at the time, but looking back, I really needed a routine and rules to follow. We ate well there, and we could smoke, not like in jail. We had chores that needed to be done and there was a chore schedule on the fridge with everyone's name on it. If your name was up for today, you had to complete the daily chores. Tomorrow would be someone else's responsibility.

There was an older lady on staff named Gail who was the house cook. She supplied a cigarette loan can that she kept in the kitchen. Anyone could take a cigarette if they were out of smokes and there was a sheet of paper that you put your name on. At the end of the week we all got paid for our chores and we would all buy cigarettes. We would see how many we owed and replace them.

Most days started with a huge breakfast, followed by individual counselling sessions. After that, we had some free time and we were encouraged to write in our journals during this time. Then we were required to participate in physical activity at the gym. In the evening, we ate a big dinner, and the evening would end with a 12 Step meeting, usually off the premises. The staff drove us.

We were allowed to choose two activities if we completed a certain amount of time in treatment. I chose parasailing and kayaking. Around week seven, a kayak instructor arrived. There were some other kids who also chose kayak lessons. We had a pool on the property, in a big building beside the treatment centre building. We all made our way over to the pool in our shorts, ready to learn how to kayak.

Our instructor was 83 years old and had been kayaking for over 60 years. The one thing I really wanted to learn from him was how to do an "Eskimo Roll." This was a maneuver where you used the strength in your hips, along with your paddle to flip yourself upright from an upside-down position. This was important to know in case you tipped over while in the river. I really enjoyed my lessons.

Most of the people in this treatment centre had either arrived from jail or had been in jail in the recent past. One of the guys in the centre befriended me. He showed me some of his "Jail Tats," homemade tattoos that he got in jail. He told me he could give me one if I wanted.

I thought this was so cool and I agreed to get a tattoo. He showed me the technique. We had a needle and we wrapped thread around the end, leaving the point sticking out a bit. The thread would absorb the ink. We used Indian ink that we bought when we were on an outing one day. I decided to do a Yin Yang design with my initials underneath. We dipped the needle in the ink. I had drawn the design on my skin, and now I just needed to make it permanent.

One dot at a time, I pushed the needle through my skin. Every time I pierced my skin, I left a tiny little permanent dot. For four days, I pierced my shoulder over and over. At the end, I had a crooked, faded Yin Yang and my initials right below it.

While I was in treatment, I started to really dive into the 12 steps. I worked on myself a lot. I took accountability for the wrong decisions I had made in my life. I vowed to change my behaviour in the future and become a better person.

If we completed eight weeks of treatment, we were permitted a weekend pass to return to our families. I got to the eight-week mark and was granted my pass. I was dropped off at the SeaBus in Vancouver. I was supposed to catch the SeaBus to North Vancouver and then get on the bus to my house. Standing on the street outside the SeaBus, I watched as the people who drove me left. I waited until the car was out of sight.

So many memories down here in Vancouver and they all involved getting drunk and high. I had freedom to choose as I wished at this point. I was eight weeks sober now. I really didn't want to ruin that. "I should really just behave myself," I thought.

After a short battle with myself, the addict won. I went to Pigeon Park to look for weed. I saw a guy with long, greasy hair that extended to his ass. He was about 5' 5", and I would say he didn't weigh more than 130 pounds. He wore a button-up shirt that was not buttoned up. Tattoos lined his bony torso. He was wearing black jeans that had many holes in them and dirty old runners, also with holes.

He was leaning up against a brick wall. As I walked by, I made eye contact. He looked right at me. "Need weed?" He asked. "Yup." I replied. "How much?" he asked. "Just a dime bag." I said. He motioned for me to follow him into the little coffee shop. "There are fucking pigs crawling all over this area!" he said. "You gotta be careful dude!" I reassured him, "You bet man, I'm cool." We completed the exchange. I thanked him and walked away.

As I got to the end of the block and turned the corner, I saw flashing red and blue lights from behind me. A cop car skidded to a stop and a cop jumped out and yelled, "Lemme see your hands!" As I raised my hands, he pushed me against the building in front of me and ordered me to place my hands behind my back. He handcuffed me and then asked me which pocket the weed was in. I told him.

At this moment I realized that I had just really destroyed any chance I had of turning my life around. I would be kicked out of treatment and I would have to face that judge again and tell him I had failed. I remembered his words, "You will see a different fate."

The officer told me the guy I bought off of was an undercover cop. I told him that I really needed a chance. I said, "Officer, I'm so sorry. This cannot be my fate. I'm so fucked! Please give me a chance." He asked, "Why do you say that? It's a dime bag of weed, not a big deal. Unless you have warrants."

I said, "No I don't have warrants. I went to jail for a bit, and then I got sentenced to a treatment centre. I'm on a pass for the weekend right now." He asked "How long have you been clean?" "Eight weeks, and I really want to stay clean, but I messed up. When I got down to the SeaBus, the temptation was too much. But maybe this can be a good lesson for me. Please, I don't want to get kicked out of treatment. I need it."

He looked at me closely. "Where are you going now?" He asked. "I'm going to stay with my mom for the weekend and then I go back to treatment on Monday." I replied. "Don't make me regret this." He said, as he unlocked one of my cuffs. He unlocked the other one and said, "Get outta here, kid. Don't come around here anymore. Good luck."

I was thinking that I just hit the jackpot. I couldn't believe it. I wouldn't be kicked out of treatment after all. Sara would have been so disappointed if I had blown my one chance to get clean and sober. And the guilt I had when I bought that dime bag was overwhelming. I was proud of my eight weeks. I didn't want to lose everything I had worked so hard for. And I really wanted Sara to be proud of me for once. I was tired of disappointing her.

I went back down to the SeaBus. This time I caught it and went to North Vancouver. I caught the bus home. It was strange being on the bus that I had taken so many times. I was back at home. It felt nice. So many emotions. I was still coming down from the adrenaline rush I got from being arrested. I was also very excited to see Sara.

Sara and I had a great talk when I arrived. She told me how happy she was that I had gone to treatment. Sara was never the type of person to say, "I'm proud of you." In fact, she never really said any words of praise. I never once heard, "I love you." But I always knew she was proud of me, and I always knew I was loved very, very much. Her actions showed it. Her English upbringing wouldn't allow her to say, "I love you." She never said that we couldn't say it; I just knew very strongly that it wasn't something that should be said. It was awkward.

Sara reminded me that the next day we would go to Granville Island where I would go parasailing. As I mentioned, in the treatment centre when we first arrived, we were asked to look at a sheet with about 30 activities on it and we could choose two of them. I wanted to choose skydiving, but the Ministry said they wouldn't allow that. So I had chosen parasailing and kayak lessons. I was excited to go.

I was picked up the next day by shuttle van. I went parasailing at Granville Island as planned. It was incredibly fun. I boarded the boat with a few others and then when it was my turn I went and sat in an elevated seat at the back of the boat. The parachute was attached to a harness. They helped me put the harness on and they clipped a carabiner onto the front of my harness. The carabiner was attached to a spool of metal wire that they would let out slowly. All I had to do now was sit back and relax.

The wind blew in my face as the boat sped up. The parachute inflated behind me and the wire slowly began to be released from the spool. I felt my butt lift out of the seat. I got further and further from the boat until the boat looked like a little speck. I couldn't see the people in it anymore. I looked out at the horizon and felt the warm summer air on my face. I put my arms out to the side like wings and pretended I was flying under my own power. "This is what life is." I thought. "I'm so grateful for that cop. Thank you, God, for helping me to stay clean and sober for eight weeks."

CHAPTER SIX

I COMPLETED 12 WEEKS OF TREATMENT. It was the longest I had ever been sober. One of the counsellors told me that if I didn't relapse, then every single day would be the longest I had ever been sober. "Pretty cool." I thought to myself. I was proud. My brother and Sara attended my graduation. When I got home, I went to my bedroom and there was a banner that said, "Welcome Home, Allan." This was Sara's equivalent to, "I love you and I'm proud of you." I felt good. In fact, I felt so good I was considering maybe staying sober. But I hadn't consumed my last drink. Not yet.

The day after I arrived home, I went out of the house and I brought with me a stereo I had received as a gift some time back. I had made my decision. I was going to sell my stereo at the pawn shop and use the money to buy some weed. I had some guilt about this, but I pushed those thoughts out of my head. After all, I had waited three whole months to smoke a joint and besides, it was only weed.

Remember my aboriginal friend Alex from elementary school? The one whose mom called me their little Indian boy? Well, as it turned out, his mom was the best known weed dealer in town. They smoked weed all day, every day, and when I went there to buy a bit of weed I would sit there and get high all day long because every 10 minutes, someone would walk in and buy a gram of weed and then roll up, and light up. After selling my stereo, I went straight there and bought two grams of weed.

When I walked in, my friend's mom said, "Holy shit! It's Allan! Where ya bin?" I said, "I went to jail for a bit then they sent me to this stupid treatment centre bullshit for like three months!" "Holy shit!" She replied. "No weed for three months! That's a bunch of crazy talk right there!" I agreed, and just like that I was right back where I left off.

The summer was coming to an end. Soon it would be time to go back to school. Sara and I looked around at alternative schools as I wasn't permitted back at my original high school. We found one in West Vancouver and I was enrolled. I would start in September. I was a bit nervous about starting at a new high school. I had fears the first time I entered high school and a lot of them came true, such as being bullied and not fitting in and not making any friends.

Every kid wants to have friends, and in my last school I was pretty much a loner until I found a couple of people who hung out with me, but I had no real connection with those kids. I've always been moderately intelligent, and the friends I made in my last school were pretty slow. I only hung out with them because nobody else would be friends with me. I didn't want to go through all of this again. I was the new kid again.

As it turned out, it wasn't nearly as scary as I thought. All the kids at my new school were delinquents, but they were all nice to me. They were like me, friendly, but just didn't fit in with kids at a regular school.

I discovered very quickly that pretty much everyone there loved to smoke weed and drink almost as much as I did. I met a few kids that I really got along well with, and it wasn't long before we were very good friends. One in particular was Donovan.

Donovan was slightly overweight, and he was half Jamaican and half Finish. His father was Jamaican and his mom was Finish. When I met him, Donovan had short, curly brown hair, but he later shaved his head, leaving a short Mohawk in the middle of his head, which he dyed purple for a bit.

We quickly became best friends. We smoked a lot of weed, and even though we were under legal drinking age, like most kids, we always found a way to get drunk.

Donovan lived with his mom and stepdad in a huge house in West Vancouver. One trip to his house told me that his parents were quite wealthy. His stepdad owned a Jaguar dealership downtown, and his mom worked at a local newspaper. Actually, it was the same newspaper that I delivered all those years earlier, when life was simpler.

I used to go to Donovan's house when his parents were out. They had a well-stocked liquor cabinet that we raided on several occasions. Donovan showed me the art of making "shit mix." We would take an empty two-litre pop bottle, and then we would pour a little alcohol from every bottle until it was full. If we had taken too much, sometimes we would water down the bottles we had stolen from, just to make it less noticeable. This worked especially well with vodka and other clear liquors. I guess most kids are quite similar, because although I was just learning the term "shit mix," this was not new to me.

Both Donovan and I received a weekly allowance. It wasn't much, we both got around $15-$20 each week, paid on Fridays. I think I did a pretty good job of playing the good kid with regards to Sara. I would tell her that we were going to the movies. We never went to the movies.

A typical Friday night consisted of getting some weed and a pack of cigarettes, which we shared between us. By the end of the evening we would stop at Subway for sandwiches and chips to kill our munchies. Subway used to have a stamp program. A six inch sub got you one stamp, and a twelve inch sub got you two stamps. Six stamps got you a free six inch and twelve stamps got you a Footlong.

Sometimes we would get this really cool sandwich artist who would give us each six or seven stamps at one time, or if we were a few stamps short for a free sub, he would just say "Let me see that card." He would put on the missing stamps and give us a free meal.

The weed smoking was pretty easy to hide from Sara. My "good kid" act started to fall apart when weed was combined, more frequently than not, with alcohol. Being high was easily hidden—being drunk, not so much.

It started to be normal for me to stumble in after curfew highly intoxicated. Sometimes I just wouldn't come home at all. Donovan and I had a lot of great times getting drunk around town. I introduced him to the Rez, where we often went to get weed, and sometimes we stayed there and got drunk.

Sara was becoming extremely frustrated with my behaviour. I was past the point of trying to hide my drinking. I stopped caring what she thought.

My opinion at this point was that she was an overprotective mom, and she needed to "chill the fuck out" because I was just being a normal teenager.

This chaotic behaviour continued for the next year or year and a half. I was getting progressively worse. I was attending school most of the time, but I was high most days and usually drinking with Donovan after class.

One day Donovan called me. He explained that he needed me to help him find a large amount of weed and he suggested I speak to some people on the Rez. "Like how much?" I asked. "Like whatever we can get for a grand." "What?" I replied. "How is it that you have a thousand dollars? You're screwing with me, right?" "Nope!" he said, "I found a stack of cash hidden in an inside pocket of one of my stepdad's suits. We should buy a ton of weed and become dealers."

Donovan and I met up that day and we went to the house on the Rez. I told my friend's mom that I needed a bunch of weed, $1000 worth. She said she would call up her cousin.

She hung up the phone and said, "Yeah he'll be here in an hour. It's $250 an ounce so you'll get a quarter pound, four ounces." Later on, I found out that this price was quite inflated, but I didn't know any better at the time, and we were just happy that we had a connection.

The cousin arrived 45 minutes later. I liked this. It's not normal to find a punctual drug dealer. Then again, he probably wanted to get there before we changed our minds. It was a good sale for him.

He pulled out the scale and four ounces of weed. An ounce is 28 grams. A couple of the ounces weighed in at 29 grams and 30 grams. He said, "That's ok bud, keep the extra couple grams!" I heard my friend's mom say, "Those are the ones they're gonna LIGHT UP! Haha haha!"

Once we paid for the weed and the deal was done, we rolled up a couple of fatties and passed them around. This was very good weed. We knew we had found the right guy. He asked us if we wanted to drive with him down to the other Rez where he lived. He said he might have a sale or two for us there and we could get high and hang out. "Sure," we agreed. He said, "Go wait in my car, I'll be right there." I'm thinking now that he was probably giving my friend's mom her cut for hooking him up with the sale.

While we waited in the car, a native guy approached the car and got in the back seat with us. He was a pretty big guy, and he had a huge scar that started from his right eye and continued down across his right cheek. He had tattoos on his neck and he wore a purple bandana.

He sat right beside Donovan. He said, "Up your weed." Donovan said, "What?" He said, "Don't play dumb motherfucker, gimme the weed you just bought!"

I was thinking "Shit! There goes $1000!" But Donovan just looked at him and said, "I'm sorry, I can't do that." The guy produced a large knife. He said, "Tough guy, hey? I'm gonna give you one more chance to hand over your weed or you're gonna get shanked right here, motherfucker!" Donovan looked at him and said, "Well I guess you'll just have to stab me because I definitely won't be able to give you my weed."

Just then, our dealer came to the car. He saw what was happening and said, "Hey, fuck off! Leave my customers alone! Get outta here, cuz!" And just like that, he got out of the car and closed the door. "Sorry about that," our dealer said. "It's ok," said Donovan.

I was happy that Donovan was holding the weed because the dude scared me so much I would have given it to him. I was looking to party, not to get stabbed. Even the thought of getting stabbed scared the hell out of me.

When we got to the other Rez, we pulled out all our weed. We had bought some foot-long rolling papers about a week earlier. We chopped up seven grams of weed and rolled it up in the giant rolling paper. We had to hold it with two hands! Needless to say, we got super-high that day!

Donovan and I also loved to use acid. We used to go downtown to get it. It was easily accessible and cheap as well. It was only five dollars per hit. Usually we would go and get two hits each, and at least one pack of smokes each, and a couple grams of weed. This would ensure a very good night.

These were the times that Donovan and I bonded. We had many deep philosophical conversations about life, the universe and any other thoughts that came up. The conversations took many twists and turns.

One time when we were on acid, I had some deep hallucinations. I saw Michael Jordan's face smiling at me in the middle of someone's lawn. Then we went to a stairwell to smoke some weed. I looked at the brick wall and saw the bricks turn into a wolf that emerged from the wall and barked at me.

During this trip I had an amazing thought. I shared this with Donovan. I remembered that I had watched this documentary about the human brain. They said we only use about 10% of our total brain.

My thoughts were that everything we see on acid—every single thing—is, in fact, always there. It's just that we are normally incapable of using the part of the brain that can see these things.

Donovan seemed to agree. It made a lot of sense to both of us. I asked Donovan, "So does this mean that acid... makes us smarter?" He looked at me inquisitively. I continued, "If we are able to use more of our brain than we are normally capable of, then we are smarter. There's no limit. If we do enough, we could get to a God-like state of consciousness. Like, we would be able to..." Donovan interrupted me, "Read people's minds?" He asked. I looked at him. We both burst into a laughing fit! We both knew that by completing my sentence, he had just proven me right. We were so smart!

Donovan had met a friend at school, and had started to hang out with him. The two of them became very close and then the three of us started to hang out together. His name was Pete. Pete was quite troubled, like us, but also a very cool guy.

Pete had a Ukrainian background. He was our age and he had brown hair. I was jealous of the fact that Pete was able to grow a full goatee. I wasn't ever able to grow much facial hair.

The three of us, Donovan, Pete and I, used to get very drunk and high together. Donovan and I were selling tons of weed. I met a new dealer who had better prices, and I started to sell ounces of weed to the house on the Rez. The same house that hooked me up to begin with. I was proud of my weed smoking. I even wrote poetry about it. One of my poems went like this:

(To the tune of Puff the Magic Dragon)

Puff the magic dragon, puffed a nice big toke
It was a very potent plant
And he couldn't help but choke (cough cough)

Puff the magic dragon
Finally exhaled

*He flicked the roach behind him
And it landed on his tail (ouch ouch!)*

*The cherry kept on burning
So, he jumped into the ocean blue
Then he called to some friends
"Won't you join me, too?"*

*They were all a bit afraid
But they all just went and joined him
Yeah, they all went in the water
Although they couldn't swim (yee haww)*

*Puff was so very cold
And he wished he had a sauna
But he said, I can't complain
For I got my marijuana (Oh yeah!)*

*All of Puff's friends
Finally lit up after
And then all night long
There was nothing but their laughter ("Ha ha ha Ho ho ho")*

*And if you listen closely
You'll hear him say to you
"Oh, my very magic friend
Won't you join me too?"*

I had other poems as well. Some of these were not as happy go lucky. Some of them were a bit more... well, disturbing. One such poem went like this:

*I find it amazing
How this great plant with green leaves
Can make me so fucked
So fucked beyond belief*

CHANGING THE STATUS QUO

You… fucking pigs
Always stealing my herb
I wanna stomp on your head
While it's still on the curb!
And don't fucking piss me off
'Cause I'm mentally disturbed!

I think you have fun arresting me
For you it's like a sport
And I know you get your jollies
By seeing me in court!

But you know me,
I don't hold a grudge
For if I did
I would've already
Killed you AND the judge!

And you say "To serve and protect"
You always arrest me for nothing
And think I'll forget
Dumb fucking pig
Don't you fucking know me yet?

I told you not to piss me off
But you still have that to learn
For one day I'll hold in my hands
A golden urn
And inside it will contain
Your dead corpse that I burned!

Now you're dead
And I still hear you telling me not to light that bowl
This time I'll just kill myself…
AND COME FOR YOUR SOUL!!!

As time went on and on, my drinking became worse and Sara was getting increasingly concerned.

Sara's big thing was to keep me occupied. She did a good job of finding things I would like. I began to carve once I found out I was native. I always wanted to, and somehow finding out I was native gave me permission to do so. Sara found a local native carver who was giving lessons at the local rec centre. He taught me how to sharpen my knife and told me this was the most important part.

I very much enjoyed carving native art. I really appreciated the guidance of a professional Aboriginal artist as well. I had lessons once a week for six weeks. Following the six weeks, Sara found me more carving lessons with another very well-known native artist.

The second set of lessons helped me even more because I learned not only carving techniques, but he also taught us about basic shapes that were used in native artwork. Shapes like split U designs and ovoids. This helped me overall because I really started to fine-tune my artwork. I had a sketch book that I drew in all the time.

Around this time, I took a trip to the lake that I spoke about earlier. During this trip, Uncle Mike was sawing up a cedar tree that had been struck by lightning in a recent storm. He asked me if I wanted some of the wood for carving. I very gratefully accepted the wood.

Shortly after I returned home from this trip is when I was enrolled in the second set of carving lessons. I brought this wood with me and told the instructor I wanted to carve a small totem pole to give to my uncle. He assisted me with this.

Carvings are meant to tell a story. I decided to tell the story of how I got this wood. There's a story in my culture of the Thunderbird. The Thunderbird is a creature much larger than an eagle who feeds on Killer Whales.

The story goes that this bird can shoot lightning bolts from his eyes. When there is a storm with thunder and lightning, a Thunderbird is feeding. He swoops down to the ocean, catches a whale and flies off. To kill his prey, the Thunderbird drops it from the sky. It is said, that the thunder we hear is in fact an Orca whale landing on the ground and then the Thunderbird shoots lightning from his eyes.

So, when I carved this totem pole from the cedar that I was given, I placed a Thunderbird at the very top. He was perched on top of an Orca. In my culture the Orca is known as "The Wolf of The Sea." It is said that the wolf transformed many years ago. This explains why the two animals have so many similar behaviours. So, below the Orca, I placed a Wolf.

On my next trip to the lake, I brought this totem pole as a gift to my Aunt and Uncle. They were thrilled. It meant so much to them. It meant just as much to me. Carving made me feel as though I was doing what I was destined for. I always knew I was not destined to be a delinquent, drinking and partying all the time.

When I carved, I felt I had found my true calling. It felt right to me. It calmed me and I thoroughly enjoyed working with the wood, shaping it into what it was meant to be. It didn't matter what it started as, I could shape it into whatever I imagined. Anything was possible.

I often thought, "What if I could shape myself into the person I wanted to be, just like I do with the wood. Perhaps this is also possible, and perhaps there is also no limit. Perhaps I can be whoever I want to be." I also carved a Sun Mask with wood from the same tree and I brought this with me as well.

These classes and activities kept me doing positive things some of the time, and I'm sure it was Sara's goal to keep me on the straight and narrow. In the end, though, there was no activity I enjoyed more than getting wasted. It didn't help that I was at that age when pretty much everyone I knew was getting drunk and high in their free time.

One night when I came home, I was extremely drunk. My brother got very upset with me when I swore at Sara. I started swearing at him as well. I have never seen him that angry. He dragged me across the street to the soccer field. He started pushing me around and screaming at me. I told him to get lost. I eventually made it back into the house and went to bed.

The next day, my brother took me for a car ride. I asked where we were going. "You'll see." He said. We ended up on skid row in downtown Vancouver. He wanted me to take a close look at my surroundings. He was trying to show me where I would end up if I continued the path I was on.

I looked out the window. I saw two people sitting on the sidewalk, one helping the other get a vein for a needle. Further down, I saw a very large female squatting with her jeans around her ankles and a big log of shit hanging from her ass. I watched as paramedics attempted to revive a man who apparently had overdosed. There was garbage everywhere, all over the streets. People were openly using needles and drinking bottles of wine.

My brother was attempting to discourage me from drinking and using drugs. But as I looked through the car window, I was fascinated. My first thought was, "Wow! What bus will bring me to this place?" It completely had the opposite affect than what he intended. I found all of this very glamorous. I wanted to come back here, without my brother, ASAP.

My drinking was getting much, much worse. I had definitely lost any control I thought I had. There were nights I came home drunk and the need for more was so intense that I drank mouthwash and vanilla extract. I was quite hopeless. Sara recognized this. I had given up on myself and was perfectly content with being an alcoholic. Thankfully, Sara would not give up on me, even after all I put her through. She couldn't give up on me. Not now when I needed her the most.

CHAPTER SEVEN

IT SEEMED THAT SARA WAS FIGHTING an uphill battle with me. She was determined for me to have a better life. She approached me one day and said that she had found a treatment centre for me to attend. She said it was six weeks long, and it was an aboriginal treatment program that focused on traditional healing while still incorporating the 12 steps of recovery. Sara said that I would have the chance to attend the sweat lodge, work on native art, and meet lots of great people, including some native elders. She did finally convince me to go, even though I didn't think I would get anything out of it.

It was a bit scary to think I would be going to treatment again. I feared failure, and at the same time, I was terrified of success. You see, being successful in recovery meant never drinking or using again… ever. All the slogans and catch phrases told me it wasn't that hard. The walls of the 12 Step meetings were lined with these phrases such as "Easy Does It" and "One Day at A Time." I always thought, "Yeah, one day at a time forever!"

I talked to Donovan and Pete, and I told them I was leaving soon. They wished me luck, and said they would see me when I returned. I packed my bag. I looked around my room. I had not spoken to my dad for a while, but I spoke to him on this evening. "Here we go," I said. I heard him say,

"You're making the right choice, son." I wasn't sure if I was. I didn't really know if I was ready for whatever would come my way.

I didn't know exactly what to expect. I was nervous, but this time, I was more willing to go through with it. It was my choice to go there. I wasn't facing the choice of treatment or jail. I really wanted to be a better person. I didn't like how alcohol made me act. Living with Sara and my brother my whole life, I knew that life was what you make it. I knew that a good life was possible, and living the life of an addict or street person was not how I was raised. I wanted a good life and I was willing to do whatever it took to get there.

The drive to Treatment was long. My brother drove me. We were living in North Vancouver, BC, and Treatment was in Creston, BC. The drive, non-stop, is about eight and a half hours, but of course, there were bathroom breaks, etc., so it took us about eleven hours.

I was greeted warmly by the staff at the Treatment Centre. A native elder was the first to approach me. He looked frail, but he had a great big smile that was contagious. His dark grey hair was tied in a ponytail that reached his lower back. He came and shook my hand. He grasped my right hand with his cold, wrinkled right hand, and at the same time, he put his left hand on my right shoulder. "Ernie," he said, introducing himself. I felt his grip get a bit stronger as he smiled and said, "Cold hands, warm heart."

Ernie's sincerity was obvious. I could tell that he truly did have a "warm heart." In just a moment, he made me feel safe and accepted. Next, there was a native lady who introduced herself. She smiled at me warmly. "I'm Mary. I'm so glad you've chosen to walk the Red Road." Mary walked up to me and wrapped her arms around me. She held me tight for a moment. She pushed her wrinkled cheek against mine and whispered in my ear, "Sorry dear, I don't shake hands."

The sincere, heartfelt greetings and the amount of love shown to me by complete strangers was overwhelming. In the first week, I went through a ton of emotions. It was very difficult to stay focused at times, and I was easily angered.

I wondered if there was some other motive that made everyone so kind. Like, maybe they received a ton of money to keep the Treatment Centre open, so they needed to make sure everyone gave it a good review or something. Clearly, my addiction was trying to find reasons for me to bolt.

I attended some 12 Step meetings and group sessions in which I had a chance to talk. One time, when I spoke, I shared the fact that I had some skepticism. I told the group that, although it was nice to see that everyone was very welcoming and everyone was super nice, I was still trying to figure out why.

Ernie looked up. He said, "I'm not sure I know what you mean." I said, "Ernie, you were so welcoming when I arrived. And Mary acted as though she loved me. I feel like if you really knew me then you wouldn't love me. YOU DON'T KNOW ME!!!"

I stopped for a moment to control myself. I took a deep breath and continued, trying hard to hold back my tears. I looked at Ernie and said softly, "Like, you don't even know me, but you seem like you sincerely want to help me. I just want to know why." Ernie sat in silence for a moment before raising his head to look at me. Sitting in the chair beside me, he put his hand on my shoulder and said, "Because somebody did it for me."

This just killed me. I could no longer control my tears. I had gotten used to a life of dishonesty. A life where I took things that didn't belong to me, lied, cheated, manipulated, and stole. Sara showed me love, but she had raised me. It was absolutely, completely overwhelming to me that these people who had only just met me seemed to genuinely care for me, even love me, and the reason they were doing all of this… their entire motivation… was that somebody had done it for them?

Wow! If this was real, and not some kind of trick, it was potentially the most beautiful thing I had ever witnessed in my short life. I wanted to believe. The thing was it made it even harder for me to relapse. I would be letting down all of these people, in addition to myself and my family. I figured I had better give this an honest effort.

In the coming weeks, I followed all the rules. I wrote in my journal, I completed the chores, I attended twelve step meetings. I also had the opportunity to smudge while I was there. We would burn sage in an abalone shell and fan it with an eagle feather. I thoroughly enjoyed this.

To this day, the smell of burning sage brings an immediate sense of calm to me. It doesn't matter what is happening in that moment. When I burn sage, the feeling is almost euphoric. It's very powerful medicine, and I am grateful to have learned this part of my culture.

I met one nice guy there who was half native, half black. He had already completed the treatment and had returned to work on himself a bit more. His name was Greg.

Greg and I became friends. Greg took me outside one day and showed me how he prayed. He brought me to a cedar tree. He had a tin with some tobacco in it. He started to speak to the tree, gently caressing its trunk. I tried really hard not to laugh. It was strange to me at first. I thought he was a bit nuts, to be honest. But I kept silent and tried to focus.

He said to me, "These are our traditions. If you speak to the trees, they will listen. I'm going to take a cedar bow to brush myself with, but first I need to ask the tree, and then I need to thank it." He opened the tin. He took a pinch of tobacco. He kneeled and sprinkled the tobacco. "Thank you for what you provide. This is my offering." With that, he broke off a small branch. He told me that it would be used in a ceremony.

I'm glad I kept quiet. I was able to see that Greg was not crazy, but rather, he was very spiritual. I remember thinking that I could learn a lot from Greg.

I had the chance to attend the sweat as well. This was quite the experience. We had to fast for 24 hours prior to entering the sweat. The elder led the sweat and asked us what we saw in there. We would describe it and he would tell us what Creator was saying to us through our visions. I did see things in there, however strict tradition forbids me from speaking of it outside the sweat.

I worked on my twelve steps while here as well. I really tried to make an honest effort at recovery. I felt it was the least I could do, after so many people had dedicated time and effort into getting me well.

I guess I would say that taking a moral inventory of myself was the hardest step I had to complete. It's not easy to admit our own part in things, especially when we are resentful at people. It's much easier to blame others for how we feel, but that is not how recovery works.

The whole point is to take ownership of the things we have done to cause harm, and do our very best to change our actions in the future. I quite enjoyed the process, but it wasn't until later on down the road that I truly began to understand it completely.

I had never been this far north, ever. One evening, it began to snow. It was mid-November now. We went to bed. When I awoke, I saw more snow than I had ever seen in my whole life. We had just received a dump of five feet of snow in one night!

We opened the front door. The cars had vanished. We all grabbed snow shovels and proceeded to dig out everybody's car from beneath the snow. At the back of the house, there was a balcony where we went to smoke, and beyond that were acres of field. There was no longer a five-foot drop to the ground from the balcony. The snow was straight, from floor of the balcony all the way across the field.

We all got our winter coats and gloves and went outside. We spent a few hours building tunnels and one giant snowman. After a while, the moisture soaked through my gloves. We were all very cold. It was time to go inside and make ourselves some coffee. I always poured a package of hot chocolate into my coffee to make a mocha. Later, we all gathered around the TV. It was Thursday night, and *North of 60* was on.

There was one elder there who was extremely tall and didn't speak any English. He spoke his native tongue. I heard him speak for the first time this Thursday night. I sat in the chair with my coffee and he was standing just behind me.

I looked up at him as *North of 60* played on the TV. He smiled. He looked at me, then nodded towards the TV and said with a chuckle, "Indian Soap Opera!" I laughed. "You do speak English." I said. He shrugged and sat down in the chair beside me. I looked at him. He just nodded towards the TV as if to say, "OK, let's watch now."

About four weeks into our stay, we had a group meeting. It was unscheduled so we were all a bit confused about what was going on. They called us all into a room and sat us down. There were three people missing. One of the staff members began to speak. "This path we're on is serious. All of us here are choosing the Red Road because we are tired of the old life."

We all looked at each other, still unsure about what was going on. He continued, "This is a matter of life and death. It's not a joke." Someone in the group spoke up, "What's going on?" The staff member told us that three of the people in the house had a pass for the weekend, and they all relapsed together. We were all shocked. We just could not believe it; it was unexpected.

Just then the three people who had relapsed walked in. A lady and two men. There was an extremely strong smell of alcohol that filled the room. The lady was crying. One of the men, shaking and holding back tears started, "I'm sorry. We screwed up guys. I'm so sorry." Apparently, they were all on a pass together and they started talking about how they could just have a few drinks. Somehow, they all convinced each other that it would be ok to just go for it.

They were driving a van that was borrowed from the Treatment Centre. The driver crashed into a guard rail and the van flipped over onto its side. He was charged with drunk driving and released with a court date. This completely changed the lives of all three of them. The driver caught a charge, and the other two were kicked out of treatment.

One of the staff members began to speak again. "We told you all when you started that the number of successful people is about 20%. There were 25 of you when you all started. That means that five from the original group will stay clean and sober permanently. This is the living proof of these odds."

The staff member then turned to the three people who had relapsed and asked if they had anything to add. The lady spoke up. She said, "I just want you guys all to know that in the moment, when you have those cravings, you tell yourself you want it. The fact is that I regretted it the moment the drink touched my lips. Nothing good comes from relapse. I hope that at least you guys will look at us and maybe it will convince you to stay on the Red Road. I wish I had."

The one person who hadn't said anything so far spoke up next. "I was driving. I could have killed us all, and I could have killed someone else. It's totally not worth it. We are not able to drink a little bit. That's why we're here. We are not capable of being responsible AND getting loaded. We have to choose one or the other."

I felt so sad for these three people. Their addictions had won. They didn't want to drink, but they did. This really hit home. I was especially affected by the statistics they gave us. Only 20% would be successful. Did I want it bad enough to be included in that 20%? I wasn't sure. I hoped that I did.

I had heard that in the native culture we had Guardian Spirits. These were spirit animals that were there to protect us. Everyone had a Guardian Spirit that was unique to them. I imagined that mine would be a wolf or perhaps an eagle.

I asked an elder at Treatment how I find out what my Guardian Spirit is. He said, "You don't find it. It finds you." "So mysterious," I thought. Whenever I spoke to a native, I could never get a simple answer. It always seemed like some cryptic riddle.

Near the end of treatment, I participated in a group meditation. We all lay on the floor and the lights were turned off. We were asked to close our eyes and be still. A meditation tape was played for us. It began with a man speaking softly. He said that we should begin with a focus on our breathing.

Next, the voice asked us to use our mind to look around. We should look around this place. What was around us? What kinds of smells were there? We were asked to start walking and continue to see and feel everything there was around us.

I was in the middle of a forest. It must have been early fall, because there were orange and red leaves on the ground. I could smell the dying leaves and that musty fall smell was in the air. A warm breeze blew across my face.

We were asked to continue our journey, but now we should travel to a place where we felt most safe and most happy in our lives. Who was there? What were we doing? What was around us? I found myself at my Aunt and Uncle's lake where I spent so many summers, back in the young and carefree days.

I was learning to dive using an inner tube again. The inner tube was sideways, and I was on top of it. My aunt was rolling me until I dove into the water. My fingers touched the water first, then I felt the water on top of my head. As I plunged beneath the water's surface, my legs started to kick, but they moved up and down simultaneously. My legs remained straight all the way to my toes and I was kicking from my hips.

After that, the magic happened. My legs transformed into a giant tail and I, myself, transformed into an Orca whale. I immediately understood that the Orca was my Guardian Spirit! Just as the elder said, he found me, not the other way around. This experience brought me much joy. I felt as though I was truly gaining something from being here.

I completed the six weeks there. I really had a lot of respect for the people that were there. I was very grateful for the opportunity. I felt as if I had the tools necessary to go out into the real world and stay clean and sober. It was time to go home now. "I got this." I said, to myself.

CHAPTER EIGHT

I RETURNED HOME TO SARA. I had Christmas with Sara and my brother. It was quite nice. They were happy to see me sober finally. I behaved myself all through the holidays and even into the New Year. I met up with Donovan and Pete once I returned to school.

I told them I was clean and sober and that I wouldn't be drinking or using weed. They respected that, although they questioned the weed smoking as we all saw that as harmless. Still, they hung out with me and respected the fact that I wasn't using anymore.

I guess that lasted about three weeks. I decided, on my own, that it would be alright to smoke weed, so long as I stayed sober from alcohol and other drugs. Besides, there were customers still wanting me to sell them weed. There was money to be made, and if I was going to sell weed, I may as well smoke it, too.

I found a little spot in the forest close to my house, where I thought would be a great place to dig a hole and hide my weed and cash, as well as my scales and so forth. I made a wooden chest in shop at school. I dug a hole big enough to accommodate the chest and placed it in there. It was off the beaten path a bit, which I thought would be less noticeable. I covered the top with leaves and dirt.

One day, I brought Donovan and Pete to my spot and we pulled out some weed, and my bong and we all got high in the forest. As we sat on a log, I asked them what was new since I left. They looked at each other as though they had something to tell me. "What?" I asked.

Donovan said, "Well… we started experimenting when you were gone." I said, "Experimenting with what?" Pete looked at me and said, "H." "H?" I asked. "What is H?" Donovan said, "You know… H." I looked at them both and asked, "heroin?" "SHHHHH!" hushed Pete. "We don't say the word like that." said Donovan.

I looked at them both. I said, "I'm not sure about this, you guys. That sounds pretty scary." Pete said, "It is, it is, if you're not smart. But we're smart. We are not junkies. We just like to indulge. We keep it in check." I had to ask, "How exactly do you keep… H… in check?" Donovan explained it to me. "We shoot up once, then wait until the track marks go away. We're not allowed to shoot up again until there's no more track marks. Then we won't be dependent on it. We won't be junkies."

"Well I guess that sounds logical, actually." I said. "I'm not ready to try that yet. I think I'm going to stick to my weed smoking." They both agreed. I never felt any pressure from them at all to partake in this. The only thing they did say was that heroin was "so fucking good." They told me it was the most incredible feeling ever. It's like, no matter what is happening in your life, or even around you at that moment, it didn't matter to you because you were in a state of complete euphoria.

This description made me think about my experience at treatment. I felt that same euphoria from smudging. It made me think about my choices in life. I could choose to walk the Red Road, or I could choose a life of addiction.

I wanted to walk the Red Road, I really did. It's just that my cravings for certain things such as alcohol and other drugs were so intense that it seemed impossible.

I limited my drug use to weed for a while and even managed to stay away from the alcohol. I was really determined to be successful and I truly believed that I could live a life free of alcohol and other drugs. In the 12 Step programs they called this the "Marijuana Maintenance Program."

It was suggested to me that this wouldn't last and that I should change the people I associated with, otherwise I would surely relapse. The old timers in the 12 Step meetings would say, "If you hang out in a barber shop long enough, sooner or later you're gonna get a haircut."

I didn't want to believe this. I didn't want to change my friends. I truly loved them. We were very close and we had shared our deepest darkest secrets with each other, especially Donovan and I. We were not just aquatinted with each other. We were best friends. For the first time in my life I felt that someone actually understood me and cared about who I was.

As much as I tried to stay sober my way, my alcoholism finally won. One day, I just decided I'd had enough of being sober all the time. I had been having some intense cravings. The day I drank, I had a good excuse, or so I thought.

I was sitting at home, having cravings. I told myself I absolutely would not give in to these cravings. I would definitely be successful at maintaining my sobriety. Then something happened that made it impossible for me not to drink; it snowed.

You may be wondering how a snowfall makes it impossible to stay sober. Allow me to explain. It doesn't snow much in North Vancouver. When it does, it's a big deal. I was sitting at home, fighting cravings and it began to snow, and I had the thought that if I didn't drink at that moment, I may very well stay sober forever, and if I did that, I would never, ever have a chance to drink a beer, by myself, in the snow; Never. I told myself I could quit again tomorrow but this chance would never come again.

I allowed myself to drink a beer, by myself, in the snow. That beer turned into several more that night, and from there, I was back to drinking regularly. My addiction tricked me into falling back to my old ways.

One day I went out with Donovan and we got drunk. I met him downtown and we went to smoke some weed. He had with him a big travel mug. He gave me a sip.

"Holy shit!" I said. "What is that?" "It's a Paralyzer," he replied. While I was away at treatment, Donovan had entered bartending school. We had both turned 19 recently, so he was of legal age and he decided this is what he wanted to do.

We drank the Paralyzer, and then I went with Donovan to find some heroin. Once he had scored, we went to a stairwell that led to a parkade and I watched him shoot up. That would be the first of many times I watched him shoot up.

Donovan's parents were concerned about his drug use. By this time, we had both finished grade 12 through the alternative school, and Donovan did a few of his last courses through correspondence, a program where you do some of the work at home. It was obvious to his parents that he was on hard drugs. The days of waiting until the track marks disappeared did not last long at all. Donovan and Pete were now daily heroin users.

Donovan's mom and stepdad gave him an ultimatum. They said he could go to live with his dad in Jamaica for a couple of months and return clean and sober to their home, or they would have to kick him out. He agreed, and he was on the next flight to Jamaica.

Around this time, I met a girl that we knew from hanging out in West Vancouver. Her name was Jen. Jen smoked a lot of weed but didn't have any issues with alcohol or other drugs. Jen and I started dating. I was at the point where I wanted to begin working. Jen worked at Walmart and said that I should apply.

I went for an interview and they hired me as a part-time sales associate for their toy department. A few days prior to the interview, I had gotten absolutely wasted and fallen on my face. The interviewer asked how I got the scrapes on my face. I said, "I was playing hockey and I got hit hard and fell onto the cement." He said, "Oh wow, I love hockey, too. Do you play on a team?" I told him that I did not belong to a team; I just played once in a while at school playgrounds and stuff.

Donovan returned from Jamaica about six weeks later. I'm not sure exactly what the whole story was with his dad, but he said his dad had given him some cash to return with and had bought him a plane ticket home. He got to the airport in Vancouver and called his mom and stepdad. He said, "I'm in Vancouver at the airport." His stepdad said, "That's great, you can stay there." And he hung up.

Donovan explained to me that it was at that moment he decided to say, "Fuck it!" He had really intended to stay clean. He wanted a better life. This rejection was too much for him. He went straight downtown and bought heroin. He called me and said he was homeless now.

I tried to help Donovan any way I could. I brought him money when I could, and I met him downtown and brought weed to smoke with him. I still hung out with Donovan and Pete. They took turns going into the various washrooms downtown to shoot up. I just hung out with them and tried to support them however I could.

Working at Walmart, I had a bit of money, and it was time to move out on my own. Since I was a permanent ward of the court, the Ministry of Children and Family Development helped me with the transition. I was placed in a basement suite apartment, and my rent there was partially subsidized by the Ministry.

There was a social worker who came by once a week and brought me grocery shopping. She helped me make a budget and helped me choose what type of food to buy. She also left me with about half a pack of smokes each week. They were menthol, but whatever, I took what I could get.

I was only in that house about two months. I had a couple of great parties there. One time, Donovan called me up and told me he was coming over with a gift. I told him I was just making spaghetti and meat sauce. He said, "No, no don't eat." But I was starving, so I ate anyway. I had a hard time telling if the meat was cooked. I'm colour-blind so I can't tell when it's pink and when it's brown. I just cooked it as long as I thought it should take.

When Donovan arrived, he had 14 grams of mushrooms. He said, we would eat seven grams each. He had four chocolate bars, too, to help with the taste. We both ate seven grams of shrooms, then I lit up a big fatty, and then we sat and chilled and waited for the shrooms to kick in.

After about 45 minutes, I started to feel a bit nauseated. I got up and went to the washroom. I barely made it to the toilet in time to puke. I saw all the spaghetti I had consumed earlier. I was on my hands and knees holding onto the toilet now, dry heaving.

I heard Donovan call out, "Are you ok?" I grunted "Siiiick!!!" I looked up at the door of the washroom. It started waving like it was watery. Then suddenly, the door and walls moved in all the way up to my face, then returned to their original position.

I tried to crawl towards the exit. As I crawled, I noticed my hands were wet and I couldn't figure out why. Then I realized. The linoleum had liquified. Every single time I put my hands down, the linoleum splashed. It had completely changed to a liquid state. I hoped there were no "deep spots," otherwise I might drown in this strange "liquid linoleum."

I eventually made it back to my feet and to the living room where I saw Donovan sitting on the couch. He looked at me and asked, "Are you ok?" I told him I was worried about the ground beef in my spaghetti. "What if it was pink and now, I have salmonella?" I asked.

He said, "Dude, I told you not to eat!" I said, "Do you think I'm poisoned from raw beef?" He replied, "I don't know. It's probably the shrooms. Yeah, it's gotta be the shrooms. I hope it's the shrooms." He said, "Tell you what, I've got a good solution for you. I brought the ENTIRE box set of Pink Floyd."

I said, "Ok… " And Donovan said, "Trust me. Here, have a cigarette, one of mine, not that menthol shit." So he handed me a smoke and told me to sit on the couch. Donovan went and grabbed the first album and put it in my CD player. Then he lit his own cigarette, brought over two ashtrays, and turned out the lights.

Donovan told me to sit and relax. He said, "Feel the music. Floyd is God." I began to feel very relaxed. I wasn't nauseous anymore. Donovan had some pre-rolled joints in his cigarette pack. He pulled one out and we smoked it. Then we had an "after-session" cigarette. That's what we called the smoke we had after we smoked weed. We sat in the dark, smoking weed and cigarettes, occasionally changing the CDs and enjoying Floyd for hours.

Quite shortly after moving into this house, my social worker helped me to find another, more permanent place to rent. The place I ended up choosing wasn't the best, but I could afford it and it would have to do. It was $350/month and for that I got a room in the basement of a house. I had to share the kitchen and bathroom.

I was happy to have my own place, even if it was a room in a basement. The owner of the house was a lady who had two teenage kids, a boy and a girl. They also had a female German Shepherd. I came and left as I wished, and I felt free.

That Christmas, Sara bought me a toaster oven and a microwave. Before that she had taken me out shopping and had bought me a coffee maker and an electric kettle, so now I had everything I needed in my little room in the basement.

I slept on a mattress on the floor. I went to a garage sale one time and found an old dresser. This is where I kept my clothes, and my toaster oven and coffee pot sat on top of this. I had an old bookcase where I kept my non-perishable food like coffee, sugar, and canned food. Looking back, it was pretty rough, but at that time I was happy as could be.

I continued working at Walmart and I continued to date Jen. I also had another friend named Mike who had recently moved out of his mom's house. Like me, he couldn't afford much so he was renting a room in a house where everyone rented a room and the bathroom and kitchen were shared. I often hung out here and we drank with all the tenants. Jen and I hung out at this house almost every weekend. It was strange for me because it was the house right beside the house I grew up in. I had sat in there before, and watched cartoons in the morning before getting a ride to school with Sara's friend.

Donovan introduced me to Heavy Metal. He was really big into Metallica, Korn, White Zombie, and many others. One time he thought it would be a great idea to take me to a Heavy Metal concert. He bought us two tickets to Pantera and White Zombie.

I got a bit nervous when he explained the "mosh pit." Basically, it's general admission at the floor level. Everyone stands up and it's just one massive crowd. When they get to the really hard songs, everyone would mosh. Moshing is when people head bang. Sometimes people would just start throwing punches and elbows. If you fall in the mosh pit it's bad news. You'll basically get trampled to death. I asked Donovan what I do if someone starts punching me. His reply was simple. "Just hit 'em back!"

We went to the concert. Of course, we took a ton of acid before we left, and obviously, we smoked a ton of weed, before and during the concert. It went ok in the beginning. I actually enjoyed the mosh pit. People were cool. We were just jumping up and down, rocking out to the tunes. Occasionally I would meet Donovan back in the seated area. We had to climb over the little wall to where the seats were. We would sit there, and smoke weed, maybe have a cigarette and then go back and mosh a bit more.

On one of these breaks, we were sitting there smoking a fat joint. The acid was really kicking in, too. Suddenly I saw this man climb onto the wall that separated the floor area from the seated area. He stood on top of the wall for a moment. He looked dazed.

The man was wearing a white t-shirt, only there wasn't much white showing anymore. The shirt was completely soaked in blood. Looking more closely I noticed that his hair and face were also covered in blood. He swayed back and forth a bit on top of the wall before spinning in mid-air and falling face down on some seats.

The man lay still briefly, and then climbed to his feet. Standing in front of us, the man swayed again, then began to cough. He leaned over, still coughing and placed his palms on his thighs with his face towards the floor. He coughed and coughed and then the coughing stopped.

He looked as though he was attempting to breathe. Just then, I noticed something rather disturbing. I saw that there was a massive blood clot, about the size of a baseball, hanging from the man's mouth, still attached, I assume, from a string of blood deep in his throat.

This blood clot slowly moved towards the ground. Then the man stood up straight, spun around and landed face up this time over the seats. His eyes were open. He did not move. I looked at Donovan. "What should we do?" I asked. Donovan replied, "I'm gonna poke him!"

Donovan walked up to the man slowly. He leaned over him, then reached out his index finger and poked the man's shoulder. There was no reaction of any kind. Just then another man ran up to us. He had a bottle of beer in one hand, and a joint in the other.

"YOU CAN'T HELP HIM!!!" The man yelled. We looked at him, both of us a bit stunned. He continued, "THAT MAN IS DEAD!!! I HAVE SEEN THIS A THOUSAND TIMES!!! DEAD DEAD DEEEEAAAD!!!" Then the man took a swig of his beer, and handed me the joint, and said, "Have a toke, brother!" And I did.

There was a security guard that was passing by a few moments later. I managed to get his attention. I brought him over to see the man. The security guard reached out his left hand and felt for a pulse on the man's neck. "He's dead, I'll get him later." He said, very casually. Donovan and I decided it was a good time to go and hit the mosh pit again.

Life was pretty good, and I was pretty happy. I had my two best friends and my girlfriend. I went for Sunday dinner every week at Sara's. I even had a job at Walmart that gave me the sense of being a responsible adult, fending for myself in the world. I was always in need of money, though, and Sara was a huge help in this regard.

Every week when I went for Sunday dinner, I would ask for a little cash. I would tell Sara that I needed smokes. This I found was the best excuse because Sara smoked, and she was quite sympathetic when I told her I didn't have enough to last me the week.

Every week when I asked for money, Sara would get upset with me at first. She would give me a short lecture on how I needed to budget my money better. In the end though, she would always say "Right then, how much will you need? Will twenty do?

Every week I felt guilty, and the butterflies would turn in my gut. I would usually reply with, "Well if you could do forty, it would sure help a lot." Sara would always blurt out, "WHAT? You're going to bankrupt me, child!" But then she would almost always do it.

I hated using Sara like this. I loved her and she very obviously loved me more than words could say. I knew she didn't have a lot of money. I knew that giving me money every week made life harder for her. But I needed to drink, smoke weed, and smoke cigarettes, and I just didn't have enough money to support these habits.

My girlfriend Jen also supported my habits quite a bit. She always had money. She was from a wealthy home in West Vancouver. Jen was in University, and she was working towards being a chartered accountant. Jen was very smart and fortunately for her, she had parents who could afford to put her through post-secondary school.

Jen was not a drinker. She really hated how drunk I got and constantly asked me to drink in moderation. She would even ask me how much I had to drink when she wasn't even with me. I guess she worried about me.

I remember that I used to buy the big bottles of beer that were only five dollars each. They were 1.5 litre bottles, and they were 7% alcohol. I thought I was so smart when I figured out that I could truthfully tell Jen that I only had three bottles of beer! Technically, this was true.

I was now 20 years old. I was living the life, so to speak. I was happy to have my own place, have a job, I was having regular sex—life was pretty good. I thought I was doing pretty well for a young man. I guess "well" is a relative term. So many different definitions, depending on your perception. I was about to turn 21. I would be of legal age in America, and boy, did Jen and Donovan have a gift lined up for me.

CHAPTER NINE

WHEN I TURNED 21, DONOVAN AND JEN had a surprise for me. They had found tickets to a concert. The concert was Rob Zombie and Korn. Donovan, being the metal head that he was, had planned this. He wanted to take me so badly. And now that I was 21 years old, I could legally buy us alcohol while we were there.

The concert also involved a road trip. It was at the Tacoma Dome in Seattle, south of the border. We piled into Jen's car and took off. Jen had already booked the hotel and Donovan had already bought our tickets. Jen didn't want to attend the concert, so we only had the two tickets, Donovan's and mine.

We left early in the morning, and when we got there, we checked into the hotel. Donovan and I stopped at the local gas station and I bought six of those 1.5 litre bottles of beer, three for each of us. By the time we finished one bottle each, Donovan and I had begun to mosh in the hotel room. He wanted to prepare for the concert.

We each finished a second bottle quickly and kept moshing. By the time we each finished our third bottle we had smashed a lamp and damaged a wall or two. Jen was getting extremely upset with us. We decided at some point that we needed to leave for the concert. Actually, I think Jen decided for us as she didn't want us at the hotel with her! Our hotel was only three blocks from the Tacoma Dome, but somehow in that short distance, trouble found us.

We stopped at a fast food restaurant for a bite to eat, since we were early. I was listening to heavy metal on Donovan's Discman. I was shouting the lyrics while I waited in line. There are parts of this time period missing from my memory, but what I remember next is looking out of the back seat of a police car, and seeing Donovan talking with a female officer.

The officer came back to her cruiser and opened the back door to speak with me. I started talking rapidly, but she looked right at me and said, "Shut up!" I said, "I'm shutting up." She said, "You have a really good friend out there." I said, "Oh, he's my best friend, he's amazing…" "SHUT UP!" She repeated, and I said, again "I'm shutting up!" The officer went on to say that Donovan was a very good friend indeed because he had somehow convinced her that she should cut me some slack and let me go to the concert.

I could not believe it. She pointed at the Tacoma Dome and said, "It's right there. That's where you are going. Go straight there and don't stop anywhere else and do not get in trouble between here and there… got it?" "Got it," I said. Then she said, "Happy birthday young man." I thanked her as she removed my handcuffs.

We got to the concert without further incident. Korn opened for Rob Zombie. Our seats were second level. We were at the edge of the second level, and there was about a ten foot drop down to where the floor was. I felt that we could go down there and mosh if we wanted to and I noticed others had the same idea.

I spoke to a guy that looked like he wanted to jump down there. I said, "Go for it man!" He stood on the edge of the wall. He crouched down, I imagine so that he could hold on and hang before dropping to the floor. I looked at him and yelled "JUMP!" Then I looked at the crowd and motioned for them all to join me in my chant.

I lead the chant and the crowd chimed in "JUMP, JUMP, JUMP!" I saw the guy gather his courage and then suddenly he threw his legs over the railing, hung on with one hand and then dropped to the floor. I saw him run through the crowd and disappear. I couldn't believe that I had inspired all of this. There was a certain power in the fact that I had asked something of the crowd, and they had all obeyed me.

Then the attention turned to me. A guy looked at me, slapped me on the shoulder and said, "OK buddy! Your turn!" I was a bit shocked and a little nervous, but the alcohol in my system helped in that regard. I said, "Oh… ok, I can go… I guess." The guy encouraged me saying "You can do it, bud!"

I looked at him and said, "Yeah!" And he repeated back to me, but much louder, "YEAH!" I screamed it out, "YEAAAHHH!!!" Then I climbed onto the wall. I turned to the crowd and yelled "Come on then, I need some encouragement!" I motioned with my hands for them to shout and I mouthed the word, "Jump," over and over again.

Soon the whole crowd within close proximity, perhaps a hundred people were all looking at me and shouting that single word of encouragement, "JUMP! JUMP! JUMP!!!" With the motivating factors of the crowd, my ego, a little stupidity, and a shit ton of alcohol, I took the plunge.

I threw my feet over the railing like the last fellow. I attempted, somewhat successfully to hang by one hand and drop, however my hand slipped, and it was a bit of a hard landing as I fell on my side. I scrambled to my feet. I looked up and saw my fans cheering. I felt like a hero.

Suddenly I saw my fans looking worried and they were pointing. I looked back and saw two bouncers running my way. I bolted towards the mosh pit. I squeezed between as many people as I could and managed to get away. Here I was, 21, in America, and moshing! This was awesome!

At the last concert, Donovan had taught me how to crowd surf. Basically, you just turn to someone and say "I'm going up." And then you lift your foot off the ground and the person will give you a boost. You fall onto the crowd and everyone raises their hands and pushes you along. The people are packed so closely together that it doesn't take a lot of effort to push you along. I was in the mood to crowd surf tonight.

I turned to the guy beside me, and said, "HEY! I'm going up, man!" He obliged and gave me a boost. Across the top of the crowd I went, my body being passed along from hand to hand. What I didn't know was how the ride ended.

At some point you reached the end of the crowd. There's a metal fence between the crowd and the stage. When you reach the end of the crowd there are bouncers waiting. They grabbed my shirt and very forcefully threw me to the cement. Once I got to my feet, they hurried me along, and back into the mosh pit I went.

After crowd surfing twice, I went for a third time. The same routine at the end, I got slammed to the cement floor between the fence and the stage. This time though, when I tried to go back into the mosh pit, I saw bouncers approaching me. They tried to grab me, and I ran for it.

I ran and ran, not knowing exactly where I was going to go. I happened to look up and noticed I was close to the wall that I had jumped off. My "fans" were reaching down, yelling at me to jump up and grab their hands. I ran towards them as fast as I could and ran up the wall. I reached up and everyone scrambled to pull me up, some holding onto my arms, others tugging on my shirt.

They got me over the wall. I stood up and looked back towards the floor. I saw the bouncers shaking their fists at me. My fans were cheering. I raised my arms in celebration and everyone was hugging me and slapping my back.

With my arms still raised, I started to walk over empty seats. I stepped on the back of one of the seats and it was wet, probably with spilled beer. My foot slipped and I fell hard, face first into the back of the seat in front of me.

My forehead hit the seat pretty hard, but I didn't stop for a second. I bounced right back to my feet and started moshing right where I was. I was singing along, head banging the whole time. A guy approached me and said, "Dude you gotta take care of your head." I said, "Oh, I'm fine, man." He said, "No dude, your head is fucked up!"

I touched my forehead and looked at my hand. There was a lot of blood. I told everyone I was just fine. "No time to stop! There's moshing to be done!!! YEAAHHH!" I was approached by a security guard. He said I would have to go with him. I asked where we were going. He said, that we needed to fix up my forehead. "But I'm moshing!" I told him. He explained that it was not a choice, I had to go with him.

I reluctantly went with the security guard. We went to the first aid room. A medic was there waiting. At this point, I had a steady stream of blood pouring from my head. It was worse than I originally thought.

The medic treated my wound as much as possible, but told me that I would need stitches and strongly suggested that I attend the hospital. I told her, "There's no way! I'm from Canada! We don't pay thousands of dollars for stitches! I don't have money to attend an American hospital." "It's up to you," she said. "But one thing is certain, you cannot stay here." With that, I was escorted from the Tacoma Dome and told to return to my hotel.

I found myself outside, walking in the direction I thought my hotel was. The music from the concert began to fade as I got further away. Soon, I could not hear the music at all. In fact, the only sounds were my own thoughts and a constant ringing in my ears that came from the loudness of the concert.

I continued to walk… and walk… and walk. I began to wonder when I would reach the hotel. I looked around. I was on the interstate. I'm not exactly sure how long I had been walking, but I estimate that it was about two hours. I looked ahead and I thought I saw a sign or something that indicated to me that I may be close to some kind of business. I hoped I was correct because I really needed to figure out where I was and how I could find my hotel.

As luck would have it, the sign I saw was a business. It wasn't just any business either, it was a bar and it was open! I didn't have money though, so buying myself a drink was out of the question. At this point I just wanted to get back to the hotel and rest my head. I was exhausted.

I walked into the bar. There was a pay phone on the wall. I picked up the receiver. I knew the phone number of Jen's parents. I dialled zero and the operator came on. I asked to make a collect call. I called Jen's parents. Her mom answered the phone.

I said, "Oh hi, it's Allan. I just have a little head injury!" She was shocked. "Oh no!" She exclaimed. I said, "Oh, no I'm sorry. I didn't want to alarm you. It's a LITTLE head injury. I'm ok. But I was hoping you could tell me what hotel I'm staying at."

She asked where I was. I said, "Well… I'm in America… and… I had to walk… and now I'm at a place where I don't know where I am." Jen's mom exclaimed, "Oh my!" She continued, "Let me tell you the name of the hotel and the address." She told me and I wrote it down with a pen I borrowed from a waitress.

I thanked Jen's mom very much. I told her I had to go now. After I hung up, I went and asked the bartender if he knew the number of the taxi service and also the name and address of where I was. He told me. I called a taxi from the pay phone and they said, it would be 15 minutes. I went to wait outside.

I waited outside for quite a while. I was wondering where this taxi was. It began to rain. I was wearing only jeans and a blood-soaked t-shirt. The rain got harder and lightning flashed in the sky. It was a full-on thunderstorm. I stood there waiting for the taxi.

I must have been standing there at least half an hour when a very drunk girl came out of the bar to talk with me. She said, "I told my boyfriend… that if you were still out here in fifteen minutes, I was going to come and get you, and that was twenty minutes ago!"

I looked at her and said, "Well I'm just waiting for a taxi." She replied, "But I don't think it's coming. Let me buy you a drink!" I was ok with that. "Well… alright," I said. We went to a table inside where the girl's boyfriend and a few other people were drinking.

They asked me where I was trying to get to. I pulled out a wrinkled napkin from my pocket. This is what I had written on when I spoke to Jen's mom. "Apparently this is the name and address of the hotel I'm staying at." The guy beside me asked "What are you doing all the way over here?" "Well…" I began, "I was at the concert tonight, but when I bumped my head, I got kicked out, and I tried to walk to my hotel, but I think I'm going the wrong way."

The people at the table erupted in laughter. A guy looked at me and asked, "Are you kidding me, bro? Are you saying you walked here on foot from the Tacoma Dome?" "Yeah, why?" I asked. The guy told me, "You are at the opposite end of the city, bro! You know how far away you are from your hotel?" I replied "Well I'm not sure, I took an exit onto the interstate or highway or whatever you call it." "ON FOOT?" Asked the guy. "Yup!" I replied.

The girl looked at her boyfriend. "Buy this man another beer!" She demanded. "He deserves it!" I finished another beer with them, and they offered me a ride home. Of course, I accepted the ride. I figured I had done enough walking for one night.

Their pickup truck was full of people, but they let me sit on the girl's lap. It briefly occurred to me that I was sitting in the back seat with no seat belt in a truck that was being driven by a guy that was very intoxicated. "Whatever!" I thought. "At least I'm not walking!"

I got to the hotel and I thanked them very much. I made my way to our room. I banged on the door harder and harder because nobody was answering. "JEN!" I yelled from the hallway. The door eventually opened. I was greeted by an extremely angry girlfriend. "What's wrong with you?" I asked.

Well, Jen was pissed! She started yelling at me about how she had called every jail and hospital in town. "Where the hell were you?" "Well, I got kicked out of the concert, but then this really nice girl kept buying me drinks at the bar across town there."

My explanation seemed to make her angrier. "You were supposed to be at the concert with Donovan," she yelled. I looked at her and asked, "Have you not been listening? I said… they kicked me out of the concert and I…" Jen interrupted, "Yes you have been drinking with a fucking little whore at the bar!" "Hey!" I said. "Don't talk about her like that."

No matter how much I tried to explain, Jen just could not understand. She was still mad even after I told her what happened. Then she looked at me strangely. "Allan…" she began. "Yeeeeesss…," I replied. "Where… where are your shoes?" I looked at my feet and sure enough, I had no shoes. "You know… I'm not sure." To this day I have no idea what happened to my shoes that night.

We went to bed. It was late, maybe 2:00 am or so. We drove back to Vancouver the next day. Jen insisted I go to the clinic and have my head looked at. By this time, there was pus in it, and it was crusty around the edges. The doctor said it was too late for stitches, but he closed it with butterfly stitches.

This was not the first time my drinking had caused concern with Jen, and not the last. I puked almost every time I drank. Jen just wanted to have a few drinks and smoke a little weed and go home and have sex. I almost always ruined these plans.

Jen tried to limit my drinking. She told me that when we went out together, I needed to stop drinking after four drinks. She didn't see any reason to drink more than that. It always sounded ok. But once I started to drink, I needed more. I just couldn't deal with the fact that at some point I would run out of alcohol. I could not control the amount I drank, ever.

Jen was losing her patience. She tried to get us to do things together that would be so much fun, I wouldn't need to drink to enjoy myself. She paid for a road trip to San Francisco. We visited Alcatraz, the San Diego Zoo, Fisherman's Wharf, and we spent a day at Disneyland.

This trip was super fun. I didn't drink much. But when we returned, I made up for that. I tried very hard to control my drinking. Sometimes I managed to be ok while we were out, and then when she dropped me off, I would race to the bar before it closed so I could get more booze in me. My drinking was definitely out of control. If Jen thought she had seen the worst of it, she was dead wrong. I had only just begun.

CHAPTER TEN

AS MY DRINKING CONTINUED TO WORSEN, Jen's patience was wearing thin. Almost every weekend I got completely wasted, and Jen would need to take care of me. I was still hanging out with Donovan and Pete. Another favourite hangout of mine was the house on the Rez.

I began to spend more and more time on the Rez, especially when Jen was busy studying for exams. I enjoyed drinking there, even though at times it got a little rowdy.

The friend that I grew up with, Alex, lived here, and he had four siblings. I became good friends with his brother, Chuck. Chuck was about two years older than I. He usually maintained a thin black moustache, but like myself, he couldn't grow a goatee. The bottom of his chin always had a few scraggly hairs.

Chuck was a really nice guy, and I always got along well with him. One day Chuck approached me with a dinner plate. There was no food on it, though. Instead, there were five fat lines of cocaine. He said if I wanted, I could buy a line off him for just $5.

I had never done coke before. I was a bit nervous, but mostly excited. I jumped at the chance to snort a line. He showed me how to do it. He said, to put the straw in a nostril and just plug the other nostril. I leaned over and snorted up the line.

I'll never forget this. I felt the slight burn in my nostril and tasted the bitterness in my throat. I was in love! It felt amazing! I felt excitement rush through me. It felt like pure happiness entered my nose, and filled my entire mind, body, and soul. I felt like there had been something missing from my life, and it was cocaine.

I immediately wanted as much as I could get my hands on. This drug was better than sex, and I didn't like anything more than sex.

I licked my fingertip and ran it along the plate, then licked the residue off my fingers. I felt my lips and tongue go numb. I asked Chuck if he had more. He said he could let me do one more line for free, but not before him. We both did another line.

It wasn't long before we were all out. I lit up a fat joint and passed it around. I told Chuck that he must have more. He said that he didn't, but if I had money, he could get me some. I asked him how much it would cost. He said that he could get us a half gram for $40, or we could put in $40 each and get a gram.

I agreed to split a gram with him. I gave him my $40 and he said he would be back soon. Chuck returned, as promised, about half an hour later. His brother Alex said, "Get outta here with that shit! Don't do it out in the open. Go to your room if you're gonna do that garbage!"

I always had a lot of respect for my friend Alex. Although he was raised in a home where there was a lot of weed, and other drugs were quite easily available, he never used any drugs, not even weed. He didn't even smoke cigarettes.

Alex was captain of his basketball team, he enjoyed lacrosse, and he seemed to be living a very healthy and productive life, in spite of his surroundings. I got the sense that his mother Eleanor was extremely proud of him. I admired him very much, and it made me sad that I was doing things that upset him.

Chuck and I went into his room together. We opened the flap of coke and poured a little on the plate. He showed me how to chop up the coke and make lines.

After a while, there was a knock on the door. Chuck opened the door and his mom Eleanor was standing there. She said, "Ok let me in for a little bit." We let her in. She said, "How about you bust out a rail for me?"

We agreed to share a little with her. We all took turns doing lines. Occasionally, Eleanor would have to go to the living room when customers came for weed. After she made her sale, she would return for more lines.

Soon, we ran out of cocaine and we all wanted more, but I didn't have any more money. Another customer arrived and bought three grams of weed from Eleanor. She said, "Holy shit! I sold out of weed."

I was still selling weed to her all the time and I had about an ounce on me. She asked if she could buy a half ounce. I sold it to her. That was $120. They both looked at me as if to say, "Ok you have cash now." I asked how much we could get for $120.

We decided in the end that we should get another gram and some beer and cigarettes. We hit the Cold Beer and Wine store just before it closed at 11:00 pm. We bought a couple of two litre bottles of cider and a couple packs of cigarettes, and then I sent Chuck to get a gram of coke.

It took him an hour this time. He said his dealer had sold out and he had to wait a bit. Regardless, he returned as promised. I was happy to see a big pile of coke on the plate. We only chopped up a little at a time. We tried to conserve it as best we could.

Through the night, more customers came for weed. I ended up selling Eleanor another half-ounce, and then we used my $120 and she threw in $80 and we got an eight-ball, which is three and a half grams.

At 6:00 am I was out of cash, and out of cocaine. We had finished the cider hours ago. Chuck said, "Well I don't know about you, but I think I'm gonna try and get some sleep. There's a couch in the room downstairs if you wanna sleep here."

I was too wired to sleep. I decided to go home. I was planning on walking the hour that it would take to get home on foot, but when I left the house on the Rez, I realized the sun was up. The streets were busy with motorists on their way to work, and the first buses had already started to run. I caught a bus and went home.

When I got home, my landlady was getting ready for work. She saw me come in. "Late night?" she asked. "Yup, I was out with friends." She said, "Ok, well, have a good day."

So, from my very first experience with cocaine, I was unable to just do a couple of lines and leave it alone. The addict in me doesn't care what substance I'm doing, as long as there's an unlimited supply. More is better. Always. I had a favourite saying, "If it's worth doing, it's worth overdoing."

Donovan invited me to his house for a party with him and Pete and one other guy I didn't know. We were drinking and smoking weed, as usual; then Pete said, "Hey, let's order up." They made a phone call and a while later, someone showed up.

They had ordered a gram of coke. They said they could give me one line, but that was all because it was only shared with people who had put in cash. They chopped up a line for me and I rolled up a five dollar bill I had and used that to snort it. It was great. Donovan and Pete disappeared into the bedroom.

I sat by myself in the living room, wishing for another line. I began looking around on the glass table hoping that maybe I missed some the last time. I used my bank card to scrape up some of what I thought was remnants of cocaine.

Just then Pete walked in. "What are you doing?" he asked. I said, "I found a little more, so I'm just gonna do this line here." He looked at the table. "Those are breadcrumbs! Don't be a junkie, man!"

I stopped what I was doing. Pete left the living room. I really wanted another line. I unrolled the five dollar bill and a giant solid chunk of coke fell onto the table. My eyes became as wide as saucers! I started to chop it up.

Pete walked back into the living room. He yelled, "I told you, don't be a fucking junkie, man! Don't snort breadcrumbs, dude!" And with that he leaned over, took a deep breath and before I could stop him, he blew away my big fat line of coke!

I told him, "I found a big chunk in the bill! What the fuck?! That was cocaine man!" Pete looked at me, "Shit, I'm sorry, bro!" I was so disappointed. In fact, even now, I can feel the loss of that line and sometimes still wish I could go back in time and protect it from being wasted.

I told Donovan and Pete that I could get cocaine on the Rez, and that I had tried it already. Donovan said, "Dude, don't do coke on the Rez. That's definitely a bad idea. You'll end up being a crackhead."

I told Donovan that it was cool. I didn't have a problem, and the people I did it with, I had known all my life. In fact, he knew them as well because

I had introduced him when we bought those four ounces of weed, and we hung out there regularly. He said, "Listen, I know they're your friends and all that. I respect them too, I really do. They're great people… I just wouldn't be doing coke with them is all."

I did not take Donovan's advice. The next time I drank with Chuck, at some point during the night he said, with a chuckle, half mumbling, "The only thing that would make this night better is if we had some lines to do! Ho ho, just kidding!"

Of course, I laughed it off, but about 10 minutes later, I said, "You know, we could get some coke, but I don't have that much money. But we could probably just split a gram if you wanna do like forty each."

Chuck hesitated. "Hmmm, yeah I don't even know. I mean I do have forty, but I was supposed to pick up weed to make some sales." We sat in silence for a moment. Chuck looked up, "Do you mean you DO have forty?" I said, "Yeah I could throw in forty."

After about an hour of talking about it we both decided it was a great idea. I gave Chuck my $40 and he went up the road. He came back in half an hour, as usual. And so it began.

We retreated to Chuck's room immediately so as not to offend his brother. It wasn't long before Eleanor joined us. The gram lasted us about two hours. Then we sat there wishing for more.

I had just been paid, but because I didn't make much money at Walmart, my spending money for two weeks was $50, and I had spent it already. The only money I had was in my bank account, and it was for rent. Rent was due in two days, on the first of the month, and I would need the entire $350 that I had in my account.

As we sat there, wishing for more coke, I couldn't shake the thought that I had this money available to me in my bank account. I eventually decided that it would be pretty easy to sell a bit of weed and make up just $40. I figured I could take $40 from my $350 and still be ok.

The problem was that I didn't have weed to sell, to make up for the $40 I would take from the bank. This was a problem. I discussed my plans with Chuck. He had a great idea.

Chuck suggested that I could easily get some weed "fronted" to me. In other words, I could get, say, an ounce of weed given to me on loan from a dealer and that way I could sell $40 worth to pay back the money for my rent, and with the rest I would have enough profit to pay back the dealer and still have some profits.

This, I thought was a great idea. Of course, a lot of things sound like a great idea when you're drunk and high on cocaine. By the time we got to the bank machine, Chuck had convinced me that we may as well get a gram, rather than a half gram because he knew someone that would do a full gram for $70 and a half gram is $40. Again, it sounded like a great idea. Besides, it was only another $30.

We got the gram of coke and went back to the Rez. By the time the coke was almost finished, I had decided that if I was going to get an ounce fronted to me anyway and I was going to pay back the money I needed for rent, and have profit, and pay back the dealer, then I may as well use my future profit, from the weed that I might be able to get fronted to me, to buy coke right now.

The entire night went like this. I kept rationalizing things and kept getting more money from the bank machine. We finished the last gram of coke at 6:00 am. I was broke. I had no rent money. Worst of all, I had no way of getting more coke, and I would need to go home.

I began to walk home. I had no money for bus fare, and I felt edgy, so I decided to walk the hour to my house. I had a lot of thoughts on the way. I decided I would stay away from cocaine for a bit. The fear of not having rent started to sink in. I didn't have any dealers that would front me weed. That was a story I made up in my head. I really had no way of getting the rent.

To make matters worse, my heart was pounding, and my chest was hurting. I was sweating profusely. By the time I got home, I was afraid I was having a heart attack. I got a couple of hours of broken sleep and my chest felt a bit better.

My phone woke me up. It was Jen. She asked how my night was. I got butterflies in my stomach. I knew she wasn't going to be happy. I was thinking maybe I could not tell her. I decided to tell her, mostly because I knew she was one person that might be able to give me rent money.

I told her that I had made some bad decisions. I told her that I had a bit too much to drink, and I ended up doing cocaine with Chuck. She was silent for a moment. Then she said, "Cocaine? What the fuck?!" I said, "I know, I know, I was going to say no, but I don't know, I just did it." I had not told her about my previous experiences with cocaine.

Jen wanted to know how much I had used the night before. I said, "Well, that's a funny story." She said, "I'm sure it's hilarious!" I said, "Well Jen, the thing is, I used quite a bit of cocaine. In fact, I kind of… well… I spent my rent money and I'm a little bit scared that I'll get evicted."

The other end of the phone was silent. I said, "Jeeen?" Then I heard Jen laughing. She laughed, and she laughed a bit more. She said, "Hahaha, yeah, you're right. That shit is fucking hilarious!" She laughed more, and I laughed as well. She said she was on her way over.

When Jen arrived, she was not laughing at all. I tried to give her a hug, and she pushed me away. She asked, "How are you going to pay your rent?" I told her I wasn't sure. I asked her if there was any way she could maybe lend me the money. She was silent for a moment.

Jen pulled out a joint and lit it up. We smoked it together. She was very mad. She told me that it just so happened that she did have enough money to pay my rent. She said, that she had saved some money and she was planning on buying us a whole ounce of weed to share. She told me I had ruined her plans, but that she would give me the cash, so I wouldn't get evicted.

Jen was angrier than I had ever seen her before. I didn't know if she would get over it or not. She certainly was not ok with me using cocaine. She made me promise not to do it ever again. I promised her and I meant it. I couldn't afford to do cocaine. Not only financially, but also it took a toll on my health and it damaged me emotionally. I was done with this drug for good. Or so I thought.

CHAPTER ELEVEN

JEN CAME AROUND AFTER A FEW DAYS. She told me that she was worried about me using cocaine because it was super dangerous and highly addictive. I agreed. "It was a stupid mistake," I said. "It won't ever happen again."

One day, Jen told me that she had seen Donovan on the bus. Jen drove, but she had been to an event downtown with her girlfriend, and they took the bus because there's no parking downtown. Jen told me that Donovan was on heroin when she saw him.

I had been hanging with Donovan and Pete on and off. Donovan had found a place to live. It was like what Mike and I had, a room with a shared kitchen and shared bathroom. He lived there with his cat, Garfield.

I decided that I wanted to know what the big deal was with heroin. I told Donovan one day that I wanted to try it. I just wanted to know what they were going through. He agreed. We went and bought $20 worth and then we went down to a parkade where he liked to shoot up.

Donovan told me to roll up my sleeve. I did. He tied me off with his belt. He dumped half of what he bought into a spoon. Next, he squirted a little water in the spoon. He pulled out a cigarette from his pack and with his teeth, tore out part of the filter.

Next, Donovan rolled up the filter into a ball and placed it in the liquid. He asked me to hold the spoon. He lit the spoon with a lighter from the bottom with one hand and with the other hand he pushed the needle through the cigarette filter. He pushed the needle around the spoon, mixing everything in as it began to bubble from the heat of the flame.

Donovan put the lighter down. It was time to load the syringe. He held the stem with one hand and pulled back the plunger with the other. Once it was loaded, Donovan held the rig, needle side up, and looked at it. He flicked it with the nail of his index finger and pushed out a bit of liquid, to eliminate any air bubbles.

It was time now. He asked me to make a fist. Donovan took a couple of tries before he found a good vein. When he was in, I knew. He pulled back the plunger and I watched as my blood flowed into the rig. Then he began to push the dope into my arm. I felt it immediately. I asked him to stop. He said, "You gotta take it all. We don't share rigs and we certainly don't waste dope."

As Donovan pushed the remaining heroin into my arm, I felt light-headed. "Woah!" I exclaimed. He said, "Ok, my turn." He did his own and then it was time to go. We left the stairwell of the Parkade and began to walk down some back alleys.

As we walked, I started to feel extremely nauseous. I leaned over and puked. Then I puked again. And again. Donovan was ahead of me. I heard him say, "Allan!" He turned around and said, "Oh."

I pulled myself together. We entered a building. I told Donovan I didn't want to see people. I asked what this place was. He said, "Don't worry; they're cool here. We're getting some free juice and stuff."

I found out it was a drop-in centre for the homeless. I had some orange juice. I had to sit on the couch that was there. Then I had to get up and go to the washroom. I thought I would get sick again, but I didn't. I just put water in my hair and on my face.

When I exited the washroom, Donovan was talking to a staff member. The guy was asking Donovan if I was ok. He said I looked rough. Donovan said, "He's fine, bro. He's my best friend. He's not the junkie, I am." That was the first and last time I ever shot up. I'm glad it was a bad experience, because I had no desire to feel like that again. It scared me.

One day, Donovan and I decided to meet up downtown. I met him on Granville Street. He had to go to West Vancouver by bus to meet a friend of his. He was buying heroin. I caught the bus with him.

The bus was full and there were no seats. As we stood beside each other, hanging onto the handles on the metal bar above our heads he began to say something to me. I couldn't understand because he was mumbling. I said, "Speak clearly man! I don't understand what you're saying."

He picked up his left arm with his right hand. He said, "Mma.. mmmaa… mmma awwwm don't wwwoook." "You mean to say that your arm doesn't work?" I asked. "Yup," he replied. "Why not?" I asked. Somehow through his mumbling I was able to ascertain that he had been hit by a car downtown—a hit and run.

I asked why he would not go to the hospital. He said, "I did. Day gabe me T-T-T Teee t-t-t treeezz." I looked at him in question. I tried to understand. "Tee treez?" Donovan laughed. He repeated himself until I understood. I was finally able to get it. "T-3s? They gave you T-3s?" "Uh-huh." He replied. "Ok. So, you went to the hospital, told them you were hit by a car, and that your arm doesn't work, and they just gave you T-3s, and then what?"

Donovan looked at me, "Day told me to go." He said. Something wasn't adding up in my mind. "Why are you mumbling. though? Did you score already?" "No!" he said. "I'm nnnawwt high." So I asked again, "Then why are you slurring your speech. Are you drunk?"

Donovan raised his one good hand and clenched his fist and said, "Rrrrr!" "What?" I'm just asking why you're slurring." He replied "I haab toed you aweady! Tee treez!" "The pain killers are affecting your speech?" I asked. "Yup!" He said.

I was upset with the hospital. I couldn't understand how they could just look at him and without further investigation, give him pain killers and send him on his way. Having said, that, I was not entirely sure that Donovan was being 100% honest with me. Somehow, I thought there might be more to the story.

Around this time, I was hanging out a fair bit with my birth mom, Lillian, and my sisters. I would catch the bus in North Vancouver, and then the SeaBus that brought me across the water to downtown, then onto another bus, and Lillian would meet me at the bus stop where I needed to get off.

Lillian and I would walk up a big hill to her house. The house was a bit older, but inside was ok. I could tell they didn't have a lot of money, but there was love in this home. Obviously, it was a lot different from the life I knew growing up, but I still knew that everyone here loved each other.

At this point, Lillian was with a new boyfriend. She had separated from the girls' father a few years earlier. Now she was with Gary. Gary was much more chill than Lillian's husband of 13 years. The girls' father was very abusive. Gary seemed pretty nice.

I went there a few times. One time, Lillian and I got there, and we were sitting on her couch, talking. I was a bit bored. We were just sitting there with nothing to do. Then she went to the kitchen and returned with an old coffee mug.

She stood in front of me for a minute. Her hands were a bit shaky. She looked nervous. She said, "Umm, Allan, I was wondering if you were thirsty or something." I thought her behaviour was weird, even for her. I said, "Sure, I could have something." She handed me the mug. She said, "Umm… I brought you some orange juice." As I took a sip, she looked over to see if Gary was watching. Then she looked back at me and put her finger to her lips and said, "Shhh."

I immediately tasted the vodka. I nodded at her. "Thanks." I said. I finished that glass rather quickly. Then she wanted to take me out. She told Gary she was going to show me around town a bit. We left and started walking down the hill.

I asked her where we were heading. She told me she knew a sports bar down the road. She said, she had $20 so we could get a couple of drinks each at least. We went there and ordered a couple pints. She also bought a pack of smokes and shared those with me.

I remember being a bit disappointed because we only had about four drinks each for the whole night. I was kind of wishing for more. I was at the point in my addiction where I definitely needed to get hammered almost every time we drank. Tonight was not one of those nights.

A few nights later, I went back and hung out with Lillian again. This time it was Welfare day and she had money. I also had about $60. She had a bottle of cheap wine that we finished before we went out as well. She told me she was going to show me a bar where her "Big wig" friends hung out.

By the time we reached the bar, I was in blackout stage. I don't remember much. I vaguely remember a huge biker guy looking down at me. He was wearing leather chaps and a leather vest. He had a super long beard. I remember getting in his face and yelling about something, but I don't remember what I was yelling about.

The next thing I remember is opening my eyes the next morning. My mouth was open, and I was sleeping face down on an old couch in Lillian's living room. There was a pool of saliva under my face. I still had all my clothes on, including my jacket. My head was pounding.

I slowly sat up. Lillian brought me a coffee. She said, "If I'd known how you are, I never would've taken you out." I was confused. I tried unsuccessfully to remember what had happened the night before. "What are you talking about?" I asked. She began to explain.

Lillian told me that the bar we went to was a biker bar. She was friends with most of the bikers. I had a feeling I knew what organization she was referring to. I asked her. When I said the name, she got really upset with me. She said, "We just say big wigs. We never ever say that name."

Lillian went on to explain that there were people there who had no problem seriously hurting or maybe even killing someone who showed disrespect. She told me I had completely disrespected some of them.

She told me I got in one guys' face and I was pointing my finger right in his face and saying, "Do you know who I am motherfucker? FUCK YOU! I don't give a fuck who you think you are, asshole! FUCK YOU!!!"

Lillian then went on to say that she had to stop him from hurting me. She told me that he said, "Lillian that boy is so lucky he's your son. You better get him out of here before he talks to someone less understanding." I was shocked. It started to come back to me in pieces, but I never did regain the full recollection of what occurred.

What I had done began to sink in a bit. What was I thinking? What on earth would possess me to challenge a guy twice my size, who was clearly a part of a biker gang? I began to feel that I was very lucky to have left in one piece.

A few days after this incident I was hanging out with Donovan again. It had been about a week since he told me he had been hit by a car. We didn't really know what we were doing. We just hung out and somehow, we ended up back at Lillian's house again.

Neither of us had any cash. We ended up sleeping on Lillian's floor. Donovan was starting to get really "dope sick." He was curled up on the floor. He started to cry. Lillian brought him a blanket, and then she pulled me away from him to talk with me. "What is wrong with him Allan?" I told her that he was out of money, and he hasn't used heroin in two days, and he's dope sick. She said, "No it's more than that. He needs a doctor. He's fucked up, Allan." I told her we would try to get some sleep and talk about it in the morning.

We had a horrible sleep that night. I was up most of the night listening to Donovan's soft cries. I was starting to get very worried. As dawn approached, we got up. Donovan and I started to talk quietly because there were others still asleep. He said, "Dude I'm so sick. I need a hit so bad. My arm hurts so bad too."

Lillian woke up and came into the living room. Then Gary came in. They sat there quietly for a minute. Then Lillian started to speak. "I think that Donovan needs to go to the hospital. We can walk there. It's not far."

Donovan said, "I went aweady." Lillian said, "I know, but you're not well, and they can help you." Then Gary spoke up. "Allan look at him! He's all fucked." Lillian turned around quickly and yelled, "Shut the fuck up! You think he wants to hear how fucked up he is? Fuck off!"

Donovan agreed to go to the hospital. We walked there together. They did an initial examination and he got in to see a doctor almost immediately, which I knew was concerning because if it wasn't bad, then we would have had to wait. Donovan went in and we waited a while. They were doing some further testing. After quite a long while, maybe an hour or so, the doctor came out to see us.

He asked Lillian, "Are you his mom? Are you related to him?" I said, "No she's my mom. He's my best friend. We're the only people he really has in his life." The doctor said, "Well ok. We have done some tests on Donovan. That young man has had a stroke."

I began to worry a lot for my friend. I asked the doctor, "Is it really bad? Will he be paralyzed or anything? Will he live?" The doctor said that he should have been treated right away. He said that the longer we wait after a stroke the more damage there is. He began to explain warning signs of a stroke.

I felt incredibly guilty for not recognizing this. At Walmart, I had completed a Level 2 First Aid course where we learned all about this. Why had I not realized what was happening? Why did the first hospital not recognize it? In both cases, we thought his slurred speech and strange behaviour was caused by heroin. I couldn't forgive myself for this.

I blamed myself for Donovan's current condition. I should have immediately recognized that he needed medical attention. I wondered how much worse he was now that we had waited so long. Perhaps if I had acted sooner he would have been ok. I feared that I had waited far too long. I feared that we were too late to help him.

Donovan went to the ICU. He spent about a week there. I called his mom and told her. She thanked me for being such a good friend. I went to visit him daily. One day I was visiting, and he said, "Dude, you wanna know something fucked up?" He pulled back his sheet a bit and showed me a tube that was about one inch thick. He said, "You see how thick that is? That's up my dick!" I felt bad for him. I said, "That must hurt a lot, bro." He said, "It's not bad right now. But sometimes they make me take it out. That hurts!"

The following day, Donovan confessed that he did not get hit by a car. He told me that he went into a washroom downtown to shoot up. He said that he had more heroin with him than he normally had. He decided to do it all in one hit. He woke up on the floor of the washroom and he realized at that time his arm wasn't working.

Donovan stayed in the hospital for about two weeks. During that time, he was allowed to have outings if someone came and took him out. I came to get him a couple of times.

The first time we took the bus downtown. We planned to go and see a new movie that had come out in the theatre. It was the original Toy Story. It was one of the first times we had ever seen computer animation. Before we went in, Donovan said, we needed to stop and see someone.

I said, to him "Who are we seeing?" He said, "We're just going to stop and find some acid." I said, "Dude, I don't think it's a good idea to do acid." He said, "OK then I guess I'll have to do it all myself." He winked at me and smiled. I said, "But dude, you just had a stroke." He had made up his mind. We were going to watch a computer animated movie in the theatre, on acid.

We dropped the acid before we went in. When we were in there, waiting for the movie to begin, Donovan reached into his jacket and pulled out a leather canister used to hold liquid. He said, it was called a Bota Bag. He passed it to me. I took a sip. I cringed a bit. It was a bit rough on the way down. I knew it was full of hard liquor. He looked at me and said, "Shit mix."

The acid started to kick in and the booze was warm in my belly. I began to have that warm glow that I was so accustomed to. Donovan looked over at me. "I love you, bro," he said "I love you too man," I replied.

When the movie finished, we exited the theatre onto Granville Street. Dusk was upon us, and it was time to take Donovan back to the hospital. We caught the bus back and I signed him back in.

My relationship with Jen around this time was up and down. When it was good, it was great. It was good when I was good. When I wasn't preoccupied with finding my next drink, Jen and I had time to connect. She would lay in bed beside me and ask me to tell her my favourite memory. I guess she wanted to know who I was. Like, who I truly was deep down inside.

I would usually tell Jen about my childhood. I would tell her funny memories about my mom, or about a best friend when I was little, and about crazy adventures we would get into. Jen helped me to remember the real me, not the alcoholic I had become.

In turn, I would ask Jen to tell me all about herself. Jen loved mathematics. She had a brain for problem solving. Jen was motivated to have a great life and wanted to have extreme wealth one day. I wanted that too, and I felt like we had the same goals in life, until one day when I discovered that not all of our goals lined up.

I always wanted to have kids. It was very important to me. I imagined that I would have a boy, who would be just like me. I would spoil him like crazy. Later, I would like to have a girl. She would be a Daddy's girl and she would adore me. Jen told me she absolutely was not willing to have children.

This was almost a deal breaker for me. I asked her why she didn't want kids. She told me that raised properly, one kid would cost upwards of a million dollars over a lifetime, which she would much rather keep for herself.

In addition to finances, she said, she just didn't like kids. She said, that they were a lot of work, and we would spend a million dollars on a pile of shit, puke, and snot! At least on this topic, Jen and I were on opposite ends of the spectrum. I was willing to look past all of this though, because I had deep feelings for Jen.

When I drank too much, she would get really upset with me. I can't say I blamed her. I was out of control and it must have been embarrassing to be around me.

Usually I would end up puking or at the very least I needed help getting from the car into the house. I tried to hold off on my drinking until Jen had studying to do and couldn't hang out with me. Those nights I really got carried away.

I started drinking on the Rez more and more. The rule they had at the house was to never ever go next door to their cousin's. Their cousin's house was the crack house. Chuck told me, "We're not junkies here. Over there, they smoke crack. Those guys are out of control. Don't be like them."

Of course, when somebody told me not to do something, it was the first thing I would do. The first chance I got, I went next door. Actually, the cousin that lived over there was in Chuck's house buying some weed one day, and I just went back to his house with him when he left.

Rudy and his dad, Robert, lived over there. Rudy was a couple of years younger than me. He was the typical crackhead, skinny, black bags around his eyes. His brown hair was usually pretty greasy.

Rudy's dad Robert reminded me of an artist I used to watch on TV, Bob Ross. Like Bob Ross, Robert was a bit older, and he had a huge dark grey afro. Robert had a kind and gentle spirit, but his weathered face told me he had been around and had a rough life.

Same deal as when I was at Chuck's house. I would give Rudy cash and he would run for me. He would come back with powder cocaine and then he would cook it up in the spoon with baking soda and water. He would stir a metal pin in there until it thickened up and formed a "rock." Just like that, we had crack.

The first time I tasted crack, I fell in love all over again. If I thought I loved snorting lines, I had not experienced anything yet! This feeling was amazing! Not only that, but the need to do more was far more intense than it was when I snorted cocaine.

I went over to Rudy's often, but only after I was drunk. Jen started to find out about this, and she was absolutely furious! One evening I was there for two full days. When the cash finally ran out, I started walking home. It was about 7:00 am, two days after I started.

I was about halfway through my hour long walk home. I was pouring sweat. I had once again spent all my rent. I talked to myself on the way. "Fuck! I need to get my life back on track."

I walked and walked and thought about this. Then I talked to myself some more… "Back on track, back off the crack!" I said, "I'm back on fucking track, back off the fucking crack!"

I started to have severe chest pains. I couldn't get a full breath. My heart was pounding out of my chest. I thought I might die. I thought about my dad, knowing that I was now experiencing what he had gone through with his heart problems. "I'm sorry, Dad." He replied, "Allan, I never ever wanted to see you go through this. You need to get well, son." I decided I had better get to the hospital. I walked into the emergency department that was on my way home.

I told the nurse I thought I was having a heart attack. She asked me if there was any reason I would be having a heart attack since I was so young. I said, "Yes well, I'll be honest, I've been smoking crack for the last two days." They brought me in to see a doctor right away.

I got a chest X-Ray and they did an ECG. After that, they had me lie on the bed and wait. The doctor came in to speak with me after about 45 minutes. He said, "Ok, I want to be clear. I'm not your parent. I won't be able to give you any form of discipline. The only reason I'm asking questions is so I can treat your symptoms appropriately."

Just then, the nurse poked her head in. "We've already had this conversation and he was super honest with me." Then I told him "Yeah, I'm on crack and have been for two days." "Thank you for your honesty. It changes how we treat you and if we don't treat you properly you could die."

The doctor returned a while later. He explained what he had found. He said that a heart attack is when the arteries get plugged with plaque and blood cannot get through. He explained that while my arteries were not plugged, the cocaine in my body had caused everything, including my arteries, to constrict. He said that when my arteries constricted, it had restricted the flow of blood, which in turn caused symptoms similar to what you feel with a heart attack.

The doctor told me as well that there was a young man who had come in the week before. He said that this young man's arteries had constricted to the point that they were fully closed, and he suffered permanent damage to his heart. He strongly suggested that I stop smoking crack.

I was released later that morning. I walked the rest of the way home. I had been treated with Aspirin at the hospital, to thin my blood. My physical symptoms were less severe; however, I was dealing with the guilt of using so much again. Once again, my rent money was gone. I had no idea what I would do this time. Jen called shortly after I got home. I was honest with her and told her everything, including all about my trip to the hospital.

Jen was furious. She told me I had better not call her for a while. She was pissed! I called her the next day and convinced her to come over. I explained to Jen that my problem was that every time I had too much to drink, I wanted to go over to the crack house. She made me promise her I would not go there. She said she would even come and get me if I needed a ride home as long as it helped me to never smoke crack again. I promised her.

The next time I got drunk without Jen was about two weeks later. She was home studying for final exams. This was a perfect opportunity to drink without Jen monitoring the amount, and acting like my mother.

I ended up on the Rez, just to hang out and to buy some weed. I definitely was not going to use cocaine, not in powder form and I certainly would not be smoking any crack. My near heart attack was still fresh in my mind. I was adamantly opposed to the use of cocaine.

The night went on and we made a couple of trips back to the Cold Beer and Wine store. We had polished off a lot of alcohol already. I began to have a strong desire to go next door and visit Robert and his son Rudy. I knew I could not. I made the right decision. I called Jen and told her I wanted to go to the crack house, but instead I was calling her to give me a ride home. She was angry but agreed she would come and get me.

Jen was about 40 minutes away. It took me about two minutes after hanging up the phone and I was sitting at the table next door. I gave Rudy $40, and he left to get some coke. He arrived back fairly quickly; I would say it was about 25-30 minutes.

Rudy opened the flap and dumped the coke into the spoon. Then he grabbed a pinch of baking soda, threw it in the spoon as well, turned on an element on the stove and squirted a little water in the spoon with a little mini water bottle he had. He looked at Robert and said, "Dad, quick give me the pin." Robert gave him the pin and Rudy got to work quickly, cooking up a big fat rock.

Rudy finished, and brought me over the rock, after breaking himself off a piece. Then he looked at me and said, "You know ya gotta give Dad a piece!" I sighed. "Ok." I said. "I know the routine." I broke off a piece for his dad, and then I broke off a piece for myself and put it in the end of a crack pipe they gave me. "This is gonna be amazing!" I thought to myself.

Just as I was about to take my first hit off the pipe there was a thunderous banging at the door. It startled all of us. We thought it was the cops. Rudy jumped up and said, "I'll go see who that is." He ran over to the door. I heard the sliding glass door open. A moment later Rudy was standing in the kitchen in front of the table where I was sitting. Standing beside him… Jen!

Well, if looks could kill, I would have been a dead man! Jen was beyond pissed. She said, "Ok I'm here to get you, let's get outta here!" I tried to tell her that I just spent $40 and I didn't even have a chance to smoke any yet. I told her ,"I'll just take this hit, and then we'll go. I promise.

This was not an acceptable answer for Jen. She looked at me with fierce conviction. "Allan… you can sit here and smoke crack or you can come with me. If you come with me we will talk and maybe just maybe we will be ok. If you stay and smoke crack, you can never, ever contact me again. Not ever. I will be done with you."

I looked down at my little pile of rocks. I picked one up and held it between my fingers. I sighed. "Well…" My pondering was interrupted by Jen's screaming. "YOU HAVE TO THINK ABOUT IT? FUCK YOU! STAY HERE, ASSHOLE!" Robert reached out his hand and slid the pile of rocks to his side of the table. "Uh, she's pretty mad, you better go there, Al!"

"Fuck!" I yelled out in frustration. I pleaded with Jen as she was halfway out the door. "Wait Jen Wait! I don't have to think about it. I'm coming with you!" I followed her to her car and got in with her.

As we drove off, she said, "One half of one second longer and you would NOT be in my car with me!" I apologized profusely. "I'm so sorry, Jen! Please, you must understand. I tried to do the right thing. Thank you for coming, you saved me from smoking crack!"

Jen did not say much for the remainder of the drive. We pulled up to my house. "I love you…" I said. "Bye," she replied. I got out and went into my house, not knowing whether she would see me again. I was afraid I might have pushed Jen too far this time. A person can only take so much.

As it turned out, Jen was not done with me. She had some more forgiveness to give. I did not tell her that after she dropped me off, I jumped on my bike and rode back to the Rez with a jar full of dimes and quarters. The crack I had bought earlier was all gone. I didn't end up getting any more that night. By the time I went back, things were quiet there.

I continued to hang out with Donovan after his release from the hospital. We hung out on and off for almost a year after his release. I went to see him close to the first of October. This was almost exactly a year after he had his stroke.

Donovan had two horns protruding from his forehead. They looked very realistic. He told me he got a bad headache, and then they just poked through his skull. Obviously, I didn't believe him. I said, "It's not Halloween yet." He raised his fist and said, "Rrrr!" I said, "Ok, ok, I'm sorry. They just didn't look real at first. But ok."

It was about a week after this when I received a call from Donovan. He said, "I just called to say I love you and I wanted to say goodbye. I'll be leaving soon." I said, "Donovan, I love you too. I just want you to know though, that suicide is a selfish decision. What about the people you leave behind that love you?"

Donovan made a very good point. He said, "First of all, suicide isn't selfish. Saying that is selfish. It's selfish because you would rather keep me with you on this earth even though you know I'm suffering. You would rather have that than let me go."

I agreed with Donovan, and I apologized. "I'm sorry. You're right. But I really don't want to lose you. I love you." He continued, "I know, bro. I love you, too. I'm not talking about suicide though. It's just my time is up here. I'm going to lay down and I'm going to break on through to the other side. I'm just leaving soon. Not by my own hand. I just know this."

On October 14th of that fateful year, I received the call from Donovan's mom. This was only a week or so after Donovan had called to say goodbye. She said, "Allan. I'm so sorry. I'm sorry. Donovan died last night."

CHAPTER TWELVE

THE SHOCK OF MY BEST FRIEND'S DEATH HIT HARD. I was in disbelief. He was 20 years old. I was only 21. Our lives were meant to be just starting, not ending. It is not an overstatement to say I was devastated. Donovan knew everything about me. I confided in him with everything, and he confided in me. I had not felt grief like this in a very long time.

I called Jen. She answered "Hello?" I said, "Hi Jen." She must have heard something in my voice. "What's wrong?" She asked. I started to cry. "What? What?" she asked. "Jen, Donovan died last night." "I'm coming over right now." She said. "Don't go anywhere."

Jen arrived less than an hour later. She came downstairs into my unfinished basement and gave me a big hug. "I'm so sorry." She said. "I brought something." She pulled out a big fat joint, lit it and passed it to me.

I was completely numb. I wasn't stupid. I knew Donovan lived a high-risk lifestyle. I mean, he had a stroke at 19 years old. Still, after everything, it still seemed unbelievable that he was gone. I looked at Jen with tears in my eyes. "It's so… final!" I cried. "This is fucked up."

Jen and I went to the Rez to pick up a quarter ounce. We sat there and smoked about two grams. Eleanor couldn't believe Donovan was dead. "I'm sorry," she offered. "That's a hard one." "It is," I said, "It really is."

I remember going to work at Walmart the next day. I tried to put on a happy face, go in and just do my job. One of my fellow associates (we were not called employees, but rather associates) noticed that I wasn't myself. He asked, "What's up with you?" I told him I was shocked and upset because the day before, I was told that my best friend had died.

This fellow associate did not have much sympathy. He said, "I've lost my fair share of friends. Best thing you can do? Forget about it! Move on! Missing him ain't gonna bring him back is it? Live your life, and don't feel sorry for yourself."

"Rather odd response," I thought to myself. He walked away and I continued my work. I still had a few hours left on my shift. I thought I would probably get some alcohol that night. I would have to leave work right on time and run as fast as I could if I wanted to reach the beer store before it closed at 11:00 pm.

This was becoming routine for me. By this time, I had been promoted from part-time Sales Associate to full time Sales Associate. I worked five days a week, 2:30 pm-10:30 pm. The closest Cold Beer and Wine store was quite far away. If I left the front doors of my work no later than 10:35 pm and sprinted as fast as possible, I could get there by maybe 10:57 pm.

This left no room for error. I would have to punch the clock at 10:30 pm exactly, run downstairs, out the front door, and sprint down the sidewalk for about seven city blocks. From there I would hit a little trail that ran along the train tracks. I would run through the forest, and eventually past the Rez. My friends on the Rez called that trail the Indian Road. At some point the trail ended and I would be back on city sidewalks again. Then a run up the hill about three blocks and I was there.

When I tell people about this, I'm often asked the logical question "Why wouldn't you just buy your alcohol before work and leave it in your fridge?" A great question for which there are two answers.

The first reason is that every day I would tell myself, "I'm not going to drink today." I really believed that every time I said, it. I was ok in the morning and had a lot of confidence that I would stay sober that day. By the time I was halfway through my shift, though, I would be thinking about it, and by the end of my shift, I knew I would drink. Now I was unprepared and would have to do my run.

The other reason is simple. I'm an alcoholic. I was unable to buy alcohol and not drink it. If I bought it before work, I would talk myself into drinking it, and I wouldn't make it to work. A few times I bought alcohol to drink in the evening, and at the same time, I purchased alcohol for after work the next day. Those nights I just got extra drunk, and woke up extra hung over with no leftover alcohol.

My work environment was close-knit. All of my co-workers were good friends. It felt nice to be out of the high school scene where bullying occurred, and nobody wanted to be friends with me. I seemed to fit in here well, and everyone accepted me for who I was… or at least who I told them I was.

Looking back, I'm sure everyone would've accepted me even if I had been honest about how much I drank. For some reason, though, I felt the need to hide my drinking from my co-workers.

Perhaps I hid my drinking because I kind of knew that those people did not drink the way I did. I knew that my drinking was different from that of the average person. Also, Jen was employed at the same store and I didn't want to embarrass her. I hid the fact that I drank as much as I did.

I started to hang out at Mike's house quite a bit. I became friends with the other roommates that lived in the three other rooms. Well, I was friends with two of the roommates.

The other roommate was pretty crazy. They used to call him "Dick-for." This came about because they used to tell this joke, "You have a Dick-for on your forehead." Of course, the person being spoken to would usually say, "What's a dick-for?" And then they would laugh hysterically and say, "Hahaha! He doesn't know what a dick is for!"

The other two rooms were each occupied by men in their 40s. Darryl was a chronic alcoholic. I got along well with him, though. He was a nice guy. I would sell them weed, which helped fund my drinking. The other guy was a bit older. He was in his late 40s, but he was so rough, he looked like he was nearing 60. His name was Jerry.

Jerry was a compulsive liar. He would tell us extravagant stories about his life. The longer I knew him, the crazier stories I heard. Jerry told me he personally knew hockey stars, famous actors, race car drivers, and many, many more.

Jerry would name celebrities and tell us about the time he cooked a four-course dinner for them, or the time some famous actor lent him their Lamborghini for a month, and so on. There was no limit to the lies. If we started to seem uninterested in his stories, the stories became even more extravagant.

Jerry told us he used to be a multi-millionaire. He told us he had travelled the world, and that's how he met all these people. When asked why he was renting a room in an illegal rental house, he said that he lost a lot of his money in a divorce, but he also has a huge settlement coming from a car accident that crippled him.

According to Jerry, he was struck by a drunk driver and that's why his hips are messed up and he walks with a cane. He said he was due to get five million dollars any day now, and then he would be out of this house. He said he would throw us all the most extravagant party ever with super models, and we could have our way with any women we want when he buys his mansion.

Sara never ever stopped trying to help me in my life. She wanted me to have a better living situation, and she hated that I lived in an unfinished basement. She knew a lot of people through foster parent meetings and various groups she was associated with. One of her contacts ended up helping me significantly.

There was a lady who worked at a community centre that had various programs, mostly related to childcare. They ran a pre-school, an out of school care program, and also a drop-in centre for special needs teens.

In addition to managing all of this, this lady was on the committee, and largely involved with a new apartment building that would be subsidized by the government.

The tenants at this new building would only need to pay one-third of whatever their monthly income was. The criteria for being accepted was that you were low income, and also you must be in some way special needs, either mentally or physically disabled. Sara approached me and told me she may be able to get me in there.

I told her that would be impossible because I was not special needs and had no disabilities. Sara said, "Well, you were born with F.A.S." I got very mad at her. She was referring to Fetal Alcohol Syndrome. I had been to so many doctors as a child because Sara was always trying to say that I had F.A.S., but all the doctors I saw said that I was normal. I didn't like being labelled as anything other than normal.

Sara said, "Listen, I can have our family doctor write a letter. It is the chance of a lifetime. It will help you in your life. It's affordable, and it will be a brand new, one-bedroom apartment with new appliances. It will get you out of that basement, Allan." Eventually Sara convinced me to swallow my pride.

I was put on a waiting list for this place. During this time, I was still living in the basement by myself. It was around this time that I began to see Pete at a local coffee shop. He worked there. He told me that he was clean, and that he was just trying to be a productive member of society. One day I saw Pete there, and he said, "I miss Donovan, dude." I said, "I know, me too. I still can't believe he's gone." It had been almost a year since Donovan passed.

Only a short while later, while I still lived in the basement, I was sitting on my bed at home in my room. I received a call from Donovan's mother. I thought it was odd that she was calling me a year after Donovan's death. I hadn't spoken to her much. She said, "Allan, I have to tell you something. I hate that I need to make this call to you. Pete is dead."

"What?" I asked. "How? I just saw him. What happened?" She said that he had jumped to his death. He got to the top of Canada Place downtown and just jumped off. "Holy shit!" I said. "What the fuck! We're barely adults. We are not supposed to be dying."

I called Jen. She again came over and brought a fat joint for us to share. I spiralled out of control again. Another death was a great excuse to get wasted. Who could blame me? I was grieving. If anyone had a problem, they could all just get lost, as far as I was concerned.

I suppose it was about a month later when Jen came to my house and said, she "needed to talk" with me. Jen had recently convinced me to stop drinking. I had been sober for about three weeks.

She came over. She reached into her purse and pulled out a fat joint. She lit it and passed it to me. I wondered what she wanted to talk about. What on earth could it be?

We each had a few big tokes off the joint as we passed it back and forth. We finished the joint and I was nice and high. "What did you wanna talk

CHANGING THE STATUS QUO

about?" I asked. "Well…" She said. "I've given this a lot of thought. I just need to break up with you." "What?" I was completely shocked. This is not anything I expected at all. Perhaps I should have. Jen said, "You can't be shocked about it. You know I've been unhappy for a long time now."

I was shocked. Yes, I understood I had made mistakes. I knew that she was frustrated with me. But I thought she loved me. "I need to go now," she said. "Ok well, can I at least get a ride up to the mall?" I asked. "Sure, I guess," Jen replied.

On the way up the street to the mall, Jen asked why I needed to go there. I told her, "Well, I thought this was the time I was going to quit drinking forever, but I guess since I have nothing good in my life now, I may as well get drunk." Jen looked over at me. "I knew you would do this," she said. I replied sarcastically, "Oh, well you can't be shocked." "That's the thing," said Jen. "I'm not."

I actually didn't buy any booze at the Mall. Instead, I took the bus down to the Rez and bought weed. I told them that I needed to get high because Jen had just left me.

I guess it was about three hours before Chuck convinced me that I should go buy some booze with him. "Just some beers, though I ain't trying to get any coke tonight," said Chuck. "Yeah, me neither," I said.

Chuck and I walked to the Cold Beer and Wine Store. We shared an 18-pack. I guess it was by about my seventh beer when we decided, "Fuck it! May as well get a gram of coke!"

Chuck and I finished that gram together, but before it was even gone, I had decided I would sneak over to the crack house. Somehow snorting lines just wasn't good enough anymore. I longed for the taste of crack. Besides, I was free now and nobody was going to tell me what I could or could not do.

I went next door to see Robert and Rudy. I ordered up a half gram. Rudy did the run and came back in 45 minutes. I had just been paid and once again I was dipping into my rent money. Of course, I told myself I would only be buying $40 worth so I wouldn't need to worry too much about the rent.

This time I was at Rudy's for three full days. As the drug use continued, I would ask what time it was. "What time is it?" Someone would answer

"3:00 am." They continued to answer me each time. "It's 6:00 am... It's noon... 3:00 pm... 7:00 pm... 4:00 am... 11:00 am..." Eventually I started asking, "What DAY is it?"

I always made sure that by early Monday morning I would call in to Walmart to let them know I was "sick." I never wanted to be a no-show. That would be irresponsible.

On the third consecutive day of being at the crack house, Rudy and I decided to go to the liquor store. It must have been about 11:00 am. We brought beers back to the house. I noticed he had stopped and bought a pop as well. I thought he was buying it for himself, but turns out he was buying it for his dad.

When we got back to the house Rudy gave his dad the pop. We sat at that same kitchen table and Rudy pulled out some more crack. As we took turns taking hits off the crack pipe, it began to sink in that I had been there for three full days.

"Fuck!" I said. "I've been here smoking crack for three fucking days now!" Robert looked at me and chuckled softly. "What?" I asked. Robert looked up. His weathered face turned to me. "Allan," he began..." I've been sitting right here at this table... smoking crack... EVERY day... for over 20 years. Three days ain't nothing."

I wondered how he was still alive. I wondered if one day I would be saying that to some new crackhead. Somehow, I didn't think my heart would last as long as Robert's had. Only time would tell, I guess.

I felt like I should show some gratitude for the hospitality Robert was showing me. I said, "Hey Robert, you can have one of my beers." Robert replied, "That's ok, I don't drink." This shocked me. "You don't drink at all?" I asked. Robert replied, "Nope. That shit'll kill ya!"

He was only half joking, but it was very funny to me considering what he had just finished telling me. Smoking crack every day for 20 years was alright, but a beer would kill him? The logic was beyond me. Regardless, I was ok with it because I really wasn't interested in giving up any of my beer.

We had just a tiny bit of cash left between Rudy and I. We really wanted to get some more beer. We began to walk toward the beer store. I had $20 in my pocket. We decided to take a short cut through the playground. The next thing I remember is being forcefully strapped down to a stretcher.

I started yelling, "What is this?! Let me go! What are you doing to me! Fuck you!!!" The paramedics explained that I was being restrained for their safety and my own safety. I looked over and saw an officer. He said, to the paramedics, "I'll meet you at the hospital."

We got to the hospital and the officer met me there. He explained that he would be taking me to the drunk tank once the doctors said I was ok. Then he said, "You know, it is extremely dangerous to be sniffing glue and huffing gas!"

I got angry with him. "You don't even know me!" I said. "Who do you think you are saying that I sniff glue! That's for losers! I don't do that!" He replied, "Well, ya did today, bud!"

I insisted, "No I did not!" He asked me, "How do you suppose you had a seizure then?" I paused. "Wait." I said. "I had a seizure?" "Yes, from sniffing glue and huffing gas. And when you came to, you were extremely violent."

I couldn't comprehend this. I told him he must be mistaken. I said, "I am not a loser. I am a good productive member of society. I have a job. I DO NOT huff gas or sniff glue!"

The officer asked, "Then why did you have a seizure in the park?" I thought about it. I answered him. "Not from huffing gas! I was smoking crack for three days! You would have a seizure too!" "I'm sure I would," he agreed.

I was transferred to the drunk tank to sober up. They finally released me about eight hours later. Now it was nighttime again. I headed straight for the crack house. I knew I had that $20 which should at least help me get a couple rocks.

As I walked, I reached into my pockets. I became alarmed. I could not find my $20. I looked in all my pockets. It wasn't there. I wondered what could have happened to it. I decided to go to Rudy's and find out.

I got to Rudy's and the first thing I asked him was if he knew what happened to my $20. Rudy looked a bit guilty. He said, "Listen! You were all fucked up, ok? I still needed to get beer. I knew you wouldn't mind, bro!" "You took it from my pocket when I was having a seizure?" I asked him. "I found people passing by and I made sure they called an ambulance for you."

I said to Rudy, "Well ok, but do you know why they said I was huffing gas?" Rudy started laughing. "Hahaha! You didn't remember, I guess?"

Rudy never really told me the story. I guessed that he had taught me how to get high off gasoline. "Well… since you took my twenty, can I get a piece of crack at least?" "I'll getcha next time bud! I'm all out now!"

I decided I should walk home. It didn't look like I was going to score any more dope tonight. So disappointing. Oh well, I really needed to get some rest anyway. I was scheduled to work tomorrow.

Speaking of work, it was going quite well. Somehow, through all of this, I managed to get promoted… twice! I went from part-time Sales Associate to full-time Sales Associate, and then I applied for and actually got the position of Department Manager of the Pet Department. I truly couldn't believe they made me a Department Manager, but they did.

As the Manager of a Department, I was responsible for scanning every label in the department every single morning. The scanner I used was a handheld computer of sorts. When I scanned a label, it would tell me how many of that item were in stock. If it said, zero, I would have to push a button to tell me the last five weeks of sales, and based on that information, I would order as many as I needed.

Some items took only three days to arrive. Those items I would order less of because I could order them every other day, if needed. Some items took three weeks to arrive. Even these items didn't need to be ordered in huge quantities, I just needed to always have a few days' worth on the way.

The goal was to never be at zero. If you ran out, you were too late. An empty spot on the shelf represents lost sales. Every empty spot represented a person who came to that spot ready to spend money, but instead, left and bought it from someone who was better at logistics.

Standards were high. There were daily tours from my managers. They would leave me with lists of stuff to fix on top of my already busy schedule, and I still needed to sell fish, and service customers, and answer the phone, and anything else that came up.

I began to feel a bit overwhelmed, but I kept on pushing through. I needed my job, desperately. It was important to me to have more money than I did when I was on Social Assistance. I tried as hard as I could at the time, but my drinking and drug use did get in the way of my motivation.

Work was one of the good things I still had going in my life. It gave me a purpose. It kept me focused on something other than alcohol and drugs. It kept me interacting with people in a positive way, not just interacting with other people who wanted to score dope. It kept me accountable to something other than my addiction.

Work was not the only great thing I had in my life. To this day, I feel forever grateful to have had my brother and Sara in my life. It would have been easy for them to turn their backs on me.

Or even if it wouldn't be "easy" per se, it certainly would have been understandable. But they did not. They were the one thing that stayed constant in my life through all of my difficulties.

The reason they never walked away from me is because of their relationship to me. Although we are not related genetically, they are, in every sense of the word, family, and I am forever grateful for them.

They hated the life I was leading, but they stood by me in hopes I would see a life they wanted to see me living. I knew this and I hoped that one day I would make them proud. In addition to my brother and Sara, I had my dad. Although he left this earth many years ago, he remained by my side. It was as though he never left, and whenever I spoke to him, he would always, always answer. I truly wanted to make my dad proud of me as well.

CHAPTER THIRTEEN

SARA'S PERSISTENCE AND HER COMMITMENT to ensuring a better life for me paid off. I was accepted into the subsidized housing and tomorrow was moving day. I had told some fellow Department Managers and they all had decided that they were going to come and help me.

I didn't really want their help because it meant that they would see the dirty, old, unfinished basement I was living in. They insisted though, and about five of them showed up at my place to help me.

They said they just needed me to have everything ready for them and they would grab it and load it and drive it to the new place and load it in for me. I accepted their help.

I thought I was pretty much done packing that night and invited them over the next morning. I'm not sure how I missed so much stuff. There was random shit everywhere. Giant wolf spiders ran across the floor as boxes and garbage bags were shuffled.

I was embarrassed to have my colleagues see the way I lived. I always went to work clean, with a nice appearance and tried to be presentable always. They were getting a glimpse into my "double life." But everyone was really cool. They focused on the positive, that I was getting my very own apartment that was brand new.

My new rent was based on my income. They only took one-third of my gross monthly income which, at the time, brought my rent to $293/month! I was currently paying $350. I had really lucked out.

I moved in and I couldn't believe how nice it was. I suppose anything would have seemed nice compared to the unfinished basement that I lived in, but this place really was nice. I was on the fourth floor and I had a balcony that had a nice view of Lion's Gate Bridge. There were marvellous sunsets in the evening. The appliances were brand new, really nice carpets, and it came with a sort of "new home smell." It was perfect

The best part of this new home? Location, location, location. I was a 10-minute walk to the crack house and directly across from the Liquor Store. I could see the Liquor Store from my balcony. It took longer to go down in the elevator than it did to walk there from my front door.

I decided to throw a housewarming party. It wasn't really a party though, it was just me and one of my best friends, Graham. Of course, we had some drinks that night. I told Graham that we were not allowed to smoke weed in there because I didn't want to be evicted as soon as I moved in. Graham found a way to smoke weed in there and have it not be an issue. He went into my bedroom and closed the window and put a towel under the door. He said, this would ensure that nobody smelled the weed, and it seemed to work.

After the beer ran out, I thought that was it for the night— Graham and I were both drunk. We decided to get some more alcohol. To be fair, I made that decision, but Graham agreed it was a good idea.

We walked across the street and returned with a case of beer. Six more each would be good. We were already quite hammered. I drank those beer quickly and started to get out of control. Graham tried to control me.

I went outside onto the balcony and lit up a joint. Graham said, "Hey, Dude, you can't smoke that here. Remember what you told me?" I looked up at Graham and said, "Woah-ho-ho, lookie here. Looks like we have the weed patrol in my own fucking house!"

Graham said, "I'm not trying to tell you what to do I just…" I interrupted him, "You just ARE! You are not trying. You ARE telling me what to do in my own fucking house! This is MY house! MY rules!"

Graham said, "I know, and it is YOUR rule that we don't smoke weed here. "You smoked weed in my bedroom, asshole!" I said. This place is mine! I can do whatever the fuck I want!" With that, I turned and faced the corner of the balcony, unzipped my jeans, and began to piss right there on the balcony.

Graham grabbed my arm and said, "What the fuck are you doing?" I blurted out "MY HOUSE!" as I tried to keep my balance. Graham was trying to reason with me, and I met him half way. I turned and faced the railing of the balcony and pissed through the bars.

"I give up!" Graham said. And he did. He did not try to tell me what to do after that. The beer was all gone anyway, and we decided to say goodnight at that point. Graham left, but I still had some cash and the Liquor Store across the street was open. I decided to go for one more six-pack of beer.

I grabbed my wallet and took off out the door. I decided that the stairs would be faster than the elevator. This was a bad choice. I lost my balance and fell down a flight of stairs. Scrambling to my feet, I steadied myself and took a step, but again was unsuccessful, and I tumbled down the next flight of stairs.

I was a bit stiff after that one, but the booze helped a lot. I managed to pull myself together in the lobby. I knew the Liquor Store wouldn't serve me if I was too drunk. I said to myself "Act sober. Act sober. Act sober."

With that, I continued across the street and somehow came off sober enough to be served. When I woke up in the morning, I regretted the decisions I'd made the night before. I had to scrub the piss smell out of the balcony outside and there were empty cans and garbage everywhere.

I must have gotten hungry in the night because there was a severely burned egg on a frying pan in the sink. I don't remember cooking, but the evidence was there.

I continued to work almost every shift at Walmart during this time. I showed up for almost every shift and was usually on time. I worked hard and tried my best when I was there. Unfortunately, my drinking and use of cocaine was getting so bad that just showing up and trying hard wasn't always enough to compensate for my actions while I was drunk and high. I was about to go on a work trip that would prove just that.

It was November and the stores were getting ready for Christmas. I was approached by my Manager and asked if I would like to go out of town for a bit, to help with a renovation in Victoria. He said we would go for about six weeks. I thought this would be a great idea and a good way to make some extra money, so I agreed.

I had made a friend at Walmart who was a fellow Department Manager. His name was Ronald. Ronald used to come over to my house each weekend to play video games and smoke weed. He didn't really drink that much, which was good because he wasn't a bad influence on me. Ronald also agreed to go on this trip and we were paired up to share a hotel room together.

We arrived in Victoria on Sunday afternoon and we were scheduled to be at the store Monday at 7:00 am. We checked into the hotel, unpacked, and then later we went for dinner.

I didn't have much of my own money, other than a bit I was using to eat, so I managed to behave myself all week. My store had given me a cash advance of $2000. This was for food and transportation, as well as a laundry allowance of $7 a day.

We were asked to keep all of our receipts. Whatever money was spent, we would provide receipts, and if there was money left over, we would give that back at the end of our stay.

We were asked to put the money in the cash office at the Victoria store. I had other plans. I just avoided that situation and hung onto the cash for "safe keeping."

I worked hard all week. We were only going to take Sundays off, so I was excited to make some extra cash. I was very engaged with my work. We were setting floor plans, moving counters, and setting up Christmas in the Seasonal Department which was giving me that warm nostalgic feeling one gets at this time of year. I was excited to be there, and the Manager had commented several times about how happy he was with our work.

When Friday came along, Ronald said, "Hey man, it's payday! We've worked hard all week, how about we get some beer after work?" I was down for that. "I think we've earned it!" I said. We worked hard all day, and after work we walked across the parking lot of the hotel to the Beer Store.

Ronald looked around. He picked up a six-pack of beer. "How about this?" he asked. "That's all you're getting?" I asked him. "No, it's not all for me. I was thinking we could share this. We still have to work tomorrow."

This was a big problem for me. I couldn't tell Ronald that one six-pack would barely be enough for just me. I could not tell him this because that would make me seem like an alcoholic. I mean, I knew I was an alcoholic, I just didn't want others to know, especially my co-workers and non-alcoholic friends.

Rather than trying to buy more, I just went with it. We left the Beer Store with just one six-pack of beer. I did manage to convince Ronald to go for the tall cans, but even still, the anxiety of knowing I only had three of those beer was setting in. I had to come up with a plan.

Ronald suggested that we go for dinner before we had our drinks. I agreed. There was a bar and grill by the lobby of the hotel. That seemed like the best place. We ordered dinner and I thought it couldn't hurt to get a drink with my meal. The plan was coming together nicely.

I ordered a pint with my burger and fries. Ronald and I sat and talked about the great week we had at work and how nice it was to get away to a new city for a bit and make some extra money from working overtime. "Maybe we can even cover our Christmas expenses with all the money we will make," Ronald commented.

Once we finished dinner, we both got receipts and went up to the hotel room. "Time to crack a beer!" said Ronald. "Great idea!" I said. Ronald turned on the hockey game that was on that night. He was a HUGE hockey fan and knew ALL statistics of almost every well-known hockey player who ever played the game.

Ronald pulled out a huge hard-cover book. It was a hockey statistics book. He wanted to test himself. He said, "Open the book to any page, choose any stat from that page, and ask me the question."

I flipped the book open. I turned to page 93. I found stats on Mario Lemieux. I asked the question: "In 1984-85 how many points did Mario Lemieux have?" Ronald replied "He had 100 points that year, which were all regular season points since they did not make the playoffs that year. The 100 points came from 43 goals and 57 assists. He played a total of 73 games that year."

I was impressed. As we drank and watched the hockey game, I continued to test Ronald. He was flawless in his answers. I must have asked him 20 questions; he nailed every single one and added in more information than was asked of him. This kept me interested for a while, but I still had to figure out how I was going to get enough to drink.

I came up with a plan. I knew I could buy alcohol downstairs, but I needed a reason to go down there so Ronald wouldn't be suspicious. I decided I should do my laundry. After all, I had been there a week and had not done laundry yet, so it made sense that I should do it.

When I had finished my first tall can of beer, I gathered up my laundry and told Ronald I would head downstairs to the laundry room. He asked if I needed help to carry some of it. "No!" I yelled. Ronald looked a bit shocked. I softened my tone. "No, no that's ok. You just relax. I'll be back before you know it."

I ran out of the room and got the elevator down to the laundry room which was one floor below the lobby. I shoved my stuff in the corner and quickly ran up the stairwell to the lobby and into the bar. I figured I would quickly get in some drinks and go back in a few minutes to put the laundry in. I couldn't be bothered now, I had my priorities and they did not include laundry.

I went into the bar. I went up to the bartender and asked for one pint of beer and one shot of whiskey. I took the shot and then drank the pint somewhat quickly. I saw the game on the TV, and it reminded me of Ronald. "Shit!" I thought. "I had better get back."

I ran out of the bar and into the elevator. I went back to the room. Ronald handed me my second tall can of beer. By this time, I had consumed the pint with dinner, the one tall can, the pint of beer, and the shot of whiskey. So really, this was my fifth drink. Ronald thought I was just starting my third.

After a few sips, Ronald asked, "So how long will your laundry take?" I jumped off my chair. "Shit!" I exclaimed. "My laundry!" Ronald was totally confused. "What is wrong with your laundry?" He asked. "Oh nothing, nothing no problem. It's just that the machines were full so I shoved it in the corner. I forgot to put it in after I…uhh…came back upstairs."

Ronald asked, "If you just left it there then how come you took so long?" I had to think quick. "Oh, because I waited and waited, but nobody came to get their laundry, so I finally just left," I said. "Ok, well you better go and put it in," he said.

I had to quickly finish my beer though, so I chugged it and ran out the door. "I'll be back!" I yelled, as the door slammed behind me. I hurried down and put my laundry in the washer.

Since I was downstairs, I felt it was an opportune time to grab a beer and a shot from the bar. I ran in and ordered a pint and a shot of whiskey. I went back to the elevator and back to the room. "Did you get a machine?" asked Ronald. "Yes, I sure did," I replied. Ronald handed me my last tall can of beer.

I started to drink my beer. Ronald began to talk about how it would be nice if we had some weed. I said, "Well, we should get some, buddy!" He said, "But we are in Victoria and I don't have a dealer here. I don't know anyone at all!" I said, "Oh come on! I can find you anything you want in any city in the world within an hour!"

Ronald looked suspicious, but also looked like he wanted me to try. "Do you really think you can find weed?" he asked. "You're talking to the mother fucking master! I can do anything!"

Ronald agreed to let me try. He gave me $10 and asked if I could go find him a gram of weed. "Buddy, give me an hour and I'll be back here smoking a fat joint with you!" "Perfect!" Said Ronald. "You're the best, man!"

I had only just started my last beer. I decided to just chug it and get out of there. I did just that. I slammed the empty can down on my nightstand and stood up from my bed. I put my shoes on and grabbed my coat.

Ronald went to the washroom. When he did, I went into my nightstand and grabbed the wad of cash. This is where I kept my $2000 that was supposed to be in the cash office at the store. I decided I better take it with me, just in case I ended up in a situation where I needed it. You never know, right?

Ronald came out of the washroom. I told him I was leaving, and I would see him shortly. The door of our room closed behind me and I went downstairs to catch a bus. Before I got on the bus though, I had to stop in and get a beer and a shot of whiskey from the bar. Now I was good.

I went outside and walked down the street until I saw a bus stop. I stood there and lit up a smoke. The bus pulled up and I walked on. "You'll have to put that out if you're getting on partner!" Said the bus driver. I looked down and saw I was still holding my lit cigarette. I pulled off the cherry and threw it outside into a puddle. "Sorry about that!" I said.

I put money in the box. I said, "This is going to sound a bit strange, but just bear with me. Just go with it!" The driver looked at me and said, "Ok…" I asked him, "Do you happen to go downtown?" He said, that he did. "Ok!" I said. "I would like you to tell me when we are in the worst area possible! Like if you have a skid row, or high crime area, that's my stop, ok?"

The driver looked less confused than I expected. "Consider it done, partner! Now have a seat and I'll tell you when we're there!" I found a seat at the back of the bus. After about 20 minutes, he stopped at a bus stop. He looked at me in his mirror. "This is your stop, partner!" I thanked him and got off.

I heard really loud music. I was outside a club. I figured I may as well go and have a drink. I went in and got a rum and coke. Everyone was dancing. I started to dance on the dance floor, alone. I was having a great old time.

A really hot girl started dancing in front of me. She was wearing a white tank top and short shorts with black fishnet stockings. She started dancing closer to me. I was loving the attention of an attractive girl. She held onto my hips. Then she reached around and grabbed my ass. "Woo!" I exclaimed. She grabbed my hand and put it between her legs. She began to grind on my fingers. Then she grabbed the back of my head and pushed my face into her chest.

I was thinking, "Yes! Yes! I'm gonna get laid!" She pulled me closer and leaned towards my ear. She spoke loudly to make sure I could hear her over the music. "Aren't ya gonna buy your girl a drink?" "Of course!" I told her. She held my hand and guided me towards the bar. I looked at the bartender. "Two of whatever she's drinking!" I yelled. We drank quickly. She pulled me close again. "How about another, honey?" I obliged. I started drinking and dancing. Then I noticed she was gone.

I looked everywhere for her, but she was nowhere. It appeared I had been played by a hot chick in a tight shirt. I wandered outside. As the cool air hit me I remembered my mission. Ronald needed weed. Suddenly the thought occurred to me that I could grab a tiny bit of cocaine while I was downtown. I decided to walk around and see what people were offering.

As I walked the downtown streets, I examined everyone. Suddenly a guy made eye contact "Up? Down?" He asked. This was street talk. "Up" is coke and "Down" is heroin. "Up." I said. "Ok how much brotha?" he asked. "Forty," I replied. "Alright I got whatcha need, brotha!" We did the exchange. I gave him $40 and he handed me a ball of white stuff tightly wrapped in plastic wrap. I went to a window ledge on the side of a building and broke it open, putting a couple of pieces on the ledge.

A guy walked up to me. "You need a pipe bro?" he asked. I realized I did. "Yeah man, I'll share some with you if you got a pipe," I said. "Deal!" said the guy. He broke off a little rock from a piece that I gave him. He put flame to the end of his glass pipe and started to take a hit. He coughed. "What the fuck is this?!" He exclaimed. "It's crack!" I said. He examined it closely. "This is fucking candle wax! It ruined my pipe! You got ripped off, bro!"

The guy asked, "Who sold you this?" I told him I would have to look around and see if I could find him. I spotted him on the corner at the end of the street. I ran up to him with the other guy by my side. I yelled at him from a distance. "Hey! Hey asshole! Get over here, motherfucker!" I ran up to him and said, "You sold me fucking wax asshole! Gimme my forty bucks right now!" The guy looked at me and said, "You best be backing off, bro!"

The guy that accompanied me said, "Dude that wax fucked up my pipe! That's not cool man!" I got really mad. I said, "You think this is a joke?!" The dude produced a knife. He said, "If you don't wanna die tonight you best be backing off NOW!"

I didn't want to die, and I didn't trust that he was bluffing. I had been around long enough to know that addicts were unpredictable. Addicts on the streets were especially unpredictable. Even more unpredictable were addicts on the streets who felt threatened. I left him alone. The guy accompanying me said, "Listen dude. My name is Jake. If you have any more money I can hook you up."

I did have more money. I had a pocket full of cash. Of course, I didn't let on how much I had. I told him I had enough to get half a gram for $40. He said, I should go back to his place because he was a dealer and sold crack but he didn't have it with him.

We walked a little way, and got to his house. He brought me into a basement door. When we walked in, we were in a laundry room. He asked me to wait there while he went to his room. While he went, I quickly reached into my pocket and separated two twenties and put them in a different pocket. I did not want him to see the wad of cash.

He came back into the laundry room. He had a new, clean pipe and a nice fat rock of crack cocaine. "That's what I'm talking about!" I exclaimed. I was happy to finally get my hands on a rock. I told Jake that I could just stay a little while because I needed to get back to my hotel. He said, "No problem bro, we will just finish this up and then you can be on your way."

I shared the half gram with Jake. We just stood there beside the washing machine, passing the crack pipe back and forth. The crack did not last long. When we were almost done, Jake said, "So you wanna buy a little more then?" I told him I really should get going. "Ok, but I have more, and I can grab it right away…"

The problem was that I was dipping into the Walmart money. I had used $40 of it to buy that wax, and now I had given Jake $40 more. I thought about that. I was thinking since I still had $1920 out of the $2000, I was ok. Plus, I had not used any of that money to eat during the week because I had used my debit card, and I had receipts for the whole week. That really meant that I had $1920 cash, plus I had over $200 in receipts so I could afford to spend more. I was still ahead as a matter of fact.

With this logic I decided to buy a gram. After that, I would definitely need to go back to the hotel. Actually, I would need to find Ronald his weed, then I would go back.

I told Jake, "Ok, well if you have a gram, then I can do that, but that's all my money." Jake said, "Ok, I'll be right back." Jake ran to the room and came back right away. "Got 80?" he asked. "Yup." I said, as I reached into my pockets and took out my carefully separated $80.

That gram seemed to go quick. I was putting huge rocks in my pipe. I almost always had to ration my crack so I would only put little rocks in each time. It was nice to indulge and throw in "Big Boulders," as I called them.

My rocks got smaller as we got close to finishing that gram. I didn't want it to run out. I NEVER wanted my crack to run out. As we got close to finishing the gram, I was beginning to rationalize in my own head. I thought that maybe I could bargain with Jake.

I said, to Jake "If I buy one more gram, could you do it for $70? Since I've been buying quite a bit?" Jake held up his index finger and motioned, "Wait," as he took a big hit off the pipe and exhaled an enormous cloud.

He stood there for a second, squinting his eyes tight. "Woah! That was a good hit!" He said. Jake looked at me and said, "I can't do one for $70, bro. But if you buy an 8-ball, I'll do it for $200." An 8-ball is an eighth of an ounce, so three and a half grams. Individually three and a half grams would have cost me $280. "Crazy not to…" I said.

I told Jake I had to use the washroom. He showed me where I could use the washroom in the other room. I didn't have to use the washroom; I just didn't want him to see how much cash I had. I pulled out my cash and separated $200.

I came back with the $200 in my hand. Jake took the money and went to his bedroom. In a minute he came back. He had powder cocaine this time. I don't think I had ever bought an 8-ball for myself at one time like that. I was kind of excited to have so much.

Jake pulled out a spoon and then went to a shelf above the washing machine and grabbed a box of baking soda. He said, "Let's cook this up!" He dumped some cocaine and some baking soda in the spoon and added a bit of water. Then he put his lighter to it and cooked it up into a huge rock.

It was getting late, and I had so much crack left. I figured I could afford to do huge hits. I packed that pipe full and filled my lungs on every hit. As the night went on, I slowly cared less and less about how much of the $2000 I was spending.

That 8-ball disappeared rather quickly, since I was doing such huge hits. I wanted more. Jake said I would need to go with him to his dealer's place because I had bought everything he had at his house. I agreed. He said, it was pretty far and he didn't drive so we should get a cab.

I paid for a cab to the dealers. Of course, he stopped the cab close to the dealer's, and I waited on the corner while he went. He said, "If you're getting another 8-ball you may as well give me $200 now so I can get more. I said, "Ok, may as well." I reached into the wrong pocket and this time he saw that I had quite a bit of cash.

He said, "Dude, if you got that much cash, we better buy a bit more. It will save us money. I can get us a quarter ounce, two 8-balls." I asked, "How much?" He said, "I can get you two 8-balls for $350 instead of $400, and remember $200 an 8-ball is already a good deal."

I agreed to get two 8-balls. When he got back, I also wanted more cigarettes so we took a cab to a 24-hour gas station and bought three packs of smokes. From there, we decided to walk back to his place because we were close.

We stopped along the way. Jake saw a house with some Christmas lights. He said, "Do you know how to make pipes with light bulbs?" "Uh, no. Can't say that I do," I replied.

He walked up to the porch of a house and unscrewed one of the bulbs. He twisted off the metal end so there was a little hole there. Then he tapped the end of it on the cement until it broke. He held it up and said, "crack pipe!" He reached into his pocket and pulled out a rock. He put it in the end and lit it up.

Soon it was my turn to try. He handed me a rock. I put it in the light bulb crack pipe and lit it up. You kind of had to burn it first, and then take a pull off it—I noticed if I put my lips to it and lit the end, I just ended up burning my lips. It wasn't the best, but it worked if you had nothing else. "What do you think?" asked Jake. "I think that's enough to get anyone in the Christmas spirit!" I replied.

We went back to Jakes' house. We finished those two 8-balls and I bought the rest of what Jake had, a gram at a time. We just kept smoking rocks and smoking rocks all night long. When he ran out, he said, "My dealers not around now. He doesn't like anyone to call after 3:00 am. But I can take you downtown." We walked downtown and found a guy that Jake knew.

I ended up buying some crack from Jakes' friend. I'm not sure how many rocks I bought downtown. All I know is that by 5:00 am I had no money left. I had spent the $2,000 and I had also used my bank card at the ATM and drained my account. I had been walking around talking with junkies downtown for a while. I was making everyone laugh with my poems and stories.

I was never afraid of being in bad neighbourhoods with addicts. Whether it was the bad part of Victoria, or Main and Hastings in Vancouver, I always felt comfortable. I fit in here. Nobody judged me. People were mostly cool. The biggest issue I had was people asking if I could share with them. Everyone was on the lookout for the guy that had some dope. When I had it, everyone was my best friend. When I didn't, everyone disappeared.

The harsh reality of my situation was beginning to sink in. I tried to rationalize things in my head. "Ok, ok...," I thought. "Two thousand dollars isn't actually that much. I have receipts. I have receipts. That will get me close. Then, when payday comes, I will have to give all of that money..." My thoughts were interrupted by someone whistling sharply. I looked and a guy on a BMX rode by quickly, racing somewhere.

"I gotta get out of here." I thought. I knew I had to call Ronald. I couldn't remember the name of our hotel, or our room number. I searched my pockets. Luckily, I had a match book with the name of the hotel on it.

I went to a pay phone. I was going to make a collect call to the hotel. I paused. I realized I needed to have a very good story about why I was gone all night. I stopped and thought about this. I decided that the only logical explanation was that I got robbed. I came up with my story, and prepared to make the call.

I returned to the pay phone. I dialled zero for the operator. I asked to make a collect call. I called the hotel and I told the front desk that I didn't know the room number, but I was looking for Ronald Styles. They put me through and I heard Ronald say, "Yes, of course... I'll accept the charges."

Ronald came on the phone. "Allan? Allan?" I replied "Yes, it's me. Ronald, I am in big trouble, man!" He said, "Are you ok? I've been so worried about you!" I told him "I will be ok, Ronald. I will be. I don't have any of my money, though." He said, "Don't worry about money. I'll lend you some cash." I realized he thought I meant MY money.

I had to explain. "No, Ronald I don't think you understand the severity of this. I'm not talking about MY money. I don't have that two thousand dollars. It is all gone!" There was a brief silence on the other end.

"What happened?" He asked. "Well...," I said. "I went to find your weed. Then I stopped to get one drink. I guess these guys saw that I had a lot of cash and they followed me out of the bar. They robbed me, Ronald."

Ronald exclaimed, "Oh no! Did they hurt you? Are you ok?" I said, "They dragged me down an alley and kicked the shit out of me!" I told Ronald that I didn't want to give up the cash, but they beat me and got it from me. I told him I was beat up, but that I should be alright.

Ronald said, "Oh man you should have just given them the cash. But it's almost 6:00 am. How come you're just calling now?" I told him "Even after they got my money they continued to kick the shit out of me, so I had to run and run, but by the time I lost them, I didn't know where I was, so I walked and walked until now, and then I decided to call you."

Ronald said, "Ok, it's ok, you just need to get back here." I told him I had no money for a cab. He told me to take a cab and he would pay for it. I told him I would do just that. Before I hailed a cab, I needed to provide some kind of evidence to back up my story.

I walked down a back alley. When there was nobody in sight, I made a tight fist with my right hand. I looked down at my fist, and then… BAM! I punched myself in the face as hard as I could. That stung. Then, with all of my might, I struck my face again. WHAM!

I continued this over and over. I even split my lip with my own fist. I punched myself in the right eye multiple times until my eye was swollen shut and I had a big shiner.

I walked out of the alley and saw a cab driving by, so I hailed him and he brought me back to the hotel where Ronald met me. When I got there and stepped out of the cab, Ronald paid the driver. As we were walking into the hotel Ronald asked me, "Allan! Where are your shoes?" I looked at my feet and sure enough, I had no shoes on. "That's crazy!" I said. "I don't know. Those fuckers must have stolen them." The truth was that I had no idea. I'm not sure what it was with me and losing my shoes when I blacked out. This was the second time this had happened.

Ronald was so cool. He didn't judge me or even suspect me of any wrongdoing at all. His only concern was my safety. I told him, "I'm so sorry, I wasn't able to find you any weed." Ronald told me he didn't care about that, and he was so happy to see me, alive.

We had to make the call to our manager in Victoria. When I got to the hotel it was pretty much time to leave for work. Before I made the call, I decided to take a quick shower. I felt extremely ill and shaky and my heart was beating irregularly, and I was pouring sweat. I thought a shower would help me out a bit.

After a few minutes I came out of the shower wearing a shirt and my underwear. I had a huge ugly bruise that ran from my hip all the way to my knee on my right leg. It was from falling down the stairs at my apartment before the trip.

Ronald looked at my leg and said, "Oh my God! Allan is that what they did to you?" I just went with it. I said, "Yeah, when they got me to the ground, they just kept kicking me over and over!" I did feel a bit bad for lying to my friend, but it was too good of an alibi to not use it.

We called the store together. Ronald vouched for me on everything. He told the store manager that I was in no shape to attend work and I should probably stay at home. "He could have been killed!" He said.

I wanted to go to work, but Ronald insisted that I should probably stay back. He said that I needed rest. I agreed. He left with the other people who stayed in the same hotel. We were carpooling every day. He said he would explain everything to the team and promised me everyone would be understanding.

Ronald left and I lay on the bed for a bit. I think I sort of dozed off a bit. I woke up a short time later. I decided to get dressed. I was looking through my drawers and could not find any clothes. I thought to myself "Where are all my clothes?"

I stood there for a moment, and then yelled out loud, "Oh shit! My laundry!" I remembered that between all my drinking I never did finish my laundry that night. I put my dirty clothes back on. I found a bit of change in the drawer and went to the laundry room. I was happy to see that my clothes were still there. They were still wet in the machine, but at least they were there.

After throwing my laundry in for another wash, I went back to the room. I decided to go for a swim in the pool. I grabbed my pants and a pair of swim shorts I had packed. I grabbed a towel and went downstairs. They had a little change room there and I went in there to change. When I took off my pants, I saw a white flap fall out of my pocket.

I guess, sometime during my crazy night I had saved a flap for later. I had completely forgotten about it. I had to snort this today. That brightened my spirits quite a bit. I figured I would still go for my swim. I went and took a dip and enjoyed the hot tub. My pool time was rushed a bit, largely because I knew there was a flap of cocaine waiting for me. I could use a little pick-me-up at this point.

I went up to the hotel lobby. I went into the eating area and found a straw. I took it and went back to my room. I sat there in the room, chopping up lines and snorting them for part of the morning. I eventually ran out of cocaine. I started to come down again and my heart was in bad shape, and I felt like shit.

I tried to sleep but that is difficult to do when you have been smoking crack all night and snorting cocaine all morning. I tossed and turned, and was unsuccessful in getting any sleep at all.

I was very concerned about my heart. I wasn't sure how much abuse my body could handle. I was pretty sure I was pushing the limits. I was also very nervous about being confronted by Walmart. I had a feeling they were not going to be nearly as understanding as my friend Ronald was.

That afternoon, Ronald arrived back at the hotel. He said he had a pretty good day at work, but there was a lot of talk about me. He said, the store manager would be talking to me in the morning.

What Ronald told me did not come as a surprise. Obviously, they would need to ask me about the two thousand dollars that I was keeping in my nightstand for "safe keeping." I was just scared about what would become of me. I didn't want to lose my job.

The next morning, we got up and met our colleagues in the parking lot. We all piled into the car, and off we went. The people we rode with were curious about my bad night. They looked at my face and one guy, Joe, said, "Oh my, they really did a number on you, didn't they?" I said, "They sure did, Joe… they sure did!"

We got to the store. I was immediately called into the office. I sat with the store manager, Frank and his co-manager. They wanted to know the whole ugly story. Frank said, "First of all, are you Ok?" I said, "Well yes, I'm ok considering everything I've been through."

Frank said, "Ok, I'm glad that you're alright, Allan. Now walk me through what happened." I said, "Well Frank, this is what happened. We worked all week. Ronald and I went for dinner. After dinner I told Ronald that I wanted to go and see a tiny bit of Victoria. Ronald didn't feel like going out, so I went alone."

Frank said, "Ok. Fair enough. So how do we go from seeing a bit of Victoria to losing two thousand dollars and going missing for twelve hours? That's the part of the story I'm very interested in." I said, "I figured you would be interested to know about that. Once I explain, I'm sure it will all make a lot of sense to you."

I took a deep breath and continued. "I stopped into a local bar. I only had one drink. I just wanted to mingle a bit, that's all. I also ordered something to eat. Then, when I decided to leave, these guys started to follow me. They ordered me to give them all my money. I refused. They dragged me down a back alley and threw me on the ground and went through my pockets. They got the money, but they still kept kicking me and punching me."

Frank interrupted me for a moment. He said, "So you mean to say they got all of the two thousand dollars?" I said, "Yes, yes unfortunately they got all of it." He said, "I guess the biggest part I'm having an issue with here is why you had ALL of the money with you, in your pocket while you went to see a bit of Victoria. Why did you not put it in the safe in the cash office like everyone else?"

This was one of my biggest obstacles. I needed to justify my actions. It wouldn't be easy. I just decided I was going to go with it and stand my ground and never ever change my story no matter how crazy it sounded. I kept telling myself "Just never ever change your story. Stand your ground."

I began to explain. "Frank…" I said. "Here's the thing, man. I really didn't feel comfortable leaving that much money in the care of anyone but myself. I just didn't feel safe doing that."

Frank said, "Ok let me stop you right there. I have a bit of a problem with that." I said, "I rather thought you would." He continued his questioning. "Do you mean to say that you felt like you had to keep Walmart's money safe and you felt that Walmart's money would not be safe in the SAFE in the cash office, where Walmart keeps ALL of the store's money?"

I adjusted my position in the office chair I was sitting in. I leaned forward a bit and put my hands in my lap, interlocking my fingers. I took a breath, and said, "Yes, that's correct." I could tell Frank was getting annoyed. He said, "Am I missing something?" I sat up in my chair. I looked left and then right, and then I looked right at Frank and said, "No I don't think so. What you said is correct."

Frank pushed a little harder with his questions. "Ok Allan. I need to know, why, if your intention was to keep the money safe, why on God's green earth would you decide to take TWO THOUSAND DOLLARS with you in your POCKET to go downtown Victoria to stroll around? WHY? Is that safer than in the safe at the store where we keep all of Walmart's money safe every day of the year?"

I paused a moment to gather my thoughts. "It seemed like the right choice at the time. You know what they say, Frank, hindsight is 20/20." He said, "Well, there's hindsight and then there is common sense, and I think you were lacking a bit with regards to the common-sense part."

Frank released me from the uncomfortable situation in his office. He asked me to head over to the Seasonal Department and find the Manager over there who would give me some direction for the day. I went over there and began work. Ronald was there too.

About half an hour later, Frank walked up and handed me a portable phone. He said, "It's the District Manager. He would like to speak with you." I took the phone and said, "Hello?" He said, "Hello Allan. This is Nick Stather." I said, "Hi Nick, how are you?" He said, "I'll be honest with you; I would be better if I had not heard about your situation. I would like you to tell me right now exactly what happened and how you lost two thousand dollars."

I said, "Nick, I didn't lose anything. It was stolen from me." He said, "Why did you have the store's money in your pocket downtown on a Friday night?" I said, "Well Nick, I didn't want to just leave it in the drawer at the hotel." Nick asked me "And what about in the safe at the store as you were instructed?" I said, "Yeah I thought that was an option, but not a mandatory requirement, and I just did not feel comfortable doing that,"

Nick asked me, "Were you hammered?" I said, "Excuse me?" He said, "Hammered, were you hammered? Drunk, intoxicated, smashed—were you hammered?!" I said, "No of course not." Nick said, "So you mean to tell me that you were not drinking?" I said, "I never said I wasn't drinking, Nick. There's a big difference between having a drink and being hammered, now isn't there?"

Nick said, "Ok, so how much did you drink?" I said, "I stopped in at a local bar and had one drink. Just one, that's all. And there were some shady guys in there that followed me and robbed me and beat me up really bad."

Nick said, "So that's your story?" I said, "It's not my story, it's just the truth. I don't know how many more times you guys want me to tell you the same thing. I got beat up and I have not done anything wrong other than making a couple of bad choices. In hindsight, I should have left the money in the safe. That was my mistake and I am sorry about that." Nick still had a couple more questions for me. He asked, "Why did you not tell the police?" I said, "I did, I did."

He said, "No, you did not. We checked and no robberies were reported that night. Not one." I said, "Yeah well I didn't call 9-1-1. I saw a cop driving and I flagged him down and I told him what happened. I gave him a description of the guys and he said he would keep a look out for them. I gave him my name and contact info and he said he would call me if he found anyone matching their description. It's not my fault if he didn't make a formal file on it."

Nick was skeptical. He asked, "What time did this happen? When were you robbed?" I said, "I don't know, around 12:00 am I suppose." He said, "Why did it take you until 5:00 am to call anyone? Why were you out all night long?" I said, "I know that looks bad. The thing is I had to run away from my attackers. By the time I lost them I was also lost." Nick said, "So then what? It took you five hours to figure out you should call someone you know for help? It didn't take Ronald that long. He was calling hospitals by 1:00 am hoping you weren't dead."

"Well…" I began. "It sounds stupid when you say it now. It shouldn't have taken five hours, I agree. But I'm pretty sure I have a concussion and I think I even lost consciousness briefly so that didn't help." Nick said, "Ok, whatever. Put Frank on the phone."

I was scared for my job at this point. I worked in fear all day. It was one of my longest shifts ever. It certainly didn't help that I had a lot of toxins in my system. I sure felt like death at that point. It seemed that death may have been easier.

At the end of the day, Frank came to get me. He asked me to come to the office. I got butterflies in my stomach. I thought for sure I was getting fired. I went into the office and sat down. Frank pulled out an envelope which I imagined had my termination papers. "This is it!" I thought.

Frank handed me the envelope and then slid a piece of paper across the desk. "Sign this." He said. "What am I signing?" I asked. He said, "You are signing to say that you received this money. There's two grand in there to replace what was stolen. Sign to say you got it and then you and I will write your name on it, and it is staying in the cash office."

I was relieved and shocked at the same time. Not only was I not getting fired, but it seemed they didn't even want me to pay the money back. I didn't know how this was possible, but I took the pen and signed the paper and said, "Thank you."

I had completely lucked out this time. I knew that this would not happen again. I knew that I would be under the microscope now. I figured I had better get my act together right away or I would be out of a job.

I had a lot of motivation to get clean and sober at this point. I wanted to stay employed, and I wanted to have a life. I knew that there was a better life waiting for me if I just did the right thing. I was also afraid of dying young, which seemed like a very real possibility these days. I had a desire to be clean. I just wasn't sure how to get there and stay there permanently. I certainly could not do it alone. I needed a lot of help.

CHAPTER FOURTEEN

SHORTLY AFTER WE RETURNED FROM VICTORIA, I went into work one day and my manager told me that he needed to speak with me in his office. I knew it couldn't be good. I went into his office and he closed the door.

He said, "I want to speak with you about your job." I said, "Ok, what about it?" He asked, "How do you think you are doing?" I said, "Well, I think I'm doing pretty good." I had been in the position about a year now and I had been employed with Walmart for about three years total at this point. I added, "Sometimes it's difficult to complete every single thing on the list that you give me, but that is due to customers interrupting me, or other unforeseen circumstances." He did not agree with my account.

He said, "You are not performing the job at a level we need you to. The department is suffering as a result." At this point I thought my days at Walmart were over. I said, "Ok, so what? You're firing me?" "No," he said. "We have a couple of options. You can try a lot harder and hopefully turn things around. If you don't succeed in your efforts, we will go through the discipline process and then you may lose your job."

That didn't sound good to me, so I asked, "What's the other option?" He said, "We can move you to night crew. You would work 11:00 pm-7:30 am five days a week and the pay is the same. Also, there's a lot less pressure and less responsibility." This was the only option for me because I knew if I didn't take this option, they would soon get rid of me. I agreed to go to night crew.

I was attending 12 Step meetings from time to time as well. Every once in a while, I would give it a really solid effort and begin to do my steps and get involved with the people there.

What I didn't like was when older guys would tell me it was so nice to see someone so young come into the program. They would say, "If only I got here at your age. I could've saved so much trouble. It's true that you need to hit your bottom to get sober, but sometimes that means bringing the bottom up to hit you!"

I hated this because they didn't know me. How the hell did they know how bad it was or wasn't for me? I felt insulted. Like I wasn't a "real alcoholic." I would think to myself, "I'll show you a rock bottom!" Then I would relapse and make damn sure it was a good one!

These times of trying to quit drinking and using were sincere. Nobody had control over me anymore. I was an adult and I could do as I pleased. I genuinely wanted to lead a clean and sober life. I had some success, however there was always a good enough reason to relapse. I was struggling immensely with my addiction.

Sara had succeeded in improving one aspect of my life, that being my housing situation. She was struggling to find a way to help me with my addiction. I still went to Sara's every Sunday for a home cooked meal and to keep a good relationship with her. She still gave me money and cigarettes each time.

One Sunday, Sara told me that she had found a really great aboriginal addictions counsellor on the Rez by my house. She pleaded with me to just go and speak with him. I was in the middle of one of my clean and sober stretches and I felt it was a great idea. I took his business card and the next day I made a call to his office and made an appointment for the following Wednesday.

By the time I went to the appointment, I had relapsed. I went to the appointment with three days clean and sober. I was met by a very kind man who introduced himself as Lorne. Lorne was a senior aboriginal gentleman. He shook my hand and invited me into his office.

I went in and sat down in the leather chair that he offered. He said this was an intake session and all he needed was a bit of information about myself. He said that I could share as much or as little as I was comfortable with. I felt very comfortable with Lorne. I could tell that he wasn't judgemental at all. He was easy to talk to.

I told Lorne that I really needed his help. I told him about my drinking, and I told him about my drug use as well. His office was just down the street from Robert's, on the same Rez. He said, "Well, we are here to help those struggling with addiction issues. From what you've told me today… you qualify."

Lorne suggested that we meet every Wednesday morning. I liked this because it worked with my schedule. After my night shift, which finished at 7:30 am, I would have enough time to get home, eat breakfast, and then walk to Lorne's office and arrive for my appointment at 9:00 am.

I struggled very much to stay clean, and I almost never missed my appointment with Lorne. Usually when I went to see Lorne, I would be about three or four days clean. This is because I typically relapsed on the weekend. Lorne would give me "homework." He wrote out a list and asked me to put it on my fridge. The list of action items for me to complete looked like this:

Allan's action items:
- Get a sponsor
- Attend 12 Step meetings several times a week
- Exercise
- When confronted with cravings, pray, call sponsor, go to a meeting.

Each week when I met Lorne and told him I was a few days clean he would ask me, "Did you use any of the tools I gave you for relapse prevention?" I would ask, "What do you mean?" He would say, "Did you get a sponsor yet?" And I would reply, "No, not yet." And he would ask, "Did you ask the Creator to remove your cravings? Did you go to a meeting? Did you call a clean and sober friend?" I would sit there and answer, "No, I did not do any of those things." And Lorne would usually say, "Hmmm. Not sure why you relapsed. Looks like you've tried nothing and you're all out of ideas."

At this time, I was using crack over at Robert's almost every weekend. My brother had given me a very expensive mountain bike a couple of years earlier. It was one of the few things I had not sold. I would use it to ride down to the Rez, and several times people tried to get me to sell it for crack. I always told them that it wasn't for sale. I was determined not to ever sell this bike.

One day, when I had about two weeks clean and sober, I was home alone and started to get some really intense cravings to drink. I tried to keep myself busy by doing some housework. I eventually gave into my cravings, as I always did. I told myself I would just get a six-pack of beer, and I definitely would not smoke crack. Just a few beers, that would be all.

I walked across the street to the liquor store. I grabbed a six-pack and went home. I opened one of the beer in the elevator on the way up to my apartment. When I got into my apartment, I put the five beer down on the counter. The phenomenon of craving began to set in. I looked at the five beer. I thought, "Once I finish the one I opened, and three more, then I'll only have two left. That sucks."

When I got down to only three beer left, I wandered downstairs to apartment 201. There was a big native guy that lived there, and we partied together. His name was Ben. Ben liked to drink as much as I did.

I brought the three drinks with me. I knocked on Ben's door. I could hear loud music. I waited a minute and knocked louder. Ben came to the door. He stood there looking at me. He was swaying back and forth a bit. He looked like he had started drinking before me.

He said, "Well, ya gonna just stand there or are ya gonna come in and drink with me?" I said, "I'm coming in, bud!" I sat down on his couch and opened one of my beer. Ben and I began to talk and listen to music together.

When I had finished all my beer, he said, "I want you to do me a huge favour and you better do it now!" I said, "What is it?" He said, "You better get off your damn ass, and go over to that big white fridge, and open it and bring me a beer, and get yourself one too!"

Well, I had no problem with that! I opened the fridge and it was full of bottles of beer. When I say full, I mean it was full! Every shelf was full of beer from front to back and he had beer in the door of the fridge, and he had another case on the kitchen table.

When I got him a beer, I said, "Holy shit Ben! You think you got enough beer?" He said, "I don't like running out!" To this I replied, "It sounds like you and I have a lot in common!"

I sat there a few more hours drinking with Ben. He drank as fast as I did so we went through countless beer in a short time. As we both got more and more drunk, I decided I should sneak some of Ben's beer back up to my place so I could drink alone later on. I stuffed beer in every pocket I could find and then told Ben I forgot something upstairs and I would be back.

I ran up to my place and put five beer in the fridge. Then I ran back down. Ben asked "Did you go somewhere?" And I said, "I couldn't find what I forgot!" We continued to drink, and I made a few more trips with Ben's beer.

Later, Ben said, "I haven't seen your apartment yet." I invited him upstairs. When we got there, I invited him in, and he sat on my couch. I said, "I've forgotten my manners! Let me offer you a beer!" I brought him a beer from the fridge, and he said, "Hey! That's my beer!" I said, "Yes, it is now, I just gave it to you! It's yours buddy!"

We got very drunk. By the time I left Ben in his apartment and went upstairs, I could barely walk. The thought occurred to me that I should sell my bike for crack. I decided to take Lorne's advice and pray to the Creator. I yelled out, "CREATOR! DO NOT LET ME SMOKE CRACK! PLEASE! I WILL NOT SMOKE CRACK! PLEASE HELP ME TO NOT SMOKE CRACK, CREATOR!!!"

With that, I lay down on my couch and passed out. I woke up a while later. I stood up trying to figure out where I was, and what I was doing. Suddenly the thought occurred to me, "Oh yeah! I can sell my bike for crack!" I ran out the door and practically flew down the stairs to the underground parking lot.

When I got there, I used my key to unlock the caged area where people locked up their bikes. I selected my bike and wheeled it out. I hopped on and rode through the parking lot, and by the time I got to the exit I was moving quite quickly.

The time was still only about 7:00 pm. The liquor store across the street was busy as it was a Friday evening. I rode my bike out of the parking lot, picking up speed as I turned right and sped onto the street. It was at this point that my problems began.

There was a car parked across the street from the liquor store in front of my building. He had his hatchback up, because he had some wood in the back that was long and extended past the end of the car.

As I turned right, onto the street, he backed out of his parking spot. His rear bumper hit my front tire. As a result of the collision, my left hand squeezed the brake, and in turn the front brake was applied, which in turn launched me in a forward, upward direction.

We must have collided with great force because my body flew up and my head hit the glass of the open hatchback with enough force that the glass shattered and my entire body went through the glass and I landed on his roof. At that point I was unconscious, and I rolled off his roof and landed flat on my chin, chomping down on my tongue in the process.

I woke up on a stretcher and the first thing I saw was that someone was cutting the front of my shirt with scissors. I freaked out. I started yelling, "What are you doing? Don't cut me! Stop it! Why are you cutting off my clothes?"

The paramedics told me that I had been in an accident. I told the lady I was fine. I said, "I'm good, this is my house! I'm home, I gotta go now." They told me I was definitely not going home. I said, "Where's my bike? I'm going down the street to sell my bike! Bring my bike!"

They told me I was definitely not going to ride my bike and I would be going with them to the hospital. I said, "I'm refusing service! You can't force me to be served!" The paramedic laughed and said, "I think you mean you're refusing treatment, and you can't because of your level of intoxication, and you have a head injury as well, and you lost consciousness, so I think you have a concussion."

I went to the hospital. Apparently, Sara came. I don't remember her being there, but she told me later that I said things that were so vulgar and so hurtful that she wouldn't repeat them. She has never told me what I said. I've always wondered what I could have possibly said that was so horrible that it couldn't be repeated.

Several hours passed, and once the hospital ruled out spinal injury, an officer kindly drove me home. I slept for a few hours. I woke up to my buzzer going off. My friend Ronald who had been with me in Victoria was at the front door. I buzzed him in, and he came up.

Ronald came in and said, "Allan, I heard about your accident and I wanted to come and make sure you're ok." I attempted to talk. I realized I couldn't speak well because my tongue was massive. It was about three times its regular size, taking up most of the space in my mouth. Sara later commented, "First time he's stopped talking in all his life!"

I managed to communicate with Ronald and told him what happened. While he was there, the phone rang. It was Walmart calling. Ronald took the phone and talked for me. He explained why I couldn't speak and said, he was here to check in with me. They asked him to let me know they would be stopping by within the hour.

I wondered why they would be coming to my house. It was the personnel manager. She showed up with a couple of department managers about an hour later. They arrived with gifts. They had sent a card around and asked everyone to sign it and give a donation. They had collected several hundred dollars.

They used the money to buy about $300 worth of groceries. They said, that they knew I wouldn't be mobile for a bit, and they didn't want me to have to go out. They had about $60 left over, which they put in an envelope and gave to me. They said, I could use that for a taxi, or whatever I needed. I thought I would try to do something good with that money, but in my heart I knew I would use it for alcohol.

The Personnel Manager then said, "Oh, there's one more thing we have for you, Allan." She handed me a giant gift bag. I opened it and laughed as I pulled out a brand-new bike helmet. She said, "Because we want to keep you safe!"

I was overwhelmed by the kindness of my colleagues. After everything I had done in Victoria, and even though the accident was entirely due to my excessive drinking, and even though I wasn't a Department Manager like them anymore, they still cared about me. They genuinely cared whether or not I was ok.

I decided I would definitely stop drinking for good now. This could be rock bottom. I didn't need to prove to anyone that I was a "real alcoholic." I figured at this point it was obvious. I didn't need to die to prove it and I didn't need things to get any worse.

I smoked a little weed with Ronald that evening. I told him I was not drinking anymore and I told him why. The following day my friend Darryl, a guy I knew from Mike's house, came over. He had a case of beer. I said, "No man, I need to chill out on the booze." I told him what happened to me. He said, "Man, after what you've been through, you DESERVE a beer!"

It took very little to convince me to drink with him. I was good this time, though, I only had three drinks. He left and I went to sleep. I guess my body had been through so much that I was able to not get wasted that night. I was just done, both physically and emotionally.

I took about a week off work to recover. I did take it easy on the drinking that week. I attended my appointment with Lorne on Wednesday morning. I told him what had happened. I told him that even though I was totally loaded at the time, I did try to follow his advice. I told him that in the middle of my drunken state, I got major cravings for crack and I yelled out to the Creator to stop me from smoking crack.

Lorne sat quietly for a moment. He eventually looked up at me, breathed deeply, and then said, "You know Allan… whenever you pray to the Creator… you should always add that you pray that this happens in a good way!"

I was confused so he continued to explain. "You prayed that you wouldn't smoke any crack, right?" I confirmed that I did. He asked, "Well, did you smoke crack that night?" I replied, "No, no I didn't." "I pray that this comes in a good way," he said, "because the Creator did what you asked. He put things in place that physically stopped you from smoking crack."

I suppose it was about a week later when I got drunk and rode my bike down to the Rez. The bike was originally bought for $1600. I figured I would get at least $200 worth of crack for the bike, so probably an 8-ball. I failed in my negotiations.

The dealer started telling me that the brakes looked horrible and he wasn't going to be able to sell it for anything at all. He said, he would give me a half gram, $40 worth. I gave in and took the offer. Of course, I had to share that $40 worth with Robert and Rudy.

At this point, I thought I had sold everything I owned. As it turns out, there's always more to sell. One weekend, a few months after the bike accident, I was smoking crack with Rudy again. I ran out of money, then spent all my rent money again. We decided to go back to my house and see if I had any stuff to sell to the dealer.

When we got there, we searched around for things of value. Rudy told me that I could get $40 for my microwave. I didn't believe him. It wasn't exactly a high-end microwave. But we called the dealer. Rudy gave me the number and I used my phone to call. He arrived 30 minutes later.

While we waited, we scrubbed the inside of it because it was nasty. When the dealer arrived, he looked at it. He said, "Oh guys, I can't give you a half for this. We pleaded with him. He looked around. He said, "I can give you a half if you throw in that vacuum over there." I said, "OK, deal!"

Rudy and I cooked it up and smoked rocks for about an hour or so. Now we needed more. I had recently received a set of two cordless phones as a gift from Sara. I told Rudy that they were worth at least $100. He said, "Well call him up!"

I grabbed the paper that had the dealer's number on it. I called the number and told him that I had these two phones for him. He said, he would stop by. 30 minutes later I was letting him back into the apartment.

I showed him the phones and told him I could let them go for $100. He immediately said, "No way, I can't do a hundred." I said, "Well, gimme a gram then, eighty." "Nope." He said. "I'll give you a half gram for those." I sighed and said, "Fine."

Rudy and I finished that in about an hour. I had nothing left to sell. The week before, I had sold my TV and a couple of lamps at the local pawn shop. I literally had nothing of value. Rudy left and I figured I would try to sleep.

About an hour later, I heard Rudy yelling up to my balcony. "ALLAN! ALLAN! ALLAN!!!" I went out to the balcony and looked down. He said, "Allan come down here!" I went down to the lobby. I opened the door, and he said, "No, no go back in! Go upstairs!"

We went up to my apartment and went in. He said, "I got eighty bucks! Let's get a gram right now!" He ran over to the table and grabbed the paper with the dealers number. He said, "Ok, no time to waste! Call him up and I'll buy a gram." I sighed.

Rudy said, "What's wrong? What are you waiting for? Let's call him up and buy a gram! I'm paying!" I said, "I can't." He said, "Why not?!" I said, "He has both of my phones!"

How ironic. I had sold every single possession to the dealer, and now that I had cash and needed to call him, I was unable to do so because he had my phones! This was a sad moment.

Rudy said, "Ok, no problem, let's go across the street to the pay phone." Luckily, Rudy had a quarter because I had nothing. We went to the pay phone and an hour later the dealer delivered a gram of coke.

Life continued like this for some time. When I wasn't using with Rudy, I was going downtown to Main and Hastings and the Pigeon Park area. Surprisingly, I continued to work, and I rarely missed a shift. I also attended my drug and alcohol counselling every Wednesday at 9:00 am with Lorne.

One day, I attended a 12 Step meeting down the street from my home. I listened to an elderly German lady talk at the meeting. She had a very calming manner. I was interested in what she had to say. She mostly spoke of the solution that we had been given and how to apply the tools that have been so freely given to us.

A day or two later, I was in the lobby at my apartment building, checking my mailbox. The lady I had seen at the meeting walked in. She opened a mailbox and collected her mail. I said, "Hi." She replied, "Hello." We didn't talk more than that, we each went to our apartments.

The next day I went to the same meeting and I saw the lady again. I approached her and said, "Hi, I think you live in my building." She looked at me and said, "No, I don't think so." I said, "Yes, you do. I saw you in the lobby yesterday." She said, "I think you're mistaken. I don't remember seeing you."

I didn't push the issue. The following day I went to the lobby for my mail and I saw her again. I looked at her and smiled. She smiled back at me. She said, "Hello. It seems you are correct. You do live in my building." I said, "Yes, yes. I thought so."

I introduced myself, "My name is Allan. I live in 403." She said, "Nice to formally meet you. My name is Angelika. I live directly below you in 303." Angelika asked if I wanted to come over for a coffee.

I accepted the offer and rode the elevator to the third floor. We went into her apartment and she brewed a pot of coffee. She asked if I would like a cigarette. I said, "If you're offering, I won't say no to that."

We sat and talked. I told Angelika that I really wanted to get sober, but I had been struggling. She said I should get a home group at the meetings and commit to going. "Get involved," she suggested. She said that she went to a meeting every Wednesday evening on the reserve. She said she would drive me there every week if I wanted. I agreed to do this.

Even though I was attending counselling every week and I had some involvement in 12 Step programs, I continued to relapse. I began to spend a lot of time at Main and Hastings and Pigeon Park.

One day, I was at Main and Hastings, and I continued to use there for a full 24 hours. I walked all over, buying and smoking crack, ten or twenty dollars' worth at a time.

A guy approached me. He said, "Hey buddy, you look like you could use some crack." I said, "Yeah buddy, I'm all out. Ya got some to share?" "I do bro." He replied.

I was excited. I couldn't believe this. Someone else was actually going to give *me* some crack for once. He leaned towards me. He was kind of getting in my personal space. He said, "You'll just do some acts of kindness for me and I'll share my crack with you." As he said this, he reached down and stroked my thigh.

I got completely freaked out. I said, "You got the wrong idea buddy." And I started to walk away. He started to follow me, calling for me to stop. I ran and ran. I felt like I was in a nightmare. I just knew I couldn't stop. I ran down some alleys and then I lay down under a car and waited there a while.

When I thought it was safe, I came out. I began wandering around the back alleys. I exited an alley onto a main road. Suddenly I heard something. I turned around and he was there. He said, "Hey bud, where were you?" I started to walk but he stopped me and said, "I'm sorry if I scared you. I can front you some crack if you want. Do you have cigarettes to share with me?"

It turned out I had a fresh pack of smokes. I said, "Well yeah, I do." "Good enough." He said. "This is my condo." He said, pointing at a building in front of me. He invited me in. I went with him.

I got upstairs and there was another guy there. He told me he just had to wait for his dealer to show up. I said, "Ok can I use your bathroom?" He showed me where it was. I went and used the washroom. When I came out I had the shock of a lifetime.

I went to the living room. I looked in front of me and saw the guy that brought me up there on his knees, performing oral sex on the other guy. My heart started racing. I got dizzy. I was so scared. He looked over and said, "I can handle two at the same time if you want to join in!"

I said, "I gotta go!" He said, "Listen, I have some crack on the way. The guy is bringing an 8-ball. If you suck me off, I'll share all of it with you." I was so nervous at this point. Nervous because I wanted to leave, and more nervous because I needed to smoke more crack, and I was considering his offer. I got butterflies in my stomach." I asked, "You'll share it all with me?" "Of course!" he replied. "Ok, let's do this," I said reluctantly.

He told me to kneel in front of him. I did. My heart was racing at this point. He moved close to me with his penis out. "Open your mouth." He ordered. As I began to open my mouth, I got dizzy, light headed, and nauseated. I jumped up and ran to the washroom.

"Hey!" he yelled, "Where do you think you're going?" I got to the bathroom and puked in his sink. When I stopped heaving, I came out and ran for the door. "I'm outta here!" I said, as I started to run down the hallway.

I ran to the end of the hallway to the elevator. I pushed the button and the door opened. I walked in and pushed the button for the lobby. Nothing happened. I was terrified. I couldn't get the elevator to work. I really felt that if I couldn't get out of there quickly, the guys would drag me back there and rape me.

The guy came out, zipping up his jeans. As he approached me, I clenched my fists, and said, "You better get the fuck away from me!" He said, "Relax, I need to use my card to make the elevator work." Apparently, all tenants had a card to make the elevator work. I guess it was a security feature.

He entered the elevator and swiped his card. The door closed. I prepared myself to fight to the death. I felt my upper lip tremble as I gritted my teeth. He said, "Don't be afraid. I'll take you downstairs." He swiped the card and pushed the button for the lobby. When we got there the door opened and he said, "If you change your mind, you know where I am, bud." "Ok." I said. And I ran out of the front door.

I ran as fast as I could. It began to rain and I was wearing only a t-shirt and jeans. It was somewhere around 2:00 am, late enough that there were no buses. I decided to sleep in a stairwell I found. I was only there about 10 minutes when a security guard came and told me to leave.

I started walking. I walked and walked and walked. I walked down a back alley and leaned up against a building. I felt the presence of a woman, and as she leaned in behind me, with her face right by my ear, I heard, very clearly, her voice. "Allan! Allan!"

I turned to look. Nobody was there. I got major shivers down my spine. The hairs on the back of my neck stood up, and my arms were rough with goosebumps. I don't know what that was, but Lorne later told me it was my spirit speaking to me.

I decided I would just walk home, all the way to North Vancouver. To do this I had to head towards Stanley Park, and walk across the Lions Gate Bridge. I didn't care. At this point I would do anything just to be back in the comfort of my own home.

As I approached the bridge, I was soaking wet from the rain. I started to shiver. I felt sick and weak. My head was spinning. I began my regular chant "Back on track, back off the crack!"

My emotions were all over the place. I reached out to my dad, who I knew was always by my side no matter what. "I'm sorry, Dad." I said. I was confronted with a deafening silence. "Dad? Dad please! Please answer me, Dad! I need you! I'm sorry, Dad! I'm so sorry!"

For the first time ever, my dad did not respond. I heard nothing. I was devastated. Dad always answered me, no matter what. Not this time. Dad was gone. I guessed that I had disappointed him so much, he could not stand it.

I got to the halfway point of the bridge. There's a lookout there. I stopped to rest. As I looked out across the water, I turned my head to look down. I thought "Perhaps I should step off right here."

After all I had been through that night, and life in general, I thought "What's the point? Why not jump off?" My addiction was so powerful that I had become willing to do almost anything to get more. Thank God I got sick and didn't follow through. I felt that if this was not my bottom, then I did not want to see what was.

I looked down again. "Death is a better bottom than whatever else awaits me in my addiction." I thought. This was a fleeting thought replaced with the thought, "Come on man! We both know you're not doing that, so let's get home!" It is a bit funny to talk to yourself as, "We both," but that's how I spoke to myself. Like two people.

I finished walking across the bridge. I was now on the North Vancouver side and still had a long walk to get home. I had a few smokes left in my package and I had a little rock of crack in there, wrapped in tin foil. I decided that I needed to make a decision. As I pulled out a cigarette, I also pulled out the rock. I looked at it and said, "You've ruined me. I'm done with you. I don't need you."

As I walked past a bush, I threw the crack in the bush. I lit up a smoke and kept walking. I eventually got back to my apartment. I was cold, soaking wet, exhausted and depressed. Not only was I still in shock from the night's events, but I was also dealing with the fear of losing my home because as usual, I didn't have the rent. My body was weak because I was sleep-deprived, and of course, because of the toxic crack I had ingested. All the alcohol I had consumed didn't help.

When I got home, I thought perhaps I should reach out to Angelika. I went down in the elevator and knocked on her door. She came to the door almost right away. I didn't even consider the fact that it was now around 5:00 am. She didn't complain or even mention the time. She just invited me in and offered me a seat at her dining room table.

I looked at her and said, "Angelika, I'm in big trouble. I have no rent money. Also, I have seen things and experienced things tonight that I don't think I can get past. I'm not ok, Angelika." She looked at me and said, with great confidence, "You will be, Allan. You will be ok. There is nothing you cannot get past."

Angelika decided the next step was a pot of coffee. She started to brew a pot. She poured a coffee into her old-fashioned china mug and brought it to me. We sat across from each other at her dining room table. She handed me a cigarette and a lighter. "Thank you." I said, as I lit the smoke.

I took a sip of the coffee and a drag of my smoke and said, "I don't know what to do. I don't have any rent. I'm very ill. I'm going to die from using drugs, Angelika."

I finished my smoke and sat there with my elbows on the table, my face buried in my hands. I started to cry. I was officially broken. I said, "I have tried to stop using. I have always attended my counselling sessions. I go to meetings. I don't understand the steps. I've tried to do the steps. I don't understand how they are supposed to keep me clean."

Angelika sat quietly and listened to me. She said, "The steps are done in order and they all need to be done. You don't need to rush through them." She reached across the table and took my hands in her hands. Her hands were frail and cold.

She grasped my hands firmly. She asked "Allan, are you an alcoholic?" I laughed out loud, crying at the same time. Through my tears I said, "Look at me! I'm completely broken! I have no control over my actions when I drink! Of course I'm an alcoholic! Of course I am!"

Angelika smiled gently and said, "Congratulations! We have just succeeded with the first step." The first step says, "We admitted we were powerless over alcohol, that our lives had become unmanageable." I had to agree, I had completed this step.

Angelika told me that I should go home and get some rest and then come back just before noon and she would take me to a meeting. I agreed. I went to my apartment, but I didn't sleep much. I thought about the night's events. I wondered "How could I let myself get to that place?" I grabbed a pen and paper and wrote my thoughts in the form of a poem. I wrote:

All us boys, we're becoming men
Sitting around the same table again
Yeah here I am, I'm back
Don't give a damn just give me some crack
Tonight I'm in for a heart attack!
Now my heart is racing fast
I don't care, just give me a blast!
Stay up all night around the clock
Money's getting tight but I need another rock
Yeah that's the way the trip goes
I got a bottle in my hand and a straw up my nose
Insanity is setting in
I keep playing this game, yet I can't seem to win
I really need to stop, but how do I begin?

Now here we are again
With the spoon and the pin
Crazy thoughts filled my head
I never listened to what she said
Fuck! I better go to bed
Or pretty soon I'll end up dead!

I followed through with my promise. I went downstairs at 11:30 am. She was ready for me. We had a smoke together, then went downstairs to the parking lot. We got in her car and drove to the meeting.

Angelika knew everyone at the meeting. She introduced me to an older man who was there. She said, "This is Allan and he's a REAL alcoholic." I loved her already. She seemed to get me. Also, she was completely non-judgmental and didn't preach to me.

I went to my appointment with Lorne on Wednesday morning. I told him what had happened. Lorne said, "Allan, I'm not sure what more I can do for you. You've been coming here for over a year now. I think you want sobriety because you have missed almost none of your appointments. You come here every week and every week you have a few days clean. But you keep coming. What can I do for you?"

I told Lorne that I didn't know anymore. I said, "Maybe there is nothing that can be done for me. I am, perhaps, beyond hope." Lorne said, "I have one last hope for you. I want to make a suggestion."

I was curious. "What is it?" I asked. He said, "There's a medication that you can take. It has no effect on you in your day-to-day life. It has no side-effects, unless you drink, in which case you will become violently ill and you could die. It reacts with alcohol and makes you super sick if you drink."

I told Lorne I would think about it and I would talk to him the following week. I finished up with my appointment and went home. I called my birth mom, Lillian. I told her the plan. She got very angry with me. She said, "Don't you dare take that! I had a friend that went on that shit and she drank when she was on it, and she died! She's dead!"

This information scared me a lot. I called Sara. I told her what Lorne wanted me to do. She wasn't sure what to say. She believed I needed help in a big way. But I think she was scared about what would happen if I drank. I pondered all of this.

The following Wednesday I went to see Lorne for my 9:00 am appointment. I had not relapsed since I saw him the week before. I told him that I didn't want to take the prescription.

I said, "Lorne, I do need to stop drinking, but I don't think I will take that prescription. I'm afraid because my birth mom had a friend who died on it. I'm scared that if I take it and I drink, then I will die."

Lorne sat silently for a bit, just breathing in and out and saying nothing. I asked what he was thinking. He said, "Allan you've been very open with me. I've been with you through your addiction. I know your story well." I said, "Yes you do."

Lorne continued, "You're afraid that if you take it and drink then you'll die?" I said, "That's correct. It scares the shit out of me." He said, "Here's the thing. If you do not take it, and you drink, you will <u>certainly</u> die. THAT should scare the shit out of you. That's the reality."

"Wow." I said. "That's profound." I thought hard about it. He said, "You drink and smoke crack without giving it much thought at all. These behaviours can and will kill you. The only thing the prescription does is make you think twice about it." I agreed to fill the prescription.

Lorne warned me. He said, "Allan the thing is that you need to know one hundred percent what is in the things you consume. You cannot use mouth wash anymore. You cannot have cough drops or cough syrup. You need to be very aware of ingredients and avoid anything that has alcohol in it."

I agreed. He wrote a letter for me to give to my doctor. I brought it to my doctor the next day and got a prescription. I filled the prescription right away. I went home and took one of the pills.

I had been sober for a while and I was feeling better, but I did get cravings. The prescription was not effective in removing cravings. The only effect it had was that it reacted with alcohol. So it was a deterrent.

I started to go to meetings with Angelika weekly. She introduced me to a guy who could sponsor me. As I got to know more and more people in the 12 Step group, I began to feel like I belonged there.

I was a member of the Wednesday night meeting. I began to do service work. I volunteered to open the meeting every week. This meant I needed to keep the key and come and open the doors, put on coffee and set up all the chairs. I rather enjoyed this.

I met with my sponsor regularly. We talked a lot and he began to walk me through the steps. Angelika drove me to meetings several times a week and kept me company when I was bored.

I often went downstairs to have coffee with Angelika. I always said, "Angelika you're not my sponsor, but you may as well have been." I told her how much she meant to me. I told her I could never repay her. She said, "The only payment I want is for you to stay sober."

So now I had a beginning. The road ahead would be challenging at the best of times. I was both scared and excited at the same time. They told me it would be hard. They told me it would be worth it. They told me my worst day sober would be better than my best day drunk. I hoped they were right. I was ready.

CHAPTER FIFTEEN

I KNEW I WANTED SOBRIETY. The problem was that I didn't know how to stay clean. I knew how to get clean and sober; I had done that many times. I didn't know how to not relapse. The people in my meetings said that the solution was in the steps. Now that I had a sponsor to guide me through the steps, perhaps I could figure it all out.

I spent a lot of time reviewing and dissecting the wording of the steps. Everyone told me that I wasn't getting sober because I didn't have Step one figured out. I did. Step one said, "We admitted we were powerless over alcohol—that our lives had become unmanageable." I admitted I was powerless over alcohol and it was impossible to deny that my life had become unmanageable. If I had Step one, then why did I continuously relapse?

I told myself many times that I was an alcoholic and I needed to stop drinking. After a brief period of sobriety, I would get strong cravings to drink. I would ultimately give in to those cravings, telling myself, "Well I admit I'm an alcoholic. Of course, I am going to drink again! I admit I'm an alcoholic and I admit I'm powerless over alcohol and I don't believe anything can change that so I'm drinking!"

But Step two told me, "Came to believe that a Power greater than ourselves could restore us to sanity." Wow. It wasn't that I didn't have the first step figured out. If I said that I was an alcoholic, but I didn't believe anything could be done then surely it meant that I didn't have Step two figured out. I needed to come to believe that my higher power, whatever that was, would be able to help.

But wait a minute. I did have Step two. I had practiced prayer many times. I had never prayed to stay sober and then gone out to drink. It worked. In fact, I remember speaking to Lorne one day. He was asking me about a relapse I had. He asked if I had prayed to stay sober. I told him I did not.

When Lorne asked me why I had not prayed I said, "I was afraid." Lorne was confused. He asked, "Afraid to pray?" I said, "Yes. I was afraid because I know it works. I knew if I prayed, I wouldn't drink. I didn't want to pray, I wanted to get loaded!"

Looking back at this, I realized I did in fact have the first two steps figured out. I didn't have Step three figured out. Step three said, "Made a decision to turn our will and our lives over to the care of God *as we understood him*." That was it! Of course, it was not my higher powers' will for me to drink. It was my will. "I didn't want to pray, I wanted to get loaded." I was not practicing the third step.

I began to realize that if I was to have any success at all I needed to not be fixated on one step. They were in order for a reason. I needed to finish one and keep moving on to the next one. Thinking about these first three steps more deeply than I ever had before, I began to feel like I was getting it. I felt excitement about it.

My sponsor told me that Step one was more than just admitting. I needed to write out my life story from the time I started drinking and using. He asked me to document all major events including how I dealt with these events, as well as how my drinking had progressed over the years.

I followed my sponsor's advice. I wrote out my story. Next, I was to complete steps two and three. My sponsor told me that in order to believe that a power greater than myself could help me, I would need to identify that power. It didn't matter what it was. I just needed to have a higher power and believe that this power could restore me to sanity.

Although I was raised as a Christian, I was struggling with whether or not I believed in a Christian God. I really gravitated towards the Creator.

This was what I had learned through the Indigenous treatment centre I attended.

Basically, the way it was explained to me was that all the religions in the world are like all the poles of a teepee. They all point to the same place. This meant that there is one God, and all faiths know him differently. An elder told me it didn't really matter what you call him. He will respond to all names. He said they believed in a loving God who wants the best for us. I went with that and began to call my higher power "Creator."

I went back to Lorne and reported my progress. He was happy for me. He was very happy to hear that I had a sponsor. He was even happier to hear that I had not relapsed and that I was attending meetings and doing my steps.

I was told that that a lot of people relapse during the fourth step. This step says, "Made a searching and fearless moral inventory of ourselves." I didn't have as much trouble with it as others. It was difficult, but I did not feel the need to relapse over it.

It was explained to me like this. Basically, I needed to start by making a list of all my resentments. Everything I'm angry about or have been angry about in the past should be on that list. Once I had a complete list of resentments, I should continue with the hard part.

I was told to make columns on a sheet of paper. The first column said, "I'm resentful at..." Here I could list all the people who have wronged me or pissed me off. The next column said, "The cause." So I could write everything they had done to make me angry. These two columns were easy. I had a long list. But the next column was more difficult to figure out. I was told to label that column "My part."

My sponsor told me that I was to be really honest. If I looked back at these relationships, there would inevitably be a time I harmed the people I was angry with. Perhaps I even instigated the disagreement. Here's an example.

Jen was on the list. I was angry that she had left me. It came out of left field. Right when I had stopped drinking, and I was struggling with that, and both of my best friends had just died—right when I needed her the most, she just left.

It didn't take a lot of digging to find my part. Let's see... she paid my rent several times. I didn't take care of my health. She rescued me from a crack house because I asked her to pick me up to stop me from using crack, and then I was reluctant to leave with her. I lied to her on multiple occasions, usually to hide my drinking or drug use. I was angry and bitter and no fun to be around, at the best of times.

Wow. I realized that SHE was the one that should be resentful. I caused her a lot of stress and anxiety. All of those things were my fault. I did that. I would have left me, too. It was hard to admit. But I had only just begun. There were many others on my list.

I continued going down the list of resentments, identifying my part in all of them. For some of them, I struggled to find my part. For example, I had my birth dad on there. I was resentful towards him. The cause of my resentment was that he was abusive to my mother, and that he was a murderer, and I guess I was resentful because I had hoped to have a dad in my life, since the dad I knew had passed away. How was any of that my part?

Working with my sponsor, I learned that in circumstances like this, my part can simply be that I had expectations of him. Having expectations of someone else is selfish and self-centred, I was told. Nobody else needs to be anything other than who they are. We should look at ourselves when discovering defects, not others.

My other part in circumstances such as this was how I reacted to situations. I was taught that nobody can MAKE me angry. Being angry is a choice. In some situations, that's the only part I had. That was ok. As long as I was honest about my part in every situation.

I worked hard at these steps while working night shift at Walmart, attending my home group meeting on Wednesday evenings, and seeing Lorne every Wednesday morning.

My friend Mike, who used to live in the house with all the other roommates, had moved. His apartment was now just down the street from my apartment. Mike was never really in the drug scene. He enjoyed a drink now and then, but he never had a problem with it. He was always very supportive of me and my efforts to stop drinking. Mike was never, ever judgmental. We became very close friends. As a matter of fact, he became my best friend.

The longer I was clean and sober, the better my life became. I began to enjoy hiking. There are so many great places to hike in North and West

Vancouver. I began to take care of my health. I never once missed my rent, and Sara began to have a little trust in me.

Work was going well, too. I was stocking shelves in the pet department. I gave it my best effort every single night. I was good at my job. I put out far more skids than anybody else. Most people were completing five skids a night in the pet department. When I worked there, I was doing 13-14 skids every single night.

Pets became my department. On my two days off, they would put two people on, and they would do 9-10 skids each night between them. My managers began to see me as exceptional. This was such a huge change compared to how they had previously viewed me.

When I spoke with my sponsor after completing Step four, he said I had done a very good job on it. He said it appeared that I had been very thorough and very honest. Next was Step five, which said, "Admitted to God, to ourselves, and to another human being, the exact nature of our wrongs."

To complete this step, I needed to find someone I could trust to say everything to. There was very personal stuff in my Step four. I had things in there that I had not told anyone before. He told me to wait and be patient. The right person would come.

I talked to Angelika about this. She said that she knew someone. He was a pastor who was also a recovering alcoholic. She said that this guy was a good friend of hers, and she gave me his number. His name was Pastor Ben.

I called Pastor Ben and made an appointment. He asked me to bring my step four with me. I met him at the church in the morning after one of my night shifts. I was ready to tell him everything on my Step four. It didn't go like that.

Pastor Ben said there was more involved with the fourth step than just listing the resentment, the cause, and my part. For every resentment, I was to list the cause and my part, but then we took it a step further; I needed to list the character defect that was the cause of my part.

For example, Sara was on the list. I was resentful toward Sara. The cause was that the last time I asked her to pay my rent, she refused. She knew I could be evicted, but she lied and said she had no money left.

My part in this was that I had lied to Sara multiple times about why I didn't have my rent. I had also stolen money from her on a recent visit to her home. So the character defects associated with my part in this were "I have been dishonest" and "I have been a thief."

Pastor Ben asked me if I could return the following morning, after updating my step four with the last column labelled "Defect of character associated with my part." I agreed. He said, "When you return tomorrow, you will also complete steps six and seven." Step six said, "Were entirely ready to have God remove all these defects of character." Step seven said, "Humbly asked him to remove our shortcomings."

Pastor Ben said, "When you come tomorrow, you will need to be entirely ready to have God remove those defects that you have listed."

I returned the next morning at 9:00 am. I went into Pastor Ben's office. I had everything ready for him. We sat in his office as I went through my list of resentments, and then I told him my part and the character defect I had identified with each one.

Once I had finished, he said, "That is very good work. Come with me now, we will go upstairs." I followed Pastor Ben. We went upstairs and through some big doors, into the church. We went up to the front pew. Pastor Ben began to speak.

He said, "We are here today in front of Allan's higher power, whoever that may be. Allan has some things to say." Then he told me to say out loud all of my character defects and while reading them he asked that I be entirely ready for my higher power to remove these defects of character.

I began. "Creator, I have been a thief. I have been dishonest. I have been cruel. I have been vindictive. I have been lustful. I have been egotistical. I have been selfish, and I have been self-centred." Pastor Ben looked at me and asked "Is that all?" I said, "I believe so."

Pastor Ben began to speak to the Creator. "I would like to address Allan's higher power. Allan and I are asking that you please remove these defects of character from Allan so that he may move forward in his recovery and his life." Pastor Ben turned to me. He said, "We are done here now. Come with me and bring your step work."

We went back downstairs. He went into a closet and found a metal bowl. I asked what it was for. "You'll see." He said. "Follow me." I followed Pastor Ben through a door that led to the back of the church. It was a garden. We walked up to a flower bed. He said, "Allan, there are ashes of over 200 saints scattered here in this garden. People who have gone before us."

I looked at him wondering what was next. He asked me to put all my Step work, everything I had written, into the metal bowl. He then pulled out some wooden matches. He asked me to light one and burn the paper. I struck the match and put the flame to the corner of one of my sheets.

The flame grew bigger, eventually engulfing all the sheets of paper. Pastor Ben let the flame extinguish itself. When all the flames were out, he said, "Time for these ashes to join the others that are already here. He passed me the bowl and asked me to spread the ashes across the flower bed. I emptied the bowl into the dirt.

After a brief moment of silent reflection, Pastor Ben turned to me and said, "Allan, the sad thing is that you came here with a ton of shit… but the nice thing is that you're not going to leave with it. Your higher power has removed your defects of character and forgiven you for your past mistakes. You have a new beginning and it starts now."

This was very powerful. I loved that I physically left all my shit there and I trusted 100% that my Creator had dealt with all of it. I thanked Pastor Ben sincerely and told him how much this meant to me.

When I left the church, I felt as though a huge weight had been lifted from me. I felt like I was truly working a program of recovery, and I was excited and motivated. I was becoming the person I was meant to be, not the person that my addiction turned me into.

I went for Sunday dinner with Sara every week. It felt nice to not be asking her for money anymore. I was self-sufficient. I had a full-time job and my rent at the apartment was less than $300/month. I could tell that Sara still worried about me relapsing because that's how it always went before. This time was different though. I could feel it.

I continued to meet with Lorne every week. He was excited about my progress, but reminded me that more steps needed to be completed, and not to get so comfortable that I stop where I am. In order for the steps to be effective, I would need to do all of them.

I had completely finished steps five, six, and seven with Pastor Ben. Now it was time to move on to the next step. Step eight said, "Made a list of all persons we had harmed, and became willing to make amends to them all."

My sponsor told me that I would already have most of my list for Step eight completed. When I did Step four, I had listed my resentments, and I had also listed "My Part." He told me I should take a look at my part on every resentment and then I would see where I had harmed others. I needed to be willing to make amends to all the people I had resentments towards, for my part in it.

Of course, I no longer had a physical copy of my Step four because I had burned it, but I remembered the list, so I wrote down all the people I had harmed, and how I had harmed them. There were others who were not on my Step four list, and I added them as well.

One of the biggest amends I owed was to Sara. I had caused her so much stress and anxiety, not to mention the fact that she paid my rent on multiple occasions and gave me money all the time. I owed her personal amends and financial amends.

The amount of money she had given me for rent and other expenses was $1100. I had no idea how I was going to pay that back, but I was determined to try. I began to put aside a little money from every cheque and hoped I could manage to save the whole amount.

Keep in mind, Step eight said, that I "became willing to make amends to them all." This was just a chance for me to identify everyone I owed amends to. Step nine said "Made direct amends to such people wherever possible, except when to do so would injure them or others."

I owed huge amends to Walmart. I had spent their $2000 on crack and I had also been extremely unproductive at work, costing them productivity. I could not make financial amends directly to Walmart because I feared that they would fire me if I was honest about Victoria.

The way I made amends to Walmart was through my work ethic. I decided I would be the best employee they had. I had to make up for all the times I was unproductive. This is why I did twice as many skids as the others. I pushed myself every single night to be the best.

As for the financial amends... well, I was able to pay it back indirectly. I skipped my 15-minute breaks. I punched out at the end of my shift and went back to the department to work for another hour, or I would start working before I punched in. I never told my managers any of this because I understood it was against policy to work off the clock, and they would never allow this. So, I did this in secret. I figured I owed them at least this much.

CHAPTER SIXTEEN

BY THE TIME I WAS ABOUT nine months sober, real changes started to happen in my life. I had my yearly evaluation at work. My manager sat with me and went over it. The ratings ranged from 1-5.

If you were a "1" it meant you were consistently not performing at a level that is regularly expected of your job. "2" meant you had some issues throughout the year, but there was some improvement. "3" meant that you consistently performed at a level normally expected of you.

Most people got a "3." It was rare to get higher than that. "4" meant that you consistently performed at a level above what is normally expected, and "5" meant that you consistently performed at a level far, far above what was normally expected.

Sitting with my Manager, I listened as he went through the whole evaluation. In every single category, he rated me a "5." I was amazed. He could not say enough good things about me. He told me I was by far the best associate he had.

At the end of my evaluation, my manager put the paper down on the desk. He said, "Ok, the formal part is done." I said, "OK..." He took off his badge and put it on the desk. He said, "I'm no longer talking as your manager. This is now a badge-off conversation. Just you and me."

I waited anxiously for what he would say. He continued. "When you were the Manager of Pets... well... let's be honest, ok? You were not ok. Over the last year, 10 months maybe... something has drastically changed. I just want you to know that I see it... I acknowledge it... and I hope you keep doing what you're doing, and I hope you keep not doing what you're not doing anymore."

I was shocked. I looked at him and said, "Thank you. Thank you so much." He had one more thing to tell me. He said, "I have the utmost respect and admiration for you, and I'm grateful that you're part of my team."

This was a major event in my sobriety. I never realized how much people knew about me, without me telling them. I did not realize it was that obvious. For my manager to acknowledge this validated for me that I was in fact a new person. It felt good.

I was hanging out with Mike every weekend now. We would usually go to his apartment down the street and play video games. Other times, I would convince him to come hiking with me. He didn't enjoy hiking that much, but he came with me because he knew I loved it. I guess that's what best friends do.

One of the hiking trips we did was the Grouse Grind on North Vancouver's Grouse Mountain. This is a very intense hike. You start at the base of the mountain and hike the switchbacks, which are appropriately named, as they are stairs that go up and to the right, then switch back and go up and to the left. This repeats over and over until you reach the top.

I had been taking about an hour and a half to do the hike, which is a moderate pace. I wasn't rushing, just a nice relaxed pace until I reached the top.

When I brought Mike, I knew we would take a bit longer, but I had no idea how long it would actually take. We began and he was having trouble right from the beginning. He wanted to go back, but I told him that would mean we gave in. We would feel defeated. He was ok with this!

I kept pushing him, and he said, "Fine I'll do it. But it's at my pace." I told him that was fine, we had all day. I tried to encourage him along the way, telling him he would have a sense of accomplishment once he finished. At one point he was lying down on the stairs.

Mike said, "I don't think I can do this." I told Mike that we had just passed the halfway marker. I said, that it was closer to go to the top now, than it is to turn back. I reminded him that it was actually a longer hike if we went back. He said, "Yeah but it's all downhill!"

I continued to encourage Mike with phrases like "Nothing worth doing is easy," and "whether you think you can, or you think you can't, you're right!" It was a long and painful process for both of us. We did succeed in reaching the top… four and a half hours later. But as I told Mike, it doesn't matter how long we took, it matters that we never gave up, a principle I place a lot of value in, in all areas of my life, not just mountain climbing.

I had been doing this hike over and over, trying to beat my personal best. I had started at 1 hour 30 minutes. The next time I did it in 1 hour 16 minutes. The next time I got it down to 1 hour 3 minutes. A while later, 58 minutes. And my best time ever was 48 minutes.

After my latest climb, I was very proud of myself. I got onto the gondola at the top of the mountain and rode back down to the bottom. On the gondola with me was an elderly man. "Good day, young man," he said. "Good morning," I replied. We began to talk.

He said, "Did you do the grind?" "Yes, I did." I answered. "I've been doing it fairly regularly these days. I enjoy it." He said, "Yes, me too. I live just at the base of the mountain, so I do it every morning after breakfast."

I was impressed. I asked him how long it took him, expecting he would say two hours or something like that because he's elderly. He said, "Well, I like to keep a good pace. It takes me just about 35 minutes." I was shocked, to say the least. "35 minutes!" I exclaimed, "That's an excellent time." He said, "Yes, I suppose it is, but like I said, I do it every day. You know, at 84, you gotta keep moving or you'll start to slow down!"

This just made me realize that there's always room for improvement. I continued to do the grind, but I never did beat my 48-minute time. I was ok with that for now, at least I was out there being active and staying in shape.

I kept pushing myself at Walmart as well. Part of our job was to make the department presentable for store opening. I was used to putting out about 10 skids a night, on average, as well as "Zoning." Zoning was the term they used for front-facing the merchandise on the shelves. We had to pull everything forward and stack it up so the shelves looked full.

I started to take this part of my job a step further. In the cat aisle, there were hundreds of cans of cat food. The really little cans were stacked five-high, and these cans stretched for 30 feet down the aisle. They sold out almost completely every day and I would need to fill them. This was much more time consuming than other items like big bags of cat litter.

Once I had finished the entire department and all my skids were done, I would pull all of the cans forward, and then I would turn every single can, so that they were all facing the same way, with the picture of the cat in exactly the same position on every single can for the entire aisle.

Multiply this by hundreds of cans, and it was a lot of work. The end result was impressive. When you looked down the aisle there was not one single empty spot and all the cats were lined up perfectly.

I began to be noticed for this work. A lot of people were amazed that I could pull this off and complete the number of skids I did. I was known for this. Sometimes I would still be at work after the store opened. Customers would say, "I feel bad about buying anything because I'll ruin the perfection."

Around this time, we got a new Store Manager. He walked past the Pet Department every morning. He never introduced himself to me or spoke to me. Not once. Until one day when he had been our manager for about three months.

It was an extremely busy night. I came to work and was confronted with 15 skids of merchandise. On top of that I had break packs to do. Break packs are reusable plastic boxes that are used to ship small items.

My break packs were full of cat collars, cat toys, and small containers of fish food. These were very time-consuming because they were all small, they were all individually wrapped in plastic, and there were lots of them. Tonight, I had 17 break packs.

I pushed hard. I skipped my breaks, and my lunch. I had to punch out for lunch and run back in because we weren't allowed to skip lunch. I worked harder than I had worked ever before in Pets. I was successful. I finished all 15 skids and every single item from the 17 break packs. I did not have time for Zoning.

At about 6:50 am, the Store Manager walked by with a couple of other Managers. He looked down the cat aisle. By this time, he was used to seeing my perfect cat aisle every day. He called me over to talk with him.

"Who are you?" he asked. I was thinking, "Man, he doesn't even know me!" I replied to him "Hi Mark. My name is Allan and I work in your Pet Department five nights a week."

Mark asked, "What happened tonight? The department looks like shit!" I began to explain. "Well Mark, what actually happened was we received a ton of freight last night. I was able to complete all of it. I put out 15 skids and 17 break packs."

Mark was unimpressed. He said, "I didn't ask you how much freight you put out. I asked you why my Pet Department looks like shit!" I replied "Yes, I understand. What I'm saying is that due to the excessive amount of freight received last night, I didn't have time to do Zoning."

He said, "Well, that's unacceptable!" His voice became louder. He started to yell. "Now I can't open my fucking store! How can I open my fucking store when it looks like shit?!"

I asked him "Did you want me to send back skids unworked so that I have time to Zone? I thought the priority was to get the skids out." He said, "It's all priority. You need to do both! That's your job!"

I was frustrated, to say the least. I said, "I'm not sure if you've noticed or not, but I zone the Pet Department perfectly every single night, and I always complete all of my freight as well. I just didn't have time tonight." He replied, "Yes well, sadly we are only as good as our latest performance. Thanks for nothing!" With that, he walked away.

I was thinking, "If I ever do another Step four, you will be at the top of my resentment list sir!" I was so angry. I had worked my ass off all night, missed all of my breaks, completed far more than two people complete when I'm not here, and you say thanks for nothing?" He didn't even know who I was.

As angry as I was, I continued to work hard every night. I reminded myself that I wasn't doing it for him, I was doing it for myself because I was striving to be the best person I could be, which happened to mean the best employee as well. I would not change my work ethic on account of this asshole.

As it turned out, Mark did not stay long. He was only there another two months before moving on. We got a new Store Manager named Rob. I just continued to do my work as I always did, minding my own business, and doing the best job I could do.

One morning, about a week after Rob became our Store Manager, he was walking through the store with the management team and happened to walk past the Pet Department. As he walked past, he smiled at me, and said, "Good morning Allan!" I was shocked that he knew my name. "Uhh, Good morning, Rob!" I replied.

He walked past the cat aisle and then suddenly stopped walking. The other managers looked, and asked why he stopped. He took a few steps backwards and looked down the aisle. "Allan!" He called. "Can you come here please?" I came over expecting some kind of criticism.

Pointing at the cat aisle, he said, "Did you do this?" Although I thought he was referring to my Zoning job, I wasn't totally sure what he meant, and I didn't want to look foolish if he was not talking about that, so I simply said, "Sorry, did I do what? I'm not sure what you are referring to." He said, "The Zoning in this aisle is perfect!" I said, "Thank you for noticing, I try to do that every night if time permits."

He was clearly in awe. He said, "Did you not have much freight last night?" I said, "Well, yes actually we had 13 skids in here last night." He said, "Oh, ok. Well, as much as I love the way this looks, I think it's more important that we put the freight out first, because now we will have items from the unworked skids that may be out of stock on the shelves."

I said, to him, "Oh no, I totally agree, my first priority is to complete the freight and then zone." He asked, "Well, how many skids did you do?" And I said, "I did all of them." And he asked "But how many skids went back? Was there overstock that couldn't go out?" I told him, "No, everything went out. I finished all 13 skids."

Rob stood there for a moment, smiling. Then he said, "Wait a second. Are you telling me that you, by yourself, put out 13 skids of Pets AND did a Zoning job that looks like this? How did you have time?" I said, "I try to keep a good pace when I'm working, I guess."

With that he said, "Ok, sorry, if you don't mind, can you stay here for a minute?" I said, "Sure, as long as you need." He told me he would be right back. He walked over to the paint desk and picked up the phone. He paged over the store's loudspeaker, "Can I please get all Assistant Managers to the Pet Department? All Assistant Managers to the Pet Department, please?"

A few moments later, there were seven Managers, including Rob, standing at the end of my cat aisle. Rob said, "Thank you guys, I know you're all busy. I just wanted us all to stop and acknowledge Allan for a moment. THIS is what a good job looks like!"

Wow! I was highly embarrassed, but tremendously elated at the same time. The Store Manager stopped what he was doing, and he stopped all managers from doing what they were doing to praise me on the job I had done. The feeling is hard to describe. I felt valued. I felt important. He had been our Manager for a week, and he knew EXACTLY who I was. I was beginning to really love my job.

I was still working my steps. I was trying to make amends to every single person on my list, one at a time. Some were easier than others. I could not make amends to Jen because she did not want to talk to me. I had a few like that. For these, I wrote my amends on paper and burned it, offering it to the Creator to take care of.

Lorne had given me some sweet grass and some sage. I had an abalone shell and an eagle feather from years before. I began to smudge regularly. I would smudge in my home, completely naked. I was told that this was the purest form of prayer, so that's what I did. I always felt peaceful after smudging.

I had told Lorne about my experience with meditation at the treatment centre, and how I discovered that my Guardian Spirit is an Orca. He said, "You will get the most healing when you pray close to water. You should smudge in, or close to the river."

I began to hike through trails that led to natural pools of glacier water and I would smudge there. I felt as though I was truly connected to the earth and all its creatures. I was becoming very spiritual.

September 3rd, 2003, was a Wednesday. Just like every other Wednesday morning, I went to my appointment with Lorne. But this was not like any other appointment.

I had been seeing Lorne for two full years at this point. When I went to see him on this morning I said, "Guess what I'm doing this evening?" He said, "I don't know, what are you doing?" I said, "I'm going to my home group meeting to celebrate my one year of sobriety." He stared at me. He asked, "You have a full year of sobriety?" I said, "Yes my sobriety date is today actually, September 3rd."

Lorne started to say, "Congratulations," but his voice cracked, and then I saw that he was wiping tears off of his cheek. Lorne was crying. I said, "Stop or you'll make me cry, too!"

We both pulled ourselves together. I said, "I guess you don't see a lot of people reach a full year of sobriety, hey?" He said, "More people will die. I work with a lot of addicts. I see more people die, than reach a year clean and sober."

I had to tell Lorne that it was because he never gave up on me. He was the reason I got a year clean and sober. He said, "No, Allan. Only you can do that. You and God, that is."

I said, "This is the longest I've ever been sober." Lorne said, "You know, as long as you don't relapse, you can say that every single day for the rest of your life." I recalled that someone had told me this before, many years ago at treatment. "I'll remember that!" I said. "Every day is the longest I've ever been sober!" Lorne gave me a great big hug when I left that morning. I think Lorne may have been even more thrilled than I was.

I attended my home group that evening. My sponsor had brought a cake for me. The whole night was about me. I was excited and amazed to see that the entire building was full, and they ran out of chairs. Everyone had come to help me celebrate my 1st year of sobriety.

The way a cake night goes is that everyone who knows you takes turns talking about you. They talk about how you were when they first met you, and the work you've done, and the person you are today. When everyone was done talking, it was my turn to speak and accept the cake.

I loved what everyone had to say, but when Angelika spoke, I cried… a lot. She had seen me at my very lowest point in life. She had sat with me and comforted me on a night when death seemed like a better option than living. She had seen me when I was completely broken.

Angelika had helped me so much through the past year, even more than my sponsor had. So, when she spoke about me in such a loving, non-judgmental way, I couldn't help but cry.

Luckily for me, my sponsor spoke after Angelika, so I had time to recover before I had to stand in front of the entire room and talk. My sponsors' words were powerful as well. He had a one-year medallion for me, and a story to go along with it.

My sponsor explained that he could really relate to my story. He at one point also felt completely hopeless. He said, that his sponsor helped guide him through the steps and when he reached one-year of sobriety he had given him this one year medallion. When my sponsor received it, his sponsor was 13 years sober. My sponsor was now 10 years sober and he was giving it to me. This medallion was 23 years old!

When I did finally stand up and walk to the front, I was so nervous. I remember my knees banging together as I stood there. I felt like I was going to pass out.

I took a deep breath and prayed. I began to tell my story. Once I started speaking, the words just kept flowing. Before I knew it I had the entire room engaged. I would tell a funny story and the whole audience would erupt in laughter. I would share stories of extreme emotion and when I looked up at the crowd there was not a single dry eye in the building.

I shared my story in full that night. I got past my stage fright quickly. I shared from the heart and just said whatever came out. When I was finished, I thanked everyone and went to sit down. That's when I was truly amazed.

Every person in the room stood up. The room was full of people shoulder to shoulder, wall to wall. Every single one of them applauded in the most thunderous standing ovation I had ever heard. I just couldn't believe this applause was for me.

I guess it had to do with the fact that these people had seen me come in and out of the program for a long, long time, never getting much sobriety. It was truly nothing short of a miracle that I was there that night, and they all knew that.

That night filled me with the hope and confidence to continue on the path I was on. I would continue walking the "Red Road," as it is called by the indigenous community.

CHAPTER SEVENTEEN

IT WAS ABOUT THREE MONTHS AFTER this day that Rob approached me with an offer. He called me into his office to talk one morning. He said, "Allan, I've been watching you closely. I love the job you do in Pets. The problem is, I think this position is a waste of your potential."

Rob went on to say, "I think you should be a Department Manager." I said, "Woah, hold on. I *was* a Department Manager and I did not do a very good job." He said, "I have a feeling you were not given a proper opportunity. Here's what I'm thinking."

He went on to say that Housewares and Small Appliances were currently under one Department Manager. He was considering splitting that up and using Small Appliances as a training department. He said, I could train there and if I didn't succeed, I could have my job on night crew back again. "You have nothing to lose and everything to gain," he said.

I told Rob that I was up for the challenge, and that I would do my very best to ensure he would not regret his decision. It was pretty unbelievable to me that I would have this opportunity, especially after the Victoria incident and all of my drinking, and also my overall lack of performance in the past. I was determined to redeem myself. I knew there wouldn't be a third chance.

I worked with a lady named Lynn in Housewares. I was given the responsibility of Managing Department 15, Small Appliances. I was determined to do well. I learned all I could from Lynn and took a lot of pride in my department.

About three weeks after I started, Lynn was involved in a car accident and was unable to work. I was now given the responsibility of managing all of it, both Housewares and Small Appliances. Rob approached me, and I told him I was a bit nervous because I had just recently started, and I felt like I was still in the learning process. He said, "It's the best way to learn. Sink or swim, buddy!"

I was not going to sink. When I was given notes from my Assistant Manager I was all over it. I completed the notes immediately, no matter what else I had going on, and I would go back to him and let him know I was finished. I was not the same Department Manager I was before. I was not the same person I was before.

I ran those departments like it was my own store. My goal was to have no items out of stock. This is literally impossible, but I was striving to get as close as possible to that goal.

I created pick lists every single day, and then went to the stock room to find all the items. Then I brought them to the sales floor and stocked them. I was constantly interrupted by customers, but I did not let that stop me. I simply helped each customer and continued stocking.

One day I was working hard in my department, and I heard Rob page me over the loudspeaker. "Allan, call 170 please!" I went to the closest phone and called him. He said, "Allan, can you come and talk to me in my office please?"

When I reached Rob's office, he invited me in and asked me to close the door behind me. I was a bit nervous. I had no idea what he was going to say. He pointed to the leather office chair, and said, "Have a seat."

"Allan, how do you think you're doing in your current position?" I immediately had a flash back to the last time a manager asked me this question.

I said, "Well, listen I know there's always room for improvement. What I can tell you is that I give one hundred percent every single day and I'm very passionate about maintaining the standards that are expected."

Rob said, "I know all of that already. That is not what I asked. I asked you how you think you are doing." I said, "Well, I think I'm doing ok. I believe I'm performing at the level that is expected of me."

Rob disagreed. "You are not performing at the level that is expected of a Department Manager." I said, "Are you serious?" Rob said, "To be honest Allan, you're performing at a level above what we would normally expect of a Department Manager. I think your potential is being wasted in this position. I believe you are capable of far more."

This was a shock. I asked, "What exactly are you getting at?" Rob said, "I think you would make an excellent Assistant Manager. I think you are currently performing at a higher level than some of my management team. I just want to know if you would be transferable, if we promoted you."

I was a bit overwhelmed. I asked where I would need to be transferable to. I wanted to know how far away I would have to move. Rob told me I would need to be transferable anywhere in Canada, but they would probably never send me out of this district. He said, "You probably wouldn't be asked to transfer further than 100 km away but you need to be willing to go further if asked."

I told Rob I would be happy to accept the offer if it came my way. He said, "Great! Keep it on the down low for now. We will work with you and train you, and you can slowly take on more responsibility until you are ready for the next step."

I was overjoyed. I simply could not believe this. A year ago, I thought I was getting fired. The future looked bright. I knew I had to work as hard as I could and never slide backwards in my productivity. I worked my ass off every single day.

I was the Department Manager of Housewares for almost a year when I was approached by Rob again. He had a position of Overnight Support Manager available. He said, that if I got this position, I would be responsible for running the entire night crew when the Assistant Manager had his two nights off. He said that this would be perfect experience for me, and would help groom me towards becoming an Assistant Manager. I agreed and I started the following week.

It worked out well because I was able to switch back to my morning meeting with Lorne on Wednesday's. I had changed our appointment time to Saturday afternoon when I came back to days, but I wasn't always able to make it.

In this new position, I had Monday nights and Tuesday nights off, so I was able to attend Wednesday morning and then get stuff done during the day on Wednesday and work that night, right after my home group meeting from 8:00 pm-9:00 pm.

The day came when Rob, our Store Manager was promoted to District Manager. He did not stay in our District, though; he was transferred to a new location. I spoke to him before he left. I told him I was afraid that the next person wouldn't care to promote me. He assured me that the Assistant Managers in the store knew the plan and that everything would be ok.

I worked hard every day, and always tried to build upon my leadership skills. I had not met the new Store Manager yet, but I was eager to make a good impression on him. His name was John.

The first thing I noticed about John was that he was absent from work a whole lot. I could see that my Assistant Manager Abdula was getting very frustrated with John. Sometimes he would vent to me. He told me one day, "I have this whole side of the store to take care of as my responsibility, scheduling, dealing with my inventory, people issues, AND I'm also doing HIS job because the asshole isn't here ever, and then he came to the store for two hours last week and wrote me up because Automotive had too many items out of stock!"

I just listened to Abdula and tried to be supportive. I felt that he must trust me a lot if he was venting to me, because he was very professional and would never talk about management issues with anyone other than management. I truly felt that it was a good sign that he was speaking to me about it.

After about a month, John started to come to work regularly. I started to see him at the end of my shifts in the morning. One day, I approached him and asked him if he had a second to talk with me. He said that he was busy, but if I wanted to walk with him and talk at the same time, then he would give me a few moments of his time.

I walked beside John all through the store, trying desperately to relay the most pertinent information as quickly as possible without rambling. I said, "Ok, so when Rob was here he was grooming me to be an Assistant

Manager and I have spent a long time working towards that goal and just wanted you to be aware and I am hoping you will help guide me in the right direction, so I can be successful."

He asked, "Was Rob supportive with your desire to be promoted?" I replied, "Yes, very much. In fact, that's how I came to be in my current role as overnight Support Manager." He said, "Yeah well, I don't like Rob. He's too fluffy. In fact, not only do I not like him, I hate that guy!"

I told him that was unfortunate. I asked that he not judge me just because he hated Rob, and Rob liked me. I asked him to give me a fair chance to prove myself to him. John definitely had a few things to say about this.

John turned the corner quickly as we walked through the toy department. He said, "Listen, I know what you're thinking. You're thinking that you will become an Assistant Manager and make fifty grand a year, and work hard and get promoted to Store Manager and make well over six figures annually, and some hot chick will dig you, and you will fall in love and make babies and live happily ever after, and yada yada yada blah blah blah!"

I was a bit shocked by John's rant but I maintained my composure. I replied "Something like that, yes." He asked, "Why? For money?" I said, "Money's good, and I always want to move forward in my life."

John stopped walking. We were now standing in front of the Infants department. He said, "Allan, if I liked someone… I mean REALLY liked someone, then I would have to be brutally honest. Let me give you a scenario to contemplate." I said, "Ok."

John said, "Let's say I promote you, and let's say you are super successful, and get promoted to Store Manager. One day perhaps you'll meet a girl and get married and have a couple kids, and you provide a good life because you make well over a hundred grand… good life, right?"

It seemed like this was a trick question. I replied, "Yes, that sounds like a great life… isn't it?" John said, "It will be. For a while. For a while, it will be great. Until one day you wake up and realize that your wife hates you because you're never home, and then one evening you'll be sitting at the dinner table for your daughter's sixteenth birthday dinner, and it will be so nice and you will be ready to give her the gift you bought, and then the phone will ring!"

John was starting to rant a bit. I just let him continue. He said, "Do you know who will be on that phone when you pick it up?" I said, "Umm… Walmart?" He shouted out loud, "FUCKING WALMART! You're right!"

John continued, "And Allan… do you know what will happen next?" I said, "No I'm not sure." He laughed softly to himself, used his thumb to wipe a little spit away from the corner of his mouth, and then said, "They will want you to go to the store. They will want you to leave your daughter on her sixteenth birthday and come into the store to deal with whatever the fuck is going on!"

John asked, "What would you do?" I was quiet for a moment. I said, "Well, I would just need to say that I'm busy and I can't come in right at that moment." John let out an enormous laugh. "HAHAHA! Are you fucking kidding me! You will say no to Walmart? You will NOT say no!" At this point he was yelling loudly in the middle of the Infants department and I could see sweat dripping off his forehead.

I said, "Well, what If I do say no?" He burst out laughing again "HAHAHAHA! You're funny!" Yelling loudly, he continued, "You don't say no to fucking WALMART! YOU CAN NOT SAY NOOOO!" I was shocked by his behaviour, to say the least. I had to think for a moment about how I would respond next.

"Well then, I suppose my wife and daughter will just need to understand, and I'll have to make it up to them later." John laughed again. "HAHAHA! They will NOT understand! They will fucking hate you! Your wife will leave, and she will take the kids and, just when you are wondering if it's all worth it, Walmart will threaten to fire you because you're not good enough! They do not fucking care about you!"

I looked at John. I said, "Ok, so what if even after all that you've told me, I still wanted to be promoted?" He said, "Listen, if I hated someone, I would just go ahead and promote them. But I like you, so I can't. There are so many ways to make a buck Al, and EVERY SINGLE ONE is better than this shit! You don't want it! It's not worth it! You don't want your daughter to hate you!"

I said, "I don't have a daughter." "I DO!" He yelled. I learned that day that if I was to be promoted, it certainly wouldn't happen through John.

I wasn't sure what was wrong with him, but I could definitely tell that he wasn't right in the head. I felt he would not be around much longer, anyway.

A while after this, I met with and spoke to my Assistant Manager Abdula. I told him about what had happened with John. It was the end of my night shift, around 8:00 am. He said, "You need to come to the office. Our District Manager, Mary, is here. You need to tell her about this."

Mary was a bigger lady, with short brown hair that was starting to show a bit of grey, as she was nearing 60 years of age. She wore glasses with thick lenses and gold frames. When she spoke, you knew immediately that she was the boss.

Sitting with Mary, I was apprehensive. I did not want to be the guy that caused someone else to lose their job. Mary said, "Listen, it is not about getting someone in trouble or not. It is about the good of the store and as the District Manager I need to know what's happening in this store and all my stores."

I agreed to tell her. I relayed the whole story to Mary. She told me she appreciated me talking with her and they would deal with that as a Management team. I got up to leave and she said, "No sit, I'm not done with you."

I sat down in the chair. Mary said, "So you want to be promoted?" I replied "Yes, very much so." Mary said, "But do you have what it takes? Can you lead people? Be accountable to tough standards? Make very difficult decisions that affect the lives of people?"

I said, "Yes, I believe so." Mary leaned forward in her chair and said, "'I believe so' doesn't cut it, young man! Do you have no confidence at all?" I sat up straight in my chair. "I have a lot of confidence and I won't be perfect at first, but you will never see me give up. I promise you I will make mistakes, and I promise you I will learn from those mistakes and be better. With a little time and some training, I will be a great Assistant Manager."

Mary leaned back and rocked her office chair a bit. She asked, "But do you really believe all that or are you just saying it?" I said, very confidently, "I believe that with all my heart, Mary!" She said, "I will tell you one thing for sure, Rob believed that very strongly."

We sat looking at each other, and then Mary said, "Alright." That's all she said. I looked at her and asked, "Alright what?" She said, "Alright! I

CHANGING THE STATUS QUO

will send you to the store of learning in Nanaimo to train for six weeks and when you return, we will assign you a store. You leave on Sunday."

I was shocked. I said, "So that means…" Mary looked right at me and said, "That means you're promoted! Now get out before I change my mind!" I scrambled to my feet and ran for the door. I was stopped by the sound of Mary's laughter.

"Get back here!" She was laughing. I turned back toward her. "Get over here!" She said. I walked towards her and when I got close enough Mary gave me a huge hug. She said, "Congratulations! If anyone deserves this, it is you, kiddo. You have been doing an amazing job here in this building. I know you will have a great career."

Once again, I was overwhelmed by the feeling of being noticed for my efforts. That acknowledgement felt amazing. She said, "I want to add one more thing. A little criticism." I said, "Ok." Mary said, "You lack confidence. We know you're amazing. Once *you* realize that, you will be even more amazing. Believe in yourself a bit more and you'll do just fine."

This was such a proud moment for me. I truly couldn't believe this was happening. Not long ago, I was just trying to not be fired. Now I was being promoted. I decided right then and there that anything was possible, and I would pursue further success with great effort and determination.

I had one more meeting with Lorne. I told him what was going on. He told me that he believed I was well on my way to having a good life. He said that I was welcome to come and see him any time, but for now, he felt we should cancel our weekly appointments. I agreed.

That Sunday, I was on the first ferry to Nanaimo. I went to the store and met with an Assistant Manager who drove me and some other trainees to some town houses. Apparently, Walmart had bought them specifically for Managers-in-training. I had a roommate named Dan. Dan was an older guy and he was pretty negative. Even though he had just been promoted, he had nothing but bad things to say about his manager and about Walmart in general.

The next morning, we went to the store and the training began. After we introduced ourselves by our name, where we were from, and what we hoped to get out of the next six weeks, we did a bunch of scenario exercises. Then we played some games that were meant to build on our management skills.

The second week we got a bit more into hands-on training. We were assigned an Assistant Manager. We would shadow that manager the rest of the time we were there. His or her job was our job. They would delegate half of their workload to us and we would be responsible for meeting the deadlines given to us.

After six weeks, I graduated and was assigned a store. I was told I was going to Chilliwack, B.C. I was a bit nervous. I did not know what to expect. I would need to move. This was the furthest away from home I had ever been. I had barely been out of North Vancouver.

I wondered how I would spend my days off if I lived in Chilliwack. My only memory of Chilliwack was from when I was very young. We would drive out to the U-Pick farms. We would get our buckets and pick berries. Then we would stop at another local farm and buy corn. Dad used to say, "Chilliwack corn is the best corn! No corn like Chilliwack corn!"

I told my friends, Graham and Mike, that I was afraid I would be spending my free time eating corn and picking berries. Sara was worried because she didn't realize there were 12 Step meetings outside of North Vancouver. I assured her that I could transfer to any country on earth, and within a day I could find a meeting.

Although I was assigned to the Chilliwack store, I did not go there right away. I went back to North Vancouver and worked there for a bit. There were some issues with Chilliwack having too many managers and they were about to shuffle some people around, so they just sent me back to North Vancouver temporarily.

I had been making a management salary the whole time I was in training. My income was now double what I was making before and I had been setting aside money. I was already saving money before I was promoted and this increase in pay helped my funds significantly. Also, when I was about nine months sober, I quit smoking, and I had been saving that money as well.

One Sunday, shortly after I got back from my management training, I went for my weekly dinner with Sara. We ate and talked about how it had been in Nanaimo over the last six weeks. At the end of the evening, when I was about to leave, I told Sara I had something for her.

I reached into my pocket. Sara was shocked to see a wad of cash. "What on earth is that?" She exclaimed. I counted out $1100. I said, "There you go, and I'm very sorry it took so long to get this back to you." She said, "What on earth are you talking about? Put that away!"

I reminded Sara that she had paid my rent on numerous occasions and lent me money and the last time we had a conversation about it, which was admittedly some time ago, she said the debt was $1100. I said, "I'm making financial amends to you, Mom."

Sara was shocked. She refused to take it. She said, "Allan, you will need to buy a car now that you are a manager and you should keep that money to help you with that." I said, "No, I can't. I need to make financial amends to you. It's necessary as part of my 12 steps. I must do this, so you need to take it."

Sara tried to reason with me. She said, "Well, ok, if you give me $100, then you'll still have a thousand. Just do that and we will call it good." I said, "No that won't do. I need to pay you back." She said, "Well, why not wait until you have the money to do so?" I said, "I have the money to do so. You're looking at it." "Oh, very funny!" she remarked. "What about buying a car? What about moving expenses? You NEED this money. What will you do?"

I said, "Here's the thing, Mom. I am practicing a program of recovery. I believe very strongly that everything… everything will just work out."

Sara was baffled. "What do you mean it will just work out?" I said, "I believe in my heart that if I do the right things in life and I follow a set of principles, then I'll be taken care of."

Sara insisted I tell her more. "Taken care of by whom?"

"Well, you know. By God, or the universe, whoever is making the big decisions. If I do good, live well, and be honest, I will just be taken care of. It's as simple as that."

Sara responded with, "What a load of rubbish! Listen, I'm glad you're sober, I truly am, but this sounds like complete nonsense! You'll just give away your money and somehow, the universe will just take care of you? Come off it, Sonny Jim!"

"Tell you what…" I said. "How about you put that cash aside. If I ever need a bit of it to help me, I will not hesitate to ask." "Right then!" Sara agreed. "I will."

This is where it gets crazy. The spiritual principles I was following paid off. Two days later, on a Tuesday afternoon, I went to my mailbox to get the mail. A brown envelope immediately caught my attention. It was from the government. I went to my apartment and opened it.

It was a cheque, along with a letter that said that they had done a reassessment of the taxes I had filed. They said that they had made an error, and as a result they were sending the additional funds owed to me. The amount was $1967.83.

Of course, I called Sara right away. I had to do the thing where I said, "I'm not going to say I told you so but…" Sara didn't know what to make of it. I think she pretty much called it an extreme coincidence. Nevertheless, she was happy that life was beginning to work out for me. I would need that money for moving expenses and maybe some stuff for the new place in Chilliwack.

A while back, I had received my learner's driver's licence and Angelika was allowing me to drive her to and from meetings once or twice a week. I had recently done my road test and received my full driver's licence. Now I needed my very first car.

I went around to some local dealerships. After shopping around a bit for the best price, I chose a Hyundai Accent, silver in colour. I was a bit nervous about the commitment. I was now fully responsible to pay $115 every single week. At the time, that was a ton of money for me. I needed to leave enough cash to pay rent and bills. It was by far, the biggest financial commitment of my life thus far.

Not long after that, I received a call telling me that I needed to go to Chilliwack. They were ready for me now. I hoped I was ready for them. Walmart booked me a hotel and I was permitted several hours a day out of my work schedule to go out and look for places to rent. But first, I would go to the store and introduce myself to the Store Manager.

As it turned out, I already knew him. The Store Manager was Martin, my very first Assistant Manager, the one who hired me as his Sales Associate in toys. It was nice to see a familiar face.

Martin introduced me to the associates at the morning meeting the first day I arrived. I spent the rest of that morning walking the store, introducing myself to each individual associate.

When I reached the front of the store I looked over and saw the Greeter. She was a short, round, older lady. As I approached her, I couldn't help but

CHANGING THE STATUS QUO

notice that she had a bit of a beard. I tried not to stare. As I walked up, she said, "Hello, my name is Norma, and no offence, but you have very big shoes to fill, Mister!"

I said to Norma, "Nice to meet you. It sounds like I'm taking the spot of someone very dear to you." Norma said, "You sure got that right! And I don't expect that someone of your young age will fill those shoes very easily!" I said, "Well all I can do is try. We will see how I do."

I met as many people as I could that day. I left halfway through the day to get settled in the hotel. The next morning, I came in early at 6:00 am so I could meet the night crew. I walked the whole store and met associates in each department. I did this because I knew how much it meant to me when daytime managers took the time to get to know me. Most wouldn't. I knew firsthand how crucial their role was to the store as a whole.

I spent half of my days searching the classifieds in the local paper and going to visit landlords. When I returned to the store, associates wanted to know where I had been looking to rent.

I remember saying to one lady, "Well I saw a place in my price range on Princess Avenue." She jumped and said, "Oh God no! You don't want to rent there! Horrible area!" I said, "Oh thanks for letting me know. I don't know Chilliwack at all."

I then told the associate that I saw another place on Bole Avenue. She jumped again. "No, no not there either. You don't want to go there." I told her I was happy that she had asked because I didn't want to make a big mistake. Then I asked her where she would suggest.

She looked me straight in the eyes and put her hand on my shoulder. She said, "Listen dear. We don't live in Chilliwack per se. We live in Sardis. You don't want to look for anything on the Chilliwack side of the tracks."

I said, "Oh really? Is it that bad over there?" She lowered her voice to a whisper and moved close to my ear so I could hear her. With her hand on my shoulder, she whispered, "There's a reserve over there!" I looked at her and whispered, "Like a reservation, you mean?" She said, "Yes dear." And I said, "Like… with Indians?" She said, "Yes, exactly dear. A reservation with Indians!"

I paused for a moment. I said, "Well how about that? I might have some family here after all! I betcha some of them Indians are my cousins!"

She looked a bit confused. My white skin sometimes allowed me to hear what people really thought. I used to say that I was an "undercover Indian." People would ramble on about their racist views until I interrupted them to say that I was a quarter native. It's always a bit awkward when they realize.

I looked at several places to rent. I went to one place and decided I would get it. I paid the damage deposit and got the key. I had a bad feeling about it though. It smelled like mould. The carpets were dirty. I could tell the landlord didn't really care much. I spoke to my brother Carl and asked his advice.

Carl asked if I thought I could get the damage deposit back since I had only put my clothes in there. I said, that I probably could. He strongly advised that I do this. I went back to the landlord and got my cash back no questions asked. The Landlord was very good about it. I told him I had looked at two places and the other people just called back.

I ended up renting the place on Bole Avenue. Sure, it was on the wrong side of the tracks and there were drug dealers on the corner, but the price was right. It was a one-bedroom apartment and it was only $700/month plus utilities. I was good with that.

Sara immediately went and ordered me a complete bedroom set, which was all real wood. It came with a long dresser, a tall dresser, two drawer nightstand, and a bed with a headboard. She had it delivered directly to my apartment. I was very grateful for this. I could tell it was built locally because I could still smell the wood stain that had been recently applied to the wood.

I made a nice little home there. I looked up 12 Step meetings in the area. I found one that was on Tuesday nights, and I made it my home group. It was actually across the parking lot from the townhouse I had originally rented and backed out of.

I attended my home group regularly and got a sponsor who was part of the same group. He was an old guy, 42 years sober. His wife was 37 years sober and also a part of the group. I got to know everyone there quite well.

Life was great. I was making more money than I had ever made or dreamed of making in my entire life. It was only an annual salary of $50,000, but for me this meant I had made it. I was almost approaching middle class, perhaps I was already lower middle class at this point.

Regardless, I did not need low income housing and I could pay all my bills without much of a problem and I even had some money for fun activities.

I was a bit nervous about attending meetings in Chilliwack because it was a small town and I didn't want anyone from Walmart to see me in a meeting. My sponsor laughed when I told him this. He said, "If someone from work sees you in a meeting guess what? They're also dealing with an addiction. Worst case scenario is that you are able to help someone."

I worked extremely hard at Walmart, trying tirelessly to prove myself. I didn't want to settle for an Assistant Manager position. I had dreams of becoming a Store Manager. I wanted that six-figure income. I doubled my income before, why not do that again?

At this point I was approaching three years of sobriety. I took my cake on September 13th, 2005. I had to choose this date because the Tuesday before already had two cakes booked for that night. In fact, our group had people celebrating every Tuesday that month. My night was shared with another person who was taking a seven-year cake.

After a few people spoke, it was time for my sponsor to get up and say a few words. He spoke about how great it was getting to know me over the last little while. He said that we had become more than just sponsor/sponsee, we had become friends. After his speech, he said "So come up here young man, I have a three year chip for you."

I got up and shared my story. This year, my story was more about what I was doing to maintain my sobriety. Of course, I did talk about the depths of my addiction and the hopelessness that accompanied that, but I wanted to focus more on the solution so others who were new might have a chance to grab onto something and maybe my story could help someone.

After that meeting, I was approached by a girl. She walked up to me and greeted me with a huge smile and said, "Hi Allan, I just wanted to say that your story really moved me. My name is Nicky." I said, "Oh thank so much. It's really nice to meet you."

Nicky and I talked for a while about work. She told me that she was a year and a half sober, and that she had found work at a hair salon about a year earlier, and that just like me, her hard work paid off and she had just been promoted to the manager position there. I was intrigued. It seemed we had a lot in common.

Other people were trying to speak to me, so she said, "Well, it looks like you gotta go, but call me sometime and we can do coffee." She handed me her number on a piece of paper.

I was thinking it would be nice to have friends outside of Walmart. I wouldn't be totally alone in this town. I did crave a social life for sure. And yes, of course, I was wondering if this would lead to something else. I was cautiously optimistic about that.

After a few days I finally decided to call Nicky. We agreed to meet at Starbucks downtown. I told myself, "Ok Allan. You're just friends. She's someone to hang out with. Don't embarrass yourself by thinking she's interested in you for anything other than a friendship."

We agreed to meet at Starbucks at 1:00 pm. I went early, at about 12:45, and I saw that she was already sitting at a table waiting for me. I saw that she had a coffee, so I said, "I'll just buy myself a coffee and then I'll come and join you."

We sat and talked for about an hour and a half. We told each other about our past a little bit and talked about doing the 12 steps and how much we had been helped by others. We laughed a lot as well. I liked her. Little did I know that this coffee would change my ENTIRE life. Things were about to become… different.

CHAPTER EIGHTEEN

I BEGAN TO HANG OUT WITH NICKY A LOT. She had some friends that she played poker with and had invited me to hang out with them a few times. One evening she invited me to her place, where she had a few friends over. She gave me the address and I went over there.

I thought the address seemed familiar and when I arrived, I realized why. It turned out that Nicky had rented the exact same townhouse that I had originally chosen and backed out of. The same unit and everything, 106. I saw this as the universe showing me a sign.

That evening, when everyone was leaving, one of her friends needed a ride. I told her that I could give her a ride home. Nicky said, "Well, why don't I come along?" I said, "Sure, why not?"

After we dropped off her friend, I invited Nicky to see my apartment. She agreed, and I brought her inside for coffee. Even though it was late, we had a great time talking and the hours just passed by so quickly. She sat close to me on the couch. One thing led to another, and I ended up waking up next to her the next morning.

So it was official. Nicky and I were dating. We often spoke on the phone for an hour or more at a time when I couldn't see her. I worked crazy hours at Walmart and often worked very late, and had to be back early the next morning. Whenever I had days off, I spent them with Nicky.

Things moved very quickly with Nicky and I. Very shortly after we began dating, I was introduced to her mother and stepfather. Nicky's parents had purchased a condo as an investment property. They said that we could move in and they would give us a great deal on the rent.

They only charged us $900 for the rent and it was a 2-bedroom apartment with two bathrooms and an in-suite laundry room. It was now January of 2006, and Nicky and I had only been dating since September of 2005.

We paid rent here for less than a year and then Nicky's mom and stepdad approached us with an opportunity. They suggested that we could buy the condo from them, so long as we were approved by the bank.

They had bought it for $130,000. They wanted to sell it to us for $170,000. Of course, I was very much opposed to this. However, when we sat with their friend, who was also a banker and would ultimately be the lady we dealt with, I was reassured.

The banker told us that the current value of the condo was $199,000. Basically, this would be perfect for both of us. Nicky's parents get to make a profit, and we also got a home with built-in equity of $30,000. It was perfect.

We were approved, and we signed the papers at the lawyer's office in the summer of 2006. I was thrilled. I couldn't believe I was purchasing my first home. I wanted a life at this point. I felt I was ready to settle down. I was, at this point, 28 years old. I decided I was going to make a big move. I was done with the dating scene.

One afternoon, I went ring shopping. Nicky and I had looked around at rings in the mall, just for fun. I got an idea of what she liked. One afternoon I went to a jewelry store and purchased an engagement ring. When the time was right, I took Nicky for a walk on the beach. I proposed to her and she happily accepted.

How my life had changed! I was very proud of myself. At times it seemed unreal. Only a few years ago I was an alcoholic, cocaine addict, almost homeless and now I was clean and sober, I was an Assistant Manager at Walmart, I was engaged, and we owned our home. I believed that anything was possible at this point.

I had made a huge impression on the associates in the Chilliwack Walmart. Everyone loved me. I was only in that store for nine months before I got transferred. When I was transferred I had only two days' notice. Fortunately, I was only being transferred to Abbotsford, which was a 20-minute drive. I walked the store the day I found out, saying goodbye to all the associates.

When I reached the front of the store, I saw Norma, the greeter standing at the door. I walked up to her. She turned away for a moment. I walked closer. She was crying. Through her tears she said, "Go away, you. I know what you're going to tell me."

I said, "Aww Norma it's ok." She asked, "Can I give you a hug please?" I said, "Of course." Norma gave me a huge hug and said, "They always take the good ones you know. It's not fair!"

Norma had one more thing to say before I left. She asked, "Do you remember what I told you when you first came here?" I said, "I think so. I believe you said I had very big shoes to fill." She cried out loud, wiped away some tears and said, "You filled them kiddo! You filled them and then some!"

Nicky and I got married October of 2007. We tried for a baby right away and she got pregnant very quickly. By early 2008, Nicky was pregnant. Our baby was due December 27th, 2008. We were both very excited.

Shortly after Nicky got pregnant, I was transferred from Abbotsford to Burnaby. It just so happened that the Store Manager here was Martin, the Manager who hired me, who I had worked with in Chilliwack. We both ended up in Burnaby and for a time, life was good again. But soon Martin was transferred, and I would get a new Store Manager.

Our new Store Manager was Roger. Roger was a very tall, very big Persian man. We immediately knew that he had a very bad temper. Roger had no problem screaming at associates and managers on the sales floor in front of customers. Everyone was terrified of Roger.

When Roger first arrived, he was pretty nice to all of the managers except for the overnight Manager. The overnight Manager was Gus. Gus was Afro-Canadian and had a thick accent.

Roger would scream at Gus every morning, and Gus would get very flustered and could not come up with explanations for why the store was not at the standards Roger expected.

I remember one day in particular clearly. I was the opening manager. I walked the sales floor with Roger until we found Gus, and then Gus walked with us, too. Walmart had a rule about features. Merchandise in the main aisles were on black pallets called stack bases. Every stack base must be eight floor tiles away from the next, so when you looked at a stack base, you would count eight floor tiles and the next stack base started on the ninth tile.

The idea of this was to allow customers space to shop. Studies had shown that customers did not like crowded aisles. The problem for the night crew was that originally the rule was six tiles between stack bases. The new rule meant that you had less room for features in the main aisles. You would lose one or two stack bases per aisle in the store. The overnight manager's job is to empty the stock room. This made it more challenging.

When we walked with Gus, we saw that the very first aisle was wrong. The very first feature at the front of the store, the very first thing Roger saw when he walked in, was wrong. There were only four tiles between the first stack base and the second. Roger brought us over to look at it.

Roger pointed at a stack base of lawnmowers and asked Gus, "What the fuck is this?" Gus replied, "Those are for cutting grass, sir!" Rogers' eyes looked like they were going to pop out of his head. He yelled, "I know what they are! I'm talking about the tiles! How many fucking tiles should be between each stack base?"

Gus replied "Eight tiles sir!" Roger yelled "Then why the FUCK are there only four tiles?!" Gus replied "My people! My people, you know? They are so stupid! I tell them! I tell them! I go get my Support Manager!" Gus walked to a phone and paged the Support Manager to come over.

The Support Manager that night was Mario. When Mario arrived, Gus started yelling at him in his broken English. He yelled, "Mario I tell you eight tiles between each stack base! Come, come, look! I tell you, eight!" Gus pointed at the tiles and yelled, "ONE, TWO, THREE, EIGHT!"

Roger started to laugh. Gus must have seen this as a good thing and started laughing too. Then Gus asked, "Ok, what? What is funny, sir?" Roger said, "One, two, three, eight. It all makes sense now. If this is how you count, then it is me who has made a mistake. Eight comes after three so, I'm sorry, they are eight tiles apart!"

CHANGING THE STATUS QUO

Gus looked confused. He smiled, then laughed awkwardly, then said, "So we good, no?" Roger yelled, "No you fucking idiot! Not unless eight comes after three! FUCK!" At this point, Roger called us into the office.

We all sat down. Roger looked at Gus. He had one simple question. He asked, "Gus, why do you not meet the standards set for you? How long do we need to talk about it?" Gus looked back at Roger and began to laugh uncontrollably. He continued to laugh for some time. Then he began to speak.

Gus said, "For a smart man, sometimes you are asking not smart questions." He continued. "You see Roger, the answer is so simple. If you would like ME to reach YOUR standards… then FIRST you must LOWER your standards. In this way, I will have SOME chance to achieve this."

I couldn't wait for Roger's response. Roger asked, "So this is MY fault?" And Gus replied, "Exactly! It is your fault because you have been making your standards TOO high! You need to expect much less of me, then you will be much less disappointed in my performance!"

Roger sat quietly for a moment. Then he started to laugh. Then Gus began to laugh. I was afraid to laugh. Roger stopped laughing. He said, "Everybody, grab your coats. We are going on a field trip."

We all got our coats and followed Roger out the front door. We had no idea where we were going. We walked about two blocks and arrived at a little corner store. We walked in. It smelled like spices.

There were boxes piled on the floor. The racks were squished so close together that one person could barely fit through. There were onions in net-like bags hanging from the ceiling.

Roger greeted the Persian owner, "Salam!" he said, and smiled. The man smiled back and said, "Salam!" We walked around briefly and then we left. As we walked back to the store Roger talked and explained the reason we went there.

He said, "That was a Persian store. Did you see how much space was between the features? Did you see all the shit hanging from the ceiling? Did you see all the unopened boxes laying all over?" We nodded our heads.

Roger continued. "That's a Persian store. I'm Persian! Those are MY standards! I don't give a fuck how many tiles there are between stack bases! If it was up to me I would hang shit off the fucking ceiling, too! Maybe it would sell better than in the fucking stock room!"

Roger kept talking as we walked and listened. "We are not in my country and we don't work for Roger-Mart. We are in Canada and we work for Walmart. If I want to keep my job, I need to follow the standards of Walmart. They tell me, I tell you, and IF you want to keep YOUR job, you execute that direction! Think about this the next time you want to tell me to lower MY standards!"

It was a little dramatic, but he made his point. We got back to the store, and he told Gus that he should go home and get some rest. He said, "When I walk the store with you tomorrow, I'd better see eight tiles between all stack bases. And you better get someone to teach you how to fucking count because eight does NOT come after three!"

I did not want to be on Roger's bad side. I worked extremely hard every single day, and when he yelled at me, I would just say, "Ok Roger, I'm sorry I'll fix that right away." I figured if I was super obedient and super hard working then he wouldn't have a chance to be upset with me.

I ALWAYS worked longer than my eight hours. In fact, most days I started at least two hours early and I would stay until that days' last task was complete. It wasn't unusual for me to work 15 hours and on a few occasions, I worked for 30 hours straight.

Having an incredible work ethic helped me at work, but it wasn't conducive to a healthy marriage. During my time in Burnaby I worked so much, and Nicky was pregnant. Nicky was getting frustrated with the long hours I was putting in. She also began to show me her jealous side.

Nicky had huge trust issues. Whenever we went out together, we had problems. One time we went out for dinner at a restaurant. The waitress came by and took our order. When she had our order, the waitress asked, "Is there anything else I can get you?" Nicky replied "No, but if you could get your tits off of my husband's plate that would be great!"

I was shocked and embarrassed. The waitress walked away. When I confronted Nicky about her behaviour, she said, "Oh yeah, because you want her tits on your plate, you fucking pervert!" This sort of event became ordinary in our marriage.

When I worked long hours, Nicky often called me, and if I didn't answer, she would call the store. I remember one time she called the store, and when I answered she said, "Who the fuck is she, Allan? Probably some fucking 18-year-old cashier right?"

We had huge fights about my work, but not because I worked long. It was because Nicky didn't believe me. She said, "Who works that much? You're full of shit! You knocked me up and now you're out fucking your Walmart whores!"

Soon Roger approached me with a question. He asked if I could go to night crew. He wanted me to be the next overnight manager. Of course, I agreed. I knew I was very competent on nights. I knew from my experience exactly what needed to be done and how to do it.

I only had a weeks' notice to switch from days to nights. The following Sunday I started at 10:00 pm. I met with the two overnight Support Managers. I was a bit nervous because I saw how the last overnight Manager was treated, but I knew I was far more competent than Gus.

My first month on nights was great. Roger made several comments about how great I was. I helped empty the stockroom. I pushed out so many skids each night, it was incredible!

I was relentless. I ran around the store giving direction to people, then I would pound out a few skids on my own, then I would follow up with the direction I had given to associates and my Support Managers.

One day we ran into a situation, and we ended up pissing off Roger very much. When I say we, I really mean Sonny. Sonny was the Assistant Manager responsible for fashion. He made a decision that would lead to a whole lot of drama.

About two months earlier when I was still on days, there was a whole conversation about rolling racks. Rolling racks are racks with wheels on them that you hang clothes on, and you can roll them around from rack to rack, stocking the clothes in the appropriate location throughout the department. Roger had an issue with these.

Roger hated these rolling racks because nobody ever actually put the clothes away. The racks would get filled with clothes and then they would sit there. These rolling racks cluttered the sales floor and Roger hated this.

Roger had all the rolling racks emptied while I was still on days and he put them in storage downstairs in our basement. (Yes, we had an underground stockroom that we called the basement.) He made a point of saying that the next Assistant Manager who uses one of these rolling racks would be fired instantly.

One evening at the beginning of my shift, I saw Sonny. He told me he wanted me to do something for him. He said that he had 30 skids of fashion in the stockroom and he needed it gone. He said, "What I want you to do tonight is go down to the basement and bring up 15 rolling racks and have your fashion associate open all the skids of fashion and fill the rolling racks with clothes."

I immediately told Sonny he was crazy. Sonny was Persian. He said, "Roger and I are both Persian. I'll talk to him don't worry. I'll deal with Roger." I told Sonny, under no circumstances could I ever bring those rolling racks upstairs, let alone fill them with fashion. "Absolutely not!" I insisted.

Sonny said, "I understand, you're scared of Roger." I said, "It's not that I'm scared, I'm just not going to disregard his direction." Sonny said, "That's ok. I'm going to get them myself and I'll have one of my own associates fill it. Just do me one favour." I was willing to hear him out.

"What do you need?" I asked. Sonny said, "I'm starting at 2:00 pm tomorrow, so when Roger comes in just tell him that I have filled all the rolling racks and you tell him that I will explain to him why, and he will understand." I said, "You got it bud!"

It was a very busy night. I worked so hard, barely stopping for two seconds. I was delegating to as many people as I could, giving each Support Manager specific tasks, and then following up with them. I had learned this over time, you can't do everything yourself, and as a Manager, if you try to do it all you will fail miserably.

One quick job I gave someone this night was to fill two skids of water that were displayed at the front of the store. It was summer and the 30 pack of water was selling like crazy. There was a spot at the front where we could park two skids. Currently, there were two empty skids sitting there and 40 skids of water in the stock room.

I called one of my Support Managers over. Joseph was his name. Joseph was very hard-working, but not very bright. As I stood beside the two empty skids, Joseph came up to me and said, "You called me?"

I said, "Yes, Joseph, I have a quick job for you. You see these two empty skids?" Joseph said, "Yes, sir." I said, "Ok, I need you to get the power jack and go to the stockroom. You will see many skids of water there. Please bring two skids of water and put them here, ok?

Joseph said, "You got it boss!" I told Joseph to call me as soon as he finished because I had other things for him to do. He said, "No problem sir, I will call you soon for my next job."

Satisfied that this one task was being taking care of, I ran around the store and continued giving people jobs and following up. I got so busy I forgot about Joseph.

About an hour had passed since I spoke with him, maybe a bit longer. I wondered why Joseph had not called me yet. I went to the front of the store to see if he was there.

When I got to the front of the store, I saw Joseph and he had sweat dripping off his forehead. In front of him, were the two spots for the two skids of water. Beside him, he had parked the two skids of water from the stockroom. One of these skids was empty, and one of the skids in the display spot was full, so it appeared that this whole time Joseph had only parked one of the two skids. I wondered why this had taken so long.

I watched Joseph as he lifted one case of water from the top of the second skid. He placed it carefully on the empty skid. He grabbed another case, and that's when I stopped him.

He said, "Boss, how come you always give me the tough jobs? I'm getting so old for this now." I said, "Joseph, jobs are as tough as you make them." He said, "I don't understand." I was thinking, "Clearly, you don't." Although I did not say it out loud.

I said, "Watch for a second." I put the case of water back on top of the full skid. Then I picked up the empty skid and moved it aside. I used the power jack to park the full skid of water in the empty spot. Joseph looked at me in awe and said, "You know… this is why you're a manager!"

This is why I had difficulty delegating for a long time. You just can't make anything foolproof. I would much rather just work faster and do most things myself.

I knew this was wrong, though. I needed to learn how to lead people to do the job the way I did it, or alternatively, just reach the same outcome in the same amount of time.

I continued to run around the store the entire night. We actually had a very productive night, and the store looked amazing in the morning. The stockroom was empty. At 6:30 am, Roger arrived. He walked the store and then came to find me.

Roger said, "Dude, the store looks amazing! Great job!" This was not like Roger. He usually had something to complain about and he was almost always angry. Not this morning. I finished collecting empty skids and crushing cardboard in the bailer machine and after the morning associates had their meeting, I was ready to leave.

Roger saw me leaving and he said, "Hey Allan! We are going to Starbucks in the mall. Why don't you join us?" I agreed. Roger got to the front of the line and asked all of us what we wanted. After taking our orders, he paid and we all sat down. Roger was in a very good mood. He was joking and laughing loudly the whole time.

At some point during the conversation somebody mentioned something about the fashion department. This triggered my memory. I had completely forgotten to tell Roger about the rolling racks. I said, "Oh crap, now that you guys mentioned fashion, I remember Sonny wanted me to tell you something."

As if sensing that he was about to be very angry, Roger stopped laughing, stopped talking , turned right towards me, blinked quickly a few times, and said, "What about fashion?"

I said, "Ok, well Sonny saw that we had a lot of fashion skids in the back room so he mentioned that he would like to bring the rolling racks upstairs from the basement." Roger interrupted me. He said, "The next words out of your mouth better be, 'Roger I didn't bring the fucking rolling racks upstairs!'"

I said, "Roger I didn't bring the fucking rolling racks upstairs!" Roger said, "Ok, good. Of course, you didn't. You wouldn't be stupid enough to do that after what I've said about rolling racks, would you?"

I said, "Absolutely not!" He laughed loudly as he slapped his hand on the table. "But Sonny might be." I said. The laughter stopped again. Roger started visibly grinding his teeth. He said, "Go on…"

I said, "Well, Sonny said he was bringing the rolling racks upstairs and he wanted me to tell you when I saw you this morning. He said, that he will explain everything when he sees you this afternoon at 2:00 pm."

Roger said, "Coffee is over. Get up. We are going back to the store and I want you to show me where they are." We all got up and marched silently back to the store, through the mall. The tension was thick. I knew something harsh was about to happen.

We got to the store and headed straight for the fashion department. I brought Roger and the rest of the managers over to the fitting rooms where 15 rolling racks were full of hanging fashion. Roger looked at me. He asked "So you had no part in this?" I said, "Absolutely not. Sonny specifically told me to tell you that he did this, and he will explain."

Roger said, "Ok that's fine. Tell me, are you able to stay a bit longer this morning or do you need to go?" I said, "I can stay if you need me for something, no problem." Roger asked again, "Are you sure? You can go home if you need to." I assured Roger that I was good to stay.

Roger said, "Great, tell you what I need. I want you to take ALL the clothes off of these rolling racks. Take the clothes and pile them in the managers office." I was confused. "In the office?" I asked. "In the office!" He replied.

Roger continued, but now he was yelling, "THROW THE CLOTHES ON THE FLOOR! PILE THEM ON THE DESK! FILL THE WHOLE FUCKING OFFICE WITH ALL THIS SHIT!!!" I said, "Ok." Roger added, "WHEN SONNY GETS HERE THIS AFTERNOON, HE WILL KNOW WHO RUNS THIS FUCKING STORE! AND HE WILL KNOW FOR SURE THAT IT IS NOT HIM!!!!"

At this point Roger was spitting when he yelled, his face was all red and sweat was dripping off his forehead. I asked "Should I put the rolling racks downstairs?"

Roger thought for a moment. "No." He answered. "Listen to me carefully. I would like you to take all the rolling racks back to the stockroom. Then, go to the maintenance room. Get the sledgehammer. Get other tools, whatever you need, and bring your tools back to the rolling racks." "And then?" I asked.

"BREAK THEM! SMASH THE FUCKING WHEELS OFF! BEND THE BARS! TWIST EVERYTHING! BREAK THE FUCKING SHIT OUT OF THOSE ROLLING RACKS!!!" When Roger was done screaming, I said, "Ok I will!" He looked at me and said, "GO! DO IT!" I started rolling some of the racks towards the office. Roger called after me "Wait!" He said. I thought for sure he had changed his mind. I was wrong.

He said, "I want you to take all the broken pieces and toss them into the office with the clothes." "Ok." I said. And with that I began to carry out the task he had given me.

I brought the rolling racks to the office and made big piles of clothes. I did not try to stack them neatly at all. I knew he wanted to make a point. I started in the back corner and I worked my way to the front door. There wasn't a lot of room left when I was done.

Now I had 15 empty rolling racks. I managed to take four at a time, so it took me four trips to get them all to the stockroom. I found a big open area in receiving where I put them all. Then I went to get a sledgehammer and a hacksaw.

I returned to the rolling racks and went to work. I put them on their side and began to smash the wheels off. I cut a couple of bars in half with the saw but it was too much work, so I stopped. I was able to dismantle them, so I had a bunch of straight metal bars.

I took one of the bars and fit it between the wall and the metal frame of the shelving units that we stored stuff on. Pushing on the end of the bar that stuck out, I was able to bend the bar in the middle. I repeated this with all of them.

When I was half done, an associate walked by and said, "Allan, what on earth are you doing?" I replied "I am breaking rolling racks." He looked at me as if I was crazy. "Why?" And I said, "So nobody will use them ever again."

When I finished, I took all of the broken pieces and piled them in the office with the clothes, like I was told. I had to shove the last of them in there to close the door. Roger was a little distance away, beside a cash register, and I heard an associate talking to him.

The associate was a lady who happened to work in fashion. She said, "Roger, I want you to know that Allan has broken all of our rolling racks and shoved all the broken pieces into the Manager's office." "Excellent!" replied Roger.

"Excellent?" asked the associate. "But our rolling racks are all broken. How will we do our job?" Roger said, "They have been downstairs for months. Have you not done your job for months?"

Frustrated, the associate said, "Of course we do our job! We bring skids to the floor and open the boxes and put the clothes away where they belong." Roger replied "Perfect! Then it seems the only way to have you actually do your job is to take the rolling racks away."

The lady was getting even more upset. "What are you talking about?" she asked. Roger replied, "When you have the rolling racks, you know what you do? You fill them, and then push them around the department and not one of you ever fucking empties them!"

The lady replied, "Ok well, all the clothes are in your office. The managers can't even go in there now!" Roger had an answer for everything. He said, "Oh boo hoo! What's the worst that can happen? The managers have to get out of the fucking office for a while? They have to go to the sales floor and work? Perfect! Looks like I finally found a way to get ALL the lazy people to actually work! Because telling you to doesn't work! I'm the guy that runs this fucking store! This works. I should do this every day!"

I figured it was time for me to leave; it was already 11:30 am. I had an hour drive to get home. I got to my car and realized I had left my phone in there all night. There were 17 missed calls and 37 text messages. Nicky was pissed!

I picked up my phone to call her, and as I was holding it, it rang. I answered it, which I was about to regret. "WHAT THE FUCK?" Is what I was greeted with. I said, "Before you start yelling, just let me explain." She did not let me explain. "WHO IS SHE???" I said, "It's not a she, it's a he." This confused her, and she stopped yelling for a moment. She asked, "What?"

I said, "It's a man. His name is Roger and I'm much more afraid of him than I am of you." This type of humour wasn't Nicky's style. Actually, humour in general wasn't Nicky's thing. She replied with "You're so full of shit! I know you're fucking some Walmart whore! You were off at 7:00 am, for fuck's sake!"

That particular day, I was not taking shit from Roger. Most days though, I was. Every single morning, he would walk in and start screaming about stuff. He would see a box on the floor in a Department, and he would kick it. One time he saw the bread rack placed somewhere it wasn't supposed to be and he pushed it over, loaves of bread scattered everywhere.

The due date for our baby came and went. The original date was December 27th, 2008. I worked Sunday night to Thursday night. My regular days off fell on December 26th and December 27th. I booked my vacation days from December 28th to January 8th, with my regular days off following that on January 9th and January 10th. I figured this would give me lots of time with our new baby.

Things did not go exactly as planned. That baby just did not want to come out on time. The doctor chose a date to induce labour if Nicky had not given birth. That day was January 6th. When the baby finally arrived, it would change my life forever.

CHAPTER NINETEEN

THE VERY BEST DAY OF MY LIFE up to this point was almost here. Nicky and I had an appointment at the hospital on January 6th, 2009. We had found out in one of the early ultrasounds that we were having a boy.

I was excited to meet my son. We went to the hospital at 6:00 am and they induced labour. Nothing happened so we were sent home and told to come back at 2:30 pm or sooner if she was having contractions.

At 2:30 pm we went back. They induced her again and we waited. Nothing happened and we were sent home and told to return at 6:00 pm. At 6:00 pm Nicky was definitely having contractions, but they were far apart.

The hospital was going to send us home, but Nicky refused. She said, "I am so pregnant right now, I'm 10 days past the due date, and I've been up since 5:00 am. I'm not leaving again. You can't make me!"

Nicky managed to convince the nurses to let us stay. They told her to pace back and forth because they had no bed for her yet. Every so often she would scream out in pain and they would bring a wheelchair over. They finally assigned a bed for her in a semi-private room.

The night went on and on for what seemed like an eternity. We were both exhausted and I was dealing with Nicky, who was miserable and almost unapproachable. At some point, the nurses came in and put sticky pads on Nicky's belly to monitor the baby's heart rate.

Several times that night, the monitor started going crazy, beeping loudly and the nurses would run in and tell Nicky to roll over onto her side. Each time Nicky changed positions like this, the beeping slowed to a regular heartbeat rhythm.

We asked what was going on. They told us they weren't sure, but they were watching us closely. They said, the heart rate was spiking at times, but they didn't know why.

After a few of these episodes, our family doctor arrived. She seemed to know what could be causing the issue. She said that the umbilical cord was most likely wrapped around baby's neck, so when the baby went down, he would get choked and move back up to relieve pressure. They presented us with a form to sign that would allow an emergency C-section. They said the baby could suffocate otherwise.

We agreed immediately and we both signed. They told us that an obstetrician was on his way and would arrive shortly. They prepped Nicky for surgery and came and asked me if I was going into the room. "Of course!" I exclaimed. They gave me a gown and mask and gloves to wear. Before we knew it, the time had come.

I went into the room and sat beside Nicky. I was at Nicky's head and they put up a sheet so I couldn't see the surgery. They said I could watch if I wanted to but I said, "I'm good!"

The freezing took affect and then they began. They started cutting. I saw them moving the light around and heard their tools. I waited anxiously, trying not to worry.

Eventually, I heard the doctor say, "Get that cord off his neck!" Another voice said, "I can't, it's too tight!" The doctor said, sternly, "You better find a way because he's choking!"

So many thoughts I had at this time, most of them bad. I tried to stay positive. I prayed hard. I was so scared for my baby. Finally, I heard a voice yell, "Got it! I got it!" Another voice said, "Ok, let's get him breathing."

I'm sure it was only a few seconds, but it seemed like forever. Finally, I heard the best sound in the whole world. The first cry from my baby boy. The doctor yelled, "Dad, you're up!" I had told them I wanted to cut the umbilical cord.

I walked around, trying hard not to peak at Nicky's open belly. I think they had covered most of it but there were bloody rags and stuff around. I walked up to my baby boy and the doctor handed me scissors. They had just left a piece long enough for me to snip. I cut it and they put a clamp on the left-over part. I was officially a dad!

Nicky went to another room and I went back to our room for a bit. They said, they needed to give the baby oxygen for a while because he wasn't breathing while the cord was around his neck.

They assured me, though, that he would be ok, and they would bring him to me soon. I said, "So I have a while?" The nurse said, "Oh yeah, for sure!" I said, "Ok then, I'm going to get a coffee!"

Our son, Eli was born at 2:32 am. It was after midnight, so rather than a January 6th baby, we had a January 7th baby. It was now after 3:00 am and I had been up for 22 hours. I went across the street to get a Tim Hortons coffee and a doughnut. I also stopped at the 24-hour convenience store, and got a Diet Coke and a bag of wine gums.

Shortly after I got back, a nurse brought Eli into the room. She said, "Mom will be recovering from surgery for a while, so it's just you and your son for a bit." Eli was fast asleep. After a while he woke up and I picked him up for the first time. What a magical moment that was!

After a little while, Nicky was brought to the room. She got to hold our baby for the first time now, too. We were both exhausted, and she was much worse off than me because, of course, she had just been through a major surgery, so she was exhausted and also hurting.

We stayed in the hospital for the rest of that day and also the next day and night. We went home on January 9th. I had to go back to work on the night of January 11th, so I really didn't have much time with my son. My first day back went well, and in the morning, Roger was pleasant, asking for details about the baby, asked how Mom was doing, etc. It wasn't long before the pressure started up again.

About a week after I got back, Roger started to walk departments in detail with me every single morning. He would ask why things were a certain way, why things were put in the wrong spot, little things that he would pick apart.

The pressure grew increasingly tense. Every day, Roger screamed at me for something. He would say things like, "Why the fuck are there 10 skids in the stockroom? The road from the stockroom to the sales floor is a one way trip! NOTHING comes back! EVER!"

Roger had increased the number of night crew associates significantly. We were supposed to get 12 people per night, and he gave us about 20, taking from other positions in the store. He used this against me. He would say, "You have twice as many people as you're supposed to, and you still can't have the store perfect."

I was losing my patience. I thought I might snap at any moment. My team did an amazing job, and I told him that. We did have twice as many people, but he had added tasks like taking all the 20 or so shopping carts that were full of merchandise and putting every item back where they belonged.

Often these carts were not just items that had been returned. People would "clean" their departments, and anything that was in their way or didn't belong to that department, they shoved in a shopping cart and left at the front of the store.

Roger also expected us to complete the price changes in each department and label everything accordingly. If it was going on rollback, we would need to go to the back and print Rollback flags and hang them up. Roger also wanted all the counters washed.

So yes, we had more people, and we still were completing the same amount of skids each night, but half my people were doing jobs that used to be Department Manager jobs. Roger began to eliminate Department Managers and he would replace them with an extra night crew every time one quit.

There is one night I remember clearly. We had two huge trucks that night. By huge, I mean huge. Every truck had a truck report showing the number of cases. The average was about 1600 pieces. On this night, one of my trucks had 2200 pieces and the other had 2400 pieces.

To add to my problems, the one truck was super late. The truck unloaders, who left at midnight, had only just begun to unload the truck when they all left. The closing manager looked at me and said, "Well I'm off now. Your call, whatever you wanna do. See ya!"

I called all my night crew to receiving for a meeting. I told them that I needed six people. I would not take anyone from foods, health and beauty, pets, or paper goods. Those were our high-volume departments and I needed them to be stocked all night. After choosing six people, I sent the rest back to their departments.

I had another issue. I had received six sick calls that night! So instead of 19 people that were scheduled, I had only 13, and now I had six on the truck, leaving only six to stock the store until we were done unloading the truck.

My saving grace was that I had three Support Managers in that night. I assigned two of them to departments and had one of them pulling skids from receiving to the sales floor.

Once the truck was empty, all the associates that had unloaded the truck helped me pull all skids to the sales floor, and immediately began stocking in their assigned departments.

I ran my ass off that night! I also had my maintenance team to follow up with. They were waxing floors in paper goods that night. I had two aisles closed most of the night. We had to blitz the nine skids for those aisles as soon as the wax was dry enough to walk on.

What an intense night! I managed to stock 15 skids myself that night, accounting for three of my missing associates because they completed an average of five skids per person per night. By doing this and by pushing my Support Managers to do the same, we put out every single skid from both trucks. I was very impressed with our performance, given the circumstances.

The only thing I had left in the early hours of the morning was to crush all the empty boxes in our bailer machine. We had cardboard bins that we used in each department for the associates to put their empty boxes. They would fold them down flat and fill the bins.

Normally we had one associate assigned to crush cardboard all night, but he spent a couple of hours with me to unload the truck and pull skids to the floor. After that, I had him stocking the furniture department to help get rid of a few more skids.

So around 6:00 am, I started crushing cardboard and making bails myself. I asked my Support Managers to walk the floor and make sure we had no empty skids and no cardboard anywhere and make sure everyone was front facing their departments, making the store look pretty.

Around 6:45 am Roger walked into receiving and saw me frantically trying to crush all the cardboard. He was furious! He asked "What the fuck is this mess?" I said, "Roger I can explain. We had two huge trucks last night. One of the trucks was very late arriving and we had to unload it ourselves. I also had six associates call in sick last night."

He said, "You didn't even begin to answer my question. Let me ask you again… WHAT THE FUCK IS ALL THIS MESS?" I said, "It's cardboard, Roger."

He said, "I can see that. What is my rule? You know what my rule is! The entire store is ready for opening when I walk in."

I said, "Yes, I know that." Roger said, "Then why are you crushing cardboard at 7:00 am?" I said, "Well the good news is that all this cardboard you see are empty boxes. Boxes that were full at the beginning of the night. We have not sent one box to the stockroom… well, we have not sent any full boxes to the stockroom."

Roger was unimpressed. He said, "I don't accept your answer. This is completely unacceptable! You can stay until all of this is done and when it is done, call me and we will walk the floor. I guarantee you, I'll find a bunch of shit that you guys fucked up and you can fix that, too!"

I said, "Listen Roger. I will finish the cardboard, but then I'm going home. I have a new baby that I spent only two days with and then came back to work. I don't know of ANY Manager that has EVER completed every single skid in a single night! To say that we completed ALL of this AFTER we unloaded an entire truck and pulled skids is nothing short of incredible! Not to mention, I was short six people! Every one of these boxes was full when it arrived last night, so I think we've done alright, thank you very much!"

He said, "Just a minute." He walked over to a phone on the wall and paged, "All Assistant Managers to Receiving please!" A few moments later all the Managers walked into receiving. He gave a little speech to everybody.

"I just wanted to remind everyone that I ask every single one of you to arrive to work every day with a plan! A plan of what you will accomplish that day. I wanted to add that so long as ALLAN is in this store, your plan should be to do his FUCKING job, because he has clearly demonstrated the he CAN'T!!!"

He continued. "Today your job will be to crush fucking cardboard! I need my store to be where it needs to be, and if I have to pay six Assistant Managers fifty thousand dollars a year to crush fucking cardboard, then that is what I will do!"

I stepped in and said, "None of these people needs to crush cardboard. I have never once asked anybody to do a single thing for me. If I need to stay until noon, then I will do that!"

Roger said, "Oh no! You cannot! Go home, your shift is over, and apparently you have a fucking baby you wanna see! Go!" I almost swore at him in that moment. Rather than argue, I said, "Kay, see ya!"

I was absolutely furious! I had everything stacked against me that night and we had a far better night than any other overnight Manager had had since I was in that store. The job we did as a team was exceptional! He had praised me on nights that were far worse than that. I didn't need praise, but I was pissed that he said, in front of everyone that I could not do my job! My blood was boiling!

I got into my car and the phone started ringing. I looked at the call display. Nicky. I picked it up. I got yelled at right away. "Where the fuck are you! You have no fucking respect for us! You were off over an hour and a half ago!"

I took a deep breath and said, "Sorry, bad reception. I can't hear you!" And I hung up. I had no patience for any more bullshit. I had to get screamed at while I was at work and again at home. That was enough. I decided the hour drive was my time.

In the 12 Step meetings, they say we must stay sober under "any and all conditions." They also say that we must deal with "life on life's terms." Life was about to get a whole lot worse before it got better. My sobriety and my sanity would be tested.

CHAPTER TWENTY

THE PHONE STARTED TO RING OVER AND OVER. I turned it off. I went to the drive-through at Starbucks and ordered my usual, a tall dark roast in a venti cup, topped up with non-fat milk and two raw sugars. If I had been in the store, I would have stirred it counter-clockwise seven times, but I was too embarrassed to say that at the drive through. That day, I also ordered an oat fudge bar.

I paid for my order and drove down the road towards the exit for the highway. As I merged onto the highway, I noticed there were cars as far as the eye could see. It seemed I was stuck in a major traffic jam "Excellent!" I said, out loud to myself.

I turned on some Bob Marley and sipped my coffee. Tapping my hands on the steering wheel, I sang along with Bob. "Don't worry, about a thing! 'Cause every little thing, gonna be alright! Singing don't worry, about a thing. 'Cause every little thing gonna be alright!"

My morning bliss came to an end when I walked through my front door. Eli was screaming and Nicky began screaming, too. "I don't know where the fuck you have been, asshole, but it's your fucking turn now! I'm going out!"

She left me with my crying son. I started to rock him a bit and he calmed down. I held him and walked around with him for a bit. Nicky wasn't gone long, maybe an hour. When she came back, I told her I was going to sleep. I still had to work that night, and I had been up since 3:00 pm the day before.

Life with Nicky was up and down. It was never great, but there were moments that gave me hope. Nicky would do her steps, and through that process she would see her part in things and make amends to me. I did the same with her.

Nicky often told me that I needed to do another full set of steps, although I remembered that Angelika had told me I only needed to do them all once. Angelika told me that Steps ten, eleven, and twelve were the "maintenance steps." These I should practice continuously, she said.

Step ten said, "Continued to take personal inventory and when we were wrong promptly admitted it." To me, this basically meant that I shouldn't slip back into blaming others. I needed to continue to take responsibility for my part in my disagreements with others, and continue with my efforts to improve my behaviour.

I practiced this step a lot in my marriage to Nicky. I always tried very hard to see my part in our disagreements, and there were a lot of disagreements. It was challenging, but I needed to continue with Step ten on a regular basis. I was told that this was critical because resentments are the main cause of relapse in alcoholics and addicts.

Around this time, I also began to look seriously at the next step. Before I explain this, I must say that this is not about religion at all. This is simply my experience, and it is not necessary for one to believe in God in order to complete the steps. In fact, as I explain later on, even agnostics and atheists can complete the steps. Again, there is no preaching happening here, it is just my experience.

Step eleven said, "Sought through prayer and meditation to improve our conscious contact with God, *as we understood him*, praying only for knowledge of his will for us and the power to carry that out."

I was struggling very much with my higher powers' identity. I had been calling my higher power "Creator" for a long time now. I was leaning towards a Christian God, but I was hesitant to believe. I had found a new sponsor recently because the one I had was extremely busy and didn't have a lot of time to work with me. He was a Christian and attended church each week. I spoke with him about it.

When I explained my struggle, my sponsor said, "You know, God will prove himself to you if you ask him to." I said, "How will he do that?" He said, "You can ask him to prove himself, however you want him to, and he will."

I didn't believe this. This was too much. I said, "If that's the case then we don't need faith. Everyone could just ask for proof." He said, "If the Christian God is for you, he will provide proof. If you don't get proof, then you'll still have your answer and you can continue to call him Creator."

I decided to follow through with this experiment. I went home that night and prayed. I said, "God, if you are in fact the Christian God I was raised to believe in, then prove yourself. I would like you to show me a rainbow. I want you to do this by my birthday. If you do this, I will refer to you as God."

My birthday was in two weeks, which is why I gave this as a deadline to God. When I woke the next morning, I turned on the TV. The Care Bears were on. The first thing I saw was a Care Bear with a rainbow on his chest. I laughed and said to God, "Nope! Nice try, buddy! That does not count."

I decided to go out looking for a real rainbow. I went for a drive. I prayed to God, saying, "I just want you to give me a sign in the form of a rainbow that you exist." Not long after this, I saw a giant sign with a rainbow on it. It read "Rainbow's End RV Park."

Again, I laughed and said, "Nope! Nice try. I did ask for a sign but that is not what I meant, and you know it! I want a rainbow!" I was unwilling to take these rainbows as proof. I needed to know, without a doubt. It would need to be much more convincing.

I got home and had given up for the day. That evening I decided to cook some steaks on the BBQ. I went out to the balcony. Right there, above the church that was behind our apartments, was a rainbow. Believe it or not, I still was not convinced. I mean, it was a rainbow, but it wasn't that bright. I told myself that God still had until my birthday.

Sara was always involved in our life. We had regular visits and she absolutely adored her grandson. As my birthday was coming up, we had planned to go visit her. Sara took us out to Earls for dinner and then we went back to her apartment. I opened a couple of gifts there and we had cake.

Before we left, Sara told me she had one more thing for me. She went to her bedroom and came back with a bag. When I opened it, I found birthday cards, art work, and Christmas cards. Sara had kept every card ever given to me, and much of the art I did in school. I thanked her and took it with me when I left.

On the hour-long drive home, Nicky and Eli fell asleep. The sky started to get very black with storm clouds. It began to rain very hard. At some point, when I was about half way home, I looked in the rear-view mirror. I was shocked to see that through the black clouds, there was an extremely brilliant rainbow. "Hmmm," I thought to myself.

If this wasn't enough, what happened next was. I got home, took off my shoes, and sat down with the bag that Sara had given me. I picked up a huge pile of cards, and as I did, one fell out onto the floor, separating itself from the rest. I picked it up and read it. I was lost for words.

On the front of this card was a teddy bear that had a paint brush in his hand. He had painted a giant rainbow across the front of the card. I opened the card and discovered that it was a birthday card to me, from my dad, Bill. The inside read "You make our life brighter." I looked at the top right hand corner of the card and saw my dad had written only one thing in the card. He had simply written "Psalm:23."

Wow! I was pretty hard to convince. I denied all other signs, but this… this I could not ignore. I had asked God for a rainbow before my birthday, then on the day before my birthday I see a brilliant real rainbow, AND I find a card from my dad who had died two decades earlier that happened to have a rainbow on it AND a bible verse written on the inside!

Not only did God prove himself to me, but my dad was back! "Thank you, Dad!" I said. He replied "You're welcome, Allan. Happy birthday! I'm so happy you're better now!" I was convinced. I was ready for the final step.

Step twelve said, "Having had a spiritual awakening as the result of these steps, we tried to carry this message to alcoholics, and to practice these principles in all our affairs."

This to me, meant that it was my responsibility to help other people. I did not rush this step though, because I wanted to be in a good place to do so. I was still working on my own recovery and once I felt the time was right, I would sponsor someone.

When I eventually did get transferred to another store, it was in Surrey. I went to Surrey with what I had learned from Roger. I was different than Roger though. My first focus was on people. I made sure I always knew everyone's name. I made sure I knew specifics about their life, and made sure they knew that I genuinely cared.

I would make a point of asking Josh how his dog's surgery went, and go see Riswana when she returned from India to ask her how her niece's wedding was. My associates loved me, and they all worked very hard. I did very well in Surrey.

Life at home was getting harder and harder. I was dealing with Nicky's anger issues and jealousy issues and aside from that, we were in trouble financially as well. Nicky had taken maternity leave, which reduced her income by about half, and then she just never went back to work.

I'm not sure exactly what happened with Nicky's employment. She said that the owner of the salon just said her position was no longer available. I told Nicky that they needed to pay her severance. She said she tried to get severance, but they refused and there was nothing she could do.

Another expense we had was our dog. Recently, Nicky had convinced me that a dog would be a great addition to our family. We went to the animal shelter and chose a small, middle-aged poodle named Wilburt. He had a couple of trips to the vet for different issues which were quite costly.

So, we had lost Nicky's income and we had the added expense of raising a baby, like diapers and formula and clothes. I was also spending a ton of money to commute back and forth from work, and there were food and vet bills for Wilburt.

My credit cards were maxed out more than once, but they kept automatically increasing my credit limit. Eventually, my one credit card had a balance of $20,000. I actually paid it down to $7,000, but it didn't stay there. It went back to $20,000 before long.

Nicky was very stressed about our financial situation. She had a plan to make some money to help with our situation. She said, she wanted to be a social worker. She would need to do some schooling though and it would cost about $6,000. We went to the bank and got approved for a line of credit for $13,000.

We used some money to pay off Nicky's credit cards, and she took out the rest in cash. She said she went to the school to pay for books and tuition, but to this day I'm very skeptical about that.

After Nicky spent the money on her schooling, she suddenly just changed her mind. She said, she didn't want to go to school after all, but there was no way for her to get the money back. In the meantime, she had maxed out her credit cards and I don't even know what she bought. Now we had her credit cards, my credit card of $20,000 and a $13,000 line of credit, and she was unemployed.

Things looked bleak. We were now in 2008-2009 and the housing market had just collapsed. The equity we thought we had in our home was gone. The apartment was now worth about $30,000 less than we paid for it.

At this time, I was approached by Walmart, and asked if I would relocate to the Okanagan, specifically Vernon, B.C., as they were in desperate need of Assistant Managers. I said I would need to ask my wife.

When I brought it up to Nicky, she was very interested in moving. I was not. I explained that we would need to sell the apartment because we had an agreement that stated we could not rent the apartment out. The owners must live there. We had gotten away with renting because Nicky was the daughter of the owners and they made an exception.

If we sold now, we would definitely lose a lot of money. Then there was the issue of all the debt. I suggested that we stay, and when the housing market bounced back, maybe we could sell the apartment at a profit and get back on track with our bills. Nicky had a different plan.

She said, "We are in so much debt that we will never pay off our bills. Why not just claim bankruptcy, and not pay anything?" I said, "Absolutely not! I am not doing that!" Nicky gave me an ultimatum. She said, "Either we claim bankruptcy and accept the transfer to Vernon and start off fresh, or I want a divorce!"

I knew Nicky was serious. Eli was just over a year old now. I thought about it hard. Neither option was desirable. In the end, I chose to keep my family together. I went back to Walmart and told them I agreed to transfer to Vernon. We started packing.

CHAPTER TWENTY-ONE

NICKY AND I TOOK THE NEXT few weeks to move. There were several trips with the U-Haul. The good news was that the expenses were all paid by Walmart. There was more good news for me as well. My store Manager in Vernon was Martin, the manager who hired me in North Vancouver, who I also worked with in Chilliwack and Burnaby. I knew he liked me a lot, and I knew I would be safe with him as my Manager.

Nicky and I were now in Vernon. Once we got settled, we went to the bankruptcy agent and declared bankruptcy. Before we did though, we went and bought a new car. We knew we would need two vehicles and we only had one, which was the one I bought when I first got sober in North Vancouver. That car was paid off, so we didn't need to make any payments on that one.

We were approved for the car and now we had two cars, one of which was brand new. When we declared bankruptcy, we simply said that we did not wish to include the new vehicle in the bankruptcy, and we would continue to make the payments for that.

Our agreement with the bankruptcy agent was based on the fact that we were a three-person family. They looked at my income and said that we could afford to pay $225/month. Once we had paid for 18 months, we would be discharged and could begin to build up our credit rating, although this would take years.

Nicky had a great idea that would save us some money. She said that we should switch over the older car to her name and put the insurance under her name because she had a longer driving record and the insurance would be less. We did this and saved about $30/month on our insurance bill. The new car was bought by both of us and we were both registered owners of that vehicle.

I should have seen the warning signs. I was so unsuspecting. I trusted my wife and took her at her word. I believed we were in Vernon to start fresh and raise a nice family. We were only in Vernon six weeks when she told me she was leaving me and moving back to Chilliwack.

I would like to believe that it happened as the result of our last fight, but looking back at it, I know it was all planned. She took the brand-new car and left me with the old one. She had no money to leave me, and actually took fifty dollars from me for gas to get to Chilliwack.

I was furious. Mostly, I was angry with myself for not seeing what she had planned. This was one of the few times I considered drinking again. I figured it wouldn't matter because my life was already destroyed. I was bankrupt, divorced, and broke, and I was living in a town where I didn't know anyone. How much worse could life get? At least if I was drinking, I could forget it for a while.

I quickly came to my senses. I knew that my life could and would get a whole lot worse if I drank. Besides, even though my son didn't live with me, I was still his father and he still needed me. During my hardest moments, I thought of him and how me relapsing would affect his life. I would not do this to him. I had a choice, he didn't, and he deserved better than that.

Nicky took Eli with her when she left, but she left our dog, Wilburt. During days of extreme loneliness, Wilburt became my confidant, and kept me company.

Whenever I got very sad, Wilburt knew, and would snuggle up under my armpit, getting as close to me as he could. I was sure grateful to have such a loyal friend during these hard times.

I found a 12 Step meeting half a block from my house and made it my home group. I began to open the meeting every Tuesday night. I made the coffee and set up the tables and chairs. I spent the rest of my time working. I worked a lot. It helped me keep my mind off things.

I needed to disclose to the bankruptcy agent that my family situation had changed. Perhaps I wouldn't have said anything, but I knew that Nicky went to them and told them she was now a single mom, and had no money to pay for bankruptcy and she wanted to be discharged right away. I went to the office and told them my situation.

Because my income was the same, but I had gone from a three-person family to a single person, they said I could now afford to pay more money. My bankruptcy fees increased from $225/month to $450/month. This added expense would hurt a lot, especially since I needed to consider travelling expenses to see my son as often as possible. The drive to Chilliwack was four hours each way. I also knew Nicky would be entitled to child support soon.

I decided the easiest and quickest way for me to save that extra money was to stop payments on the new car. I said, "Fuck her! Why should I pay for Nicky to drive a brand-new car?" I went to the bank and paid them $40 to stop the automatic withdrawals from my account.

I sent Nicky an email. I told her that I could no longer afford to make the car payments. I said she could keep driving the new car, but she would need to make arrangements to make the payments, otherwise it would get repossessed. She flipped out. I mean she completely lost her mind!

My phone rang about 10 minutes after I sent the email. Nicky was on the other end, screaming at me. I tried to calm her down for a minute and then I said, "Wait a second. I just realized something. It doesn't matter if you're mad anymore!"

Nicky said, "What the fuck are you talking about?" I said, "I'm always so afraid that you'll be mad. But it doesn't matter now. You already left me!"

Right after this conversation, I took a trip down to see my son. I stayed with Mike, who over the years had become my best friend. He said Eli and I, as well as Wilburt, were always welcome at his home. Nicky was still pissed about the car situation, but I didn't care. I couldn't afford to pay for it.

While I was with Eli at Mike's house, my phone rang. It was the police. The officer told me that Nicky had reported her car stolen and had told them I was the one who stole it. I said, "No, no officer. It's my car. I made every single payment and it's paid off and I own it." He said, "Well, you don't own it. She showed us papers that have her as the only registered owner. You need to return it or she's going to charge you with theft. But she said she has your other car and will be happy to just switch with you!"

If I wasn't raging before I was now! This is when I began to realize that all her previous actions had alternate motives. She put the car in her name, so she owned it! Not to save us a few bucks on the insurance! I felt so stupid.

I met Nicky, and switched cars with her. Eli was with me and when we left, I still had a day left on my visit with him. But now he had seen his mom and was crying for her. We spent the rest of the visit with him crying that he wanted his mommy.

So now I had to go back to the bank and tell them to resume payments on my new car. Nicky kept calling me and telling me to get her name off of the car because she had already been discharged from bankruptcy, and she said that if I couldn't make the payments she didn't want to be responsible in any way for that car. She called many, many times and yelled at me about this.

The only way I could pay for the car now and pay child support in the near future was if I moved. I began looking around for an affordable place to rent. The Produce Manager at Walmart said he might know of a place. He rented the basement in a house and said that his landlord had a brand-new suite upstairs that was about to go up for rent.

I took the guy's number and went for a meeting with him. The house was half a block from the place I was living. The guy agreed to rent me the suite for $825/month, including utilities and internet. I was currently paying $1400 plus utilities, so I was pretty happy with the new price.

I moved right away. I cleaned the house I was in perfectly and got my damage deposit back, which I gave to my new landlord for the first month's rent and the damage deposit there.

The new place wasn't much, but it was good for me. It had laminate floors that looked like hardwood. It had a kitchen, a bathroom that had a shower only, no bath, a laundry room with a washer and dryer, small living room and a small bedroom. That's all I needed, and the price was right.

I began to dive into work. I decided I was going to push as hard as I could at my job. I had dreams of being a Store Manager. I figured that was my best shot at having a good life with a good income. First though, I would need to overcome the court battles that lay ahead of me.

With everything that had happened before and after my separation, I wasn't exactly taking care of myself physically. I began to eat fast food a lot, and at night I would eat chips and drink pop. Right across the street from me was the best pizza in town and they sold it by the slice. I went there several times a week. I started to gain a lot of weight and people noticed.

I was 210 pounds when I decided to make a change. Across the street from my house, right beside the best pizza in town, was a gym. I decided it was time to put the pizza down and step on the treadmill.

I knew from doing research that there are 3500 calories in a pound of fat. I decided that if I burned 500 calories per day then I could lose one pound per week if I went every day. I knew if I ate less or at least made better choices then I would lose even more.

I completely changed my diet. I cut out pop and all junk food and greatly reduced my consumption of bread. I went to the gym every single day. I would run on the treadmill and I would put Eli's photo in front of me. This reminded me that part of being the best dad I could be was taking care of myself. I would do this for him.

In addition to running on the treadmill at the gym, I began to jog with Wilburt. He accompanied me on my runs around town. I remember he made me laugh so hard one day when I let him off his leash.

It was wintertime now, and we had just received a huge dump of snow. I let Wilburt off the leash on a trail close to my house. He ran off the trail and tried to pounce on a big stick. It was soft snow and Wilburt completely disappeared into the middle of it.

This didn't stop Wilburt, though. He came flying out of the snowbank and charged towards me. He tried to grab a stick from the ground, but didn't stop running. His ass flipped over his head, he landed on his feet and continued to run to me, smiling the whole time.

I did not miss a day at the gym for 59 days. On the 60th day, I worked 16 hours and the gym closed before I got off. In those 59 days, I went from 210 pounds to 170 pounds. I felt great.

Life was actually pretty great at this point in my life. My boss loved me, I lost a bunch of weight, and Wilburt kept me company, listening to me each night, without prejudice.

Although life was going well, I was about to learn that life is full of ups and downs. I would soon go through a fairly major life event. I would suffer a loss and be faced with more challenges to overcome.

CHAPTER TWENTY-TWO

I WAS HAVING A SOMEWHAT NORMAL life at this point. I was making regular trips to Chilliwack to see my son, and to visit my brother and Mike. It was now summertime and I was due for a vacation.

I booked some time off and made plans to bring Eli to my Aunt and Uncle's lake that I had loved so much as a child. I wanted Eli to experience this as well, and I wanted my Aunt and Uncle to get to know my son, too.

When the day came, I packed the car and left very early with Wilburt to pick up my son in Chilliwack. I got Eli around 9:00 am and went to pick up Sara, who was going to come up with us. I got Sara around 11:00 am and we went to catch the ferry.

I spent four days at the lake, loving every minute of it. I went out water skiing and showed Eli how to catch little bullhead fish and crawfish with a small hook, on two feet of fishing line, baited with pieces of hotdog.

We lay down at the edge of the dock, where the water was shallow and put our hook in. We caught several fish and crawfish and Eli loved it. Eli was two and a half, and didn't speak a whole lot, but he pointed at our bucket, laughing, and saying "Fish!"

When the four days were up, it was time to go home. We said our good-byes and Sara, Eli, Wilburt and I got into the car and headed for the ferry.

I dropped off Sara first, and then went to Chilliwack and dropped off Eli with his mom.

The date was July 11th, 2011 or 7-11-11. For me, this set of numbers is very important. I happen to believe in numerology, or at least, I am a bit superstitious, and my lucky numbers are 3, 5, 7, and 13. The numbers 1 and 9 are known by many as "magical" numbers. Most people also know about the belief that if you look at a clock and it's 11:11, then you can make a wish.

Whether these numbers had anything to do with it or not, the events that happened that day made me one of the luckiest people alive. It started with an extremely unfortunate event, but the result I can only describe as a miracle.

July 11th means something else to the 7-11 franchise. Because it was the seventh month and the eleventh day, the store had a special promotion that I noticed when I stopped for gas. They had free Slurpees and $1 Pizza slices. I decided to have pizza and a Slurpee for lunch, and I bought some chips for the drive back to Vernon as well.

Before I hit the highway, I stopped at Starbucks, as I always got a Grande dark roast, in a Venti cup, topped up with non-fat milk and two raw sugars, and stirred counter clockwise precisely seven times, when I was on the road.

Once I had my food and my coffee, and I had taken my buddy Wilburt for a short walk, we started our drive back to Vernon. It was a beautiful summer day; I had the air conditioning on and the tunes blasting as I cruised the Coquihalla highway.

Sometimes I would stop in Merritt to let Wilburt pee again, but he was sleeping peacefully in the back seat, so I decided to keep going to save time. I still had daylight, but it's a long drive, and I wanted to make sure I got home before dusk.

There were no cars on the road at all, and I began to pick up speed. I remember looking at the speedometer and reading 160 km/hr. I thought, "Crap that's fast, I had better slow down a bit." But before long, my heavy foot won, and I was back at that speed again.

Suddenly, the whole car began to shake violently. In the next second, my steering wheel cranked hard to the right by itself and the whole car started spinning in circles in the centre of the highway.

After three or four spins, the car stopped spinning. The front of my car was pointed slightly to the left, facing 11:00, but the car was sliding very fast, sideways and the passenger side of the vehicle was headed straight for the ditch.

One of the last things I remember was looking at the ditch and thinking, "Ah FUCK!" The car hit with such force that my whole body felt the blow, just for a moment, and then I lost consciousness.

When I regained consciousness, I was sitting in my seat and the first thing I noticed was a large amount of dust in the air. The next thing I noticed was a dull, aching pain in my ribs on the left side.

I noticed my seatbelt was bothering me, so I pushed the button to release it. When I released my seatbelt, I suddenly fell down, to the passenger seat. This is because the car was on its side, passenger side down.

Completely dazed, I believe I acted impulsively, and at that moment I just wanted out of that car. I crawled out on my hands and knees through the sunroof, which was completely smashed. My palms got cut a little bit as I crawled across the broken glass.

I scrambled to my feet. I was so dizzy I almost fell over again. The whole world was spinning uncontrollably. I saw a car skid to a stop on the side of the highway, and a man jumped out and ran towards me.

As he approached, the man said, "Hi, I'm James. I'm not on duty at the moment, but I'm a firefighter and I can help you. What's your name?" He asked. "Allan," I replied. Then he asked, "Are you hurt anywhere?" All I could manage to get out of my mouth was one word over and over, "Dizzy! Dizzy! Dizzy! Dizzy!" James looked at the car, then looked at me and said, "Yeah, you're gonna be dizzy, bud!"

He asked me to walk with him to a cement barricade on the side of the road. As I walked with him, I saw the lifeless body of my dog Wilburt. I got very upset. "WILBURT!" I yelled. James said, "Allan I'm sorry, he didn't make it. We can't look at him now though, you need to sit down."

I tried to walk over to my dog, yelling, "Wilburt! No, oh no! No, no, oh please!" James stopped me, saying, "I'm sorry Allan, but you have been in a serious accident. You may have a spinal injury. If you keep moving, you could become paralyzed for life."

Photo of accident scene July 11th 2011

That got my attention and I followed his instructions. I sat on the side of the road and I leaned up against the cement barricade. I looked back at Wilburt for a moment and started to cry. "Fuck!" I yelled. "No, no, oh fuck! That really sucks!" I said.

James told me again not to move. At this point another car had stopped and a man and his teenage son got out. James asked them to make sure that I didn't move, as he ran to his car to get a first aid kit.

James came back right away with an ice pack and bandages. After James wrapped my head, I noticed my music was still blasting from the car. "I want my… I want my M-TV. Money for nothin' and the chicks for free!"

I said, "Hey if we have to wait for an ambulance, at least I brought good tunes!" James laughed and said, "Speaking of the ambulance, where the hell are those guys?" I said, "James, be patient! You just called them. You can't expect them to arrive in three minutes!"

What James said next surprised me. He said, "Dude, I've been sitting here on the side of the highway talking with you for 45 minutes now!" "REALLY?" I asked. "What did we talk about?" James said, "The same two or three things… over and over again! You have a concussion."

The ambulance eventually arrived on scene. The paramedics put me on a backboard and put a collar on my neck to keep my spine straight. A police officer arrived and wanted to ask me a few questions.

The cop said, "Allan I'm Officer Johansen. I have some questions for you. First of all, do you remember what happened to cause the accident?" I told him what I could remember and explained that I didn't know why my car started to spin. He wanted me to answer a few more questions.

"And what was the speed of your vehicle at the time of the accident?" "Pardon me?" I asked. He said, "How fast were you going?" I told Officer Johansen, "Most highways have a speed limit of a hundred kilometres per hour, but here it says a hundred and ten."

Officer Johansen said, "Yes, that's correct. But I'm wondering how fast YOUR vehicle was going at the time of the accident." I said, "They say you should never use cruise control in the winter time. I rarely use my cruise control anyway!"

Very patiently, Officer Johansen asked, "Allan, do you recall how fast you were driving when you crashed?" I said, again "You know, most highways have a speed limit of a hundred, but here it says a hundred and ten."

Now it is true that I was concussed, but I also kind of played that card a bit because I really didn't want to tell him I was driving at 160 km/hr. He said again, "Allan I know what the speed limit is. How fast were you driving?"

I said, "Officer, you know, most highways have a speed limit of a hundred but here it says a hundred and ten!" He began to ask one more time. "Allan how fast…" He stopped and smiled at me. He said, "You know what? I'm just going to say a hundred and ten." I smiled back at him and said, "Thank you!"

Next, he told me that he was very sorry about my dog. He told me that he attends many car accidents. He said that the dogs rarely survive. He said, "I live on an acreage. I have buried over a hundred dogs there. If you want, I can bury your dog there, with the other dogs."

I was very moved by this, but I was still trying to process my loss. I said, "I'm not sure right now. Can I decide later?" "Of course," replied Officer Johansen. He gave me his card and said I could call him any time.

The paramedics cut our conversation short. The female medic said, "Ok sorry, we gotta roll!" The doors of the ambulance shut, and we began the trip to the Kelowna hospital. We were driving so fast! I was actually very scared. Every corner we took, metal cabinet doors opened, and I heard the tools slam back and forth.

At some point during the ride, the one paramedic informed me of what was going to happen next. She said, "Ok Allan, here's what's gonna happen. Firemen are racing our way. When they reach us, we are going to stop and open the doors. A fireman will get in, we will close the doors, and we will start driving again!"

Of course, I had only one question. "Why?" She said, "Because your left chest is very swollen, and if it's what we think it is, then we need to perform a procedure. Firemen are a higher level of care and we need their help."

"What procedure?" I asked. She said, "Don't worry about that right now." I said, "If you're worried my lung is collapsed you probably want to put a tube in my chest! Are you going to cut a hole and shove a tube in there?" "Only if we need to!" She said.

Not long after that conversation I saw flashing lights behind us, and we stopped. As promised, the doors flew open, a fireman jumped in, the doors closed and we started driving again.

I was very chatty. The fireman said, "Sorry Allan, can you not talk just for a few seconds while I listen to your chest?" I nodded my head. He listened. Then he laughed and said, "He doesn't have a flail chest! It's just bruised!" "OH, THANK GOD!" I exclaimed, "I did not want a hole in my chest!"

When we arrived at the hospital, the paramedics rolled me in through emergency. They put me to the side of the hallway. I saw the female paramedic walk up to a doctor and show him a few photos of my car she had on her cell phone.

The doctor examined the photos, and said, "Oh no! That's horrible! How many casualties was that one?" She said, "None, actually!" He said, "What? How many injured? They must be in very critical condition!" Pointing my way, she said, "Only the one, and he's right over there!"

The doctor walked over to me. He asked the paramedic, "What is his chief complaint?" She said, "Sore ribs and the bump on his head!" The doctor said, "I want x-rays of his chest and spine right away, but… wow! He looks good!"

He asked me, "Were you really driving that car, young man?" "Yes, I was," I replied. He said, "You're so lucky that I can't even begin to explain. I've seen several accidents like yours. I haven't ever seen anyone survive a crash of that magnitude."

Next, the doctors wanted to know if there was someone I wanted to call. I really wanted to call my mom; Sara, that is. They dialled the number for me, but there was no answer. She was out.

I wanted to call my brother, but I didn't know his number. I had it in my phone, which paramedics retrieved from the car, but the battery had died. I decided I had better tell Nicky because she would find out soon anyway.

I managed to remember Nicky's number and they dialled it for me. She answered. I told her I had been in a horrible car accident. I told her the car was completely destroyed. She said, "Who cares about the car! Are you seriously injured?"

I told Nicky that they were going to do a spinal x-ray. I thought of Wilburt, and started crying. "What?" asked Nicky. I said, "Wilburt didn't survive!" She said, "I'm sorry to hear that." The doctors ended my call because they wanted to get my x-rays done.

After confirming that my spine was intact, and my chest was only bruised, they finally removed my neck brace. I had been waiting for hours for that uncomfortable thing to be removed. Next, they wanted to know if there were any other calls I needed to make. I knew I needed to inform my work.

I told them that I didn't know the number, but I worked at the Walmart in Vernon, and they would know me there because I was a manager. I said, "I can't remember my shift for Monday so if you can ask them what I'm working that would be great."

I dozed off a little bit and I woke up to a nurse standing over my bed. She said, "Allan, your cousin is here. He came to drive you home!" I was very confused. "Cousin?" I asked. "Yes," she said. "Your cousin Martin from Vernon."

Just then Martin peeked around the corner and put his finger to his lips, indicating for me not to blow his cover. "Oh, Martin!" I exclaimed. "Thanks for coming, cuz!"

As we walked out, I asked Martin what the hell he was doing. He said, "You're only allowed to be released to a family member. How else were you going to get home?"

I thanked Martin very much for coming to get me. He asked, "Is there anything you need right at this moment? Anything at all?" There was something. I said, "Yes. Yes, there is." "Name it and I'll make it happen," he said.

I pointed to my jeans. "See that stain all over my jeans?" I asked. He said, "Yes, but I'm sure it will come out. If it doesn't, I can take you to get jeans tomorrow." "I don't care about the jeans!" I said. "Oh, what do you want then?" he asked. I said, "That stain is from a Venti dark Roast! I only had half of it and the other half spilled on my jeans when I crashed!! I want another coffee from Starbucks, please!"

Martin found this very humorous. "I'll remember this!" he said. "I tell Allan he can have anything he wants, anything he needs, anything at all, and he requests a Starbucks coffee!"

Martin very kindly brought me to Starbucks and even paid for my coffee. I enjoyed that coffee very much as we made the 45-minute drive back to Vernon.

When Martin dropped me off, it was around 10:00 pm. I had to wake the Landlord to let me in because my keys were in my car. Martin said he would call the next day and we could go to the place they took my car, to get my stuff. "Now get some rest," he said.

As promised, Martin called the next day around 11:00 am, and he asked me to be ready within the hour. I got dressed and waited for him to arrive. I was hoping to retrieve most of my stuff from the car, but I wasn't sure what was still in there.

The car had been towed to a place in Merritt. Martin and I had a three-hour drive there, and a three-hour drive back. Martin picked me up around 11:30 am and we went to the wreckers in Merritt.

During the drive, Martin and I had lots of time to talk. He asked where my black hat was. I told him I must have lost it in the crash. It was a black Nike hat that I called my "Lucky Black Hat." I called it this because I always just felt like it was a lucky hat.

When we arrived at the wreckers, a man asked us the make and model of the car and when it was brought in. I told him it was the Toyota Matrix that was brought in the night before. He said, "Oh that one! Are you guys family members of the driver?"

"No," I said. "I AM the driver!" The man looked at me in disbelief. He said, "YOU? Are you trying to tell me you walked away from that mess?" "I did," I said. All he could say was, "Wow! You better go buy a lottery ticket buddy!"

He got us to follow him to the back 40 where the car had been left. When we approached the car, Martin said, "Holy shit, Al! This is unreal!" I walked around the car. When I got to the driver's side, I saw that my lucky black hat was in the driver's door. It was slammed in there, as if someone opened the door, placed the hat there, and closed the door on the hat.

Due to the excessive damage to the door, I was unable to open it. I pulled the hat until it came free, then brushed off the dust with my hand and put the hat on my head. "Found my lucky black hat!" I said to Martin, who had been watching the whole time.

Martin stopped me. He said, "Wait just a minute. That hat was on your head at the time of the accident?" "Yes," I said, "Why?" He said, "Because it was slammed into the door. Why is your head not slammed in the door?" I said, "Well there's only one explanation. It really is a lucky black hat!"

I rummaged through the car, collecting the clothes that I had packed for my trip to the lake, and a few other possessions, and then we left. Martin said, "I'm far from being a religious man, but the fact that you walked away from that accident is nothing short of miraculous."

On the drive back to Vernon I told Martin that nobody had told me what my shift was for Monday, which was the following day. He said, "You don't have a shift tomorrow." I said, "I do, but I can't remember if it's 7:00-4:00 or 9:00-6:00."

Martin told me I would be taking the next week off to get better. I said, "Absolutely not!" He said, "I'm your manager and I'm telling you that you're not allowed to work this week."

When I got home that evening, I charged my cell phone; it had died on the trip to Merritt. I had voicemails from Nicky telling me to call her ASAP. Nicky had also sent multiple text messages. They read, "Call me back please!" and,

"Allan it won't help to ignore me!" and "You best be calling back pronto!" I wondered what she wanted. I made a coffee and called her back.

Nicky answered right away. She said, "I've been trying to call you!" I said, "I saw that, and I'm calling you back. What can I do for you?" She said, "I want to know if you ever removed me from the title of the car when I asked you to."

I said, "No, I never got around to it. Why?" She said, "So it shows we are both registered owners?" "Yes," I said, "Why?" She said, "I just want you to know… I just want you to know that I'm half owner of that fucking car, and when you get your insurance money, ya best be giving me half of that fucking cheque or I'll sue you for it!"

I said, "What's that? Am I ok? Yes, I am still grieving the loss of my dog, and no, I'm not paralyzed—thank you so much for asking!" Nicky replied, "Go fuck yourself!"

I was very angry that I had almost died, and the first thing Nicky wanted to know was if she was getting money as a result. I know we didn't like each other, but I was still her child's father.

I did call the insurance company. About a week later, they came up with an amount of $15,000. The amount left owing on the car was $19,000, so they said they would be sending a cheque for $15,000 directly to the lender, and I would still owe $4,000.

I called Nicky. I said, "So the insurance company called, and they're writing a cheque for fifteen grand." She said, "I'm entitled to half!" I said, "Do you really want to split the amount?" "Yes!" she exclaimed.

I said, "Ok, great, WE still owe nineteen thousand on it. They sent the cheque directly to the lender. WE are responsible for the remaining four thousand dollars. When can I expect the two grand from you?"

Nicky was furious. "What the fuck are you talking about?" She asked. I replied, "You said, you wanted to split it. So, your half of the remaining debt is two thousand dollars. Did you want to make payments to me?" "Fuck you!" she replied.

Right around the same time I received a call from Officer Johansen. He wanted to know if he should bury Wilburt with the other dogs on his property. I told him that I had a chance to think about it and I would like very much if he could do that. He agreed.

Officer Johansen also had something else to tell me. He said that they had completed the accident scene investigation. He said that they were able to determine that my car had rolled six times. I was shocked to hear this, but not as shocked as I was when I heard what he said next.

Officer Johansen said, "Your car spun around and then came out of the spin and hit the ditch. Between the initial impact and the second impact, you were airborne for twenty-seven metres! Then you rolled five more times!"

I couldn't believe this. Officer Johansen added, "I wrote that you were driving a hundred and ten kilometres an hour, like we talked about. Between you, me, and the fence post, nobody gets airborne for twenty-seven metres when they are traveling at a hundred and ten kilometres an hour. Just slow down a bit, ok?" I have slowed down a lot since then.

I managed to convince Martin to let me work on Wednesday. I felt up to it, although my body was still sore, and my left side hurt for the next few weeks. I just felt better working than sitting around doing nothing.

CHAPTER TWENTY-THREE

I BEGAN TO GET MORE INVOLVED with 12-step meetings in Vernon. I started to attend meetings other than my home group, and I began to meet some new people.

One evening after a meeting, a man approached me. He introduced himself as Dale. Dale was new to recovery. He had about one month sober at this point. He asked me if I would be willing to sponsor him. I agreed.

Dale told me right from the start that he had a big problem with some of the steps. Dale did not believe in God at all. In fact, he was a strong atheist, meaning he believed in the non-existence of God. I told him that was fine. I still wanted to guide him through the steps, and I made sure he knew that it didn't matter that he was an atheist.

Speaking with Dale over coffee one day, I was shocked to find out that he had a similar story to mine. Dale told me that like me, he was a quarter native, and that he was adopted. He told me that he was in touch with his biological mother who was alcoholic, and that he and his adopted father were close, but that his adopted father had died quite a while back. Wow! We definitely had a few things in common. In fact, all of this matched my story.

Dale chose to use his adopted father as his higher power. He didn't believe that there was a God or an afterlife, but he felt comfortable calling his father his higher power, and even told me that for years, he spoke to him as a form of prayer. This was crazy to me. Another huge similarity! It was almost as though our two dads had worked together to pair us up!

I walked Dale through each and every step in the exact same way I was walked through it. He completed his step four in the same fashion and one evening at the end of that process, we went to a park where he burned his step work. The whole process of the 12 steps took us several months. I was able to witness Dale get a year of sobriety, and I gave him his cake at my home group.

I got up and shared about the growth I had seen in Dale, and what a pleasure it was to know him. After speaking for a while, I told him I had a one-year medallion for him. I was now nine years sober, and I decided to give him the medallion that was given to me by my sponsor.

I said, "Dale, this one-year medallion was given to my sponsors' sponsor when he had one year sober. After keeping it for thirteen years, he gave it to my sponsor when my sponsor had one-year sober. My sponsor kept it until he had someone to give it to. When he was ten years sober, I took a one year cake, and he gave it to me. I've never had anyone to give it to—until now. I'm now nine years sober and I would like you to have my one year medallion—it's now at least thirty-two years old."

I was so happy to be able to do this for Dale. Helping him helped me so much. It helped me because I felt like I was completely finishing the 12 steps. I had been thorough and honest, and I got clean and sober, and as a result, I was able to be of help to someone else. I was now practicing the 12th step.

Although work kept me busy, I was longing for something more in my life. I was getting a bit lonely. I desired the companionship of a woman. I just wasn't sure that I wanted to be in a committed relationship yet. I was looking for something more casual.

I started looking online at various dating sites. I found one that was free, and I joined. I created my profile with a picture and a description and then started scrolling through the endless list of available women near me.

I chatted with a few online, sending messages back and forth and talking in very general terms about myself, and reading what they had to say about themselves.

Some, I knew right away that I wanted no part of. They had drama written all over them. I did chat with a few and some were nice. I went on two dates, and I was very disappointed both times. Both had crazy written all over them.

I confided a lot in the Personnel Manager. Her name was Brenda. She was very easy to talk to. She would often ask me about my son, and ask for gossip about the ex. She always asked me "How's your love life? Any lucky ladies?" I told her I had given up on dating. "No offence," I said, "but women are nuts!"

One day, when I was speaking with Brenda, she decided to play matchmaker. She had someone in mind that she thought was a perfect match for me. What happened next would change my entire life.

The girl that Brenda had in mind came as a shock to me. She said, "What about Margaret?" "Who's Margaret?" I asked. She said, "You know, little Margaret from Produce." I was confused. "You mean Margaret, the blonde girl in Produce? The girl who used to be my associate in the Toy Department?" "Exactly!" she said.

"But she's an associate and I'm a manager," I said. Brenda said, "So what?" I told Brenda that if anyone should know, she should know that it is against policy for a manager to date an associate. She said, "No, it's against policy for you to date one of YOUR associates. Produce is not one of your departments."

I was apprehensive. Brenda asked, "Ok, forget that she's the Produce girl. What if she wasn't an associate? Then how would you feel about dating her?" I said, "I don't really know her!" Brenda asked "What about her looks? And what about the little that you do know? Would she be a match?"

I said, "She's very attractive. She's cute, for sure. And she seems like a very nice girl. But none of that matters, because I can't date her! I work with her!" Brenda said, "I think you should ask her out!"

I said, "Wait just a minute! Slow down here! Even if I did decide to ask her out, there's no way she will agree to date a manager in the same store she works in! Plus, I highly doubt she would be interested in me. She would never go on a date with me! Then it will be awkward when I see her at work because she has said no to me, and I'll feel like a fool."

Brenda said, "She won't say no!" I asked, "How can you be so sure?" She replied, "Because people trust me. They come into this office and they close the door and they talk to me. I happen to know that she won't say no!"

Brenda added that I already knew her whole family. As it turned out, Margaret was one of several family members who worked in the store. Her mother worked in Deli, her sister was the Front-End Manager, her brother was on the overnight maintenance team, and her aunt worked overnight as well, stocking shelves in the bedding department.

Now I was getting nervous. Could I really ask Margaret, the Produce girl to go on a date with me? I was terrified she would reject me, even after reassurance from Brenda. I decided to go for it. I was shy, but I wasn't completely lacking in self-esteem. I did believe I deserved a girl like Margaret. I just wasn't sure if Margaret wanted a guy like me. I was so scared to approach her.

I looked at Margaret's schedule to see when she worked. It seemed that she worked mostly 2:30 pm-10:30 pm shift. I wondered when she usually took her lunch, as I would need to speak to her when she was off the clock, not while she was working. I needed everything to be very professional and I wanted to make sure I wasn't being inappropriate in any way.

I pulled up Margaret's time clock punches on the computer. I noticed that she always took her lunch at the exact same time. She punched out for lunch every single day at 6:00 pm. I wanted to speak to her today, but I was off at 4:00 pm. I decided I would just go home, get a bite to eat, and come back at 6:00 so I could talk to her on her lunch break.

I was so excited to speak to Margaret that I returned at 5:00 pm. I was afraid I would miss her, or I would be late, and she would leave the store for lunch, or somehow I would miss my chance. I decided I should start shopping and casually approach her while she worked.

I carefully selected some bananas from her department. I strolled around, taking great interest in the vast selection of produce. My heart literally skipped a beat when I saw Margaret coming out of the back room, pushing a cart full of vegetables.

I knew this was my chance. I got extremely nervous. My hands began to shake. My stomach turned around and around. I felt like I would pass out at any moment, and I had not even approached her yet. How would I manage to actually say words to her?

I eventually got up the courage and approached Margaret. I walked up behind her and said, "Hi Margaret!" She looked over at me briefly and said, softly, "Oh, hi." She put her head down and focused on what she was doing.

I said, "I was hoping to speak to you, but it actually has absolutely nothing to do with work, so I was wondering if I could speak to you when you're off the clock, maybe on your lunch?"

She looked up at me and said, "Umm, sure that will work." I asked "Will you be taking a lunch any time soon?" Margaret looked at her watch and said, "Yes, actually I'll be taking my lunch in just a little bit, at six o'clock." I thought to myself, "Yes I know you will. I've done my research!" I told Margaret that I would meet her at the front doors, and she agreed.

It was now only about 5:30 pm. I went to the front to pay for my produce. The cashier that was ringing me through said, "Are you alright today Allan? You look very pale!" I said, "Yes, yes, I'm ok. Maybe just a bit tired."

I went to my car. I still had time to burn so I drove across the street to Tim Hortons. I did not want coffee. I walked into the bathroom and threw water on my face. I took some deep breaths, looked at my wet face in the mirror, and said, "You got this! YOU GOT THIS!"

I went back across the street to Walmart and parked. I was early. I knew Margaret wouldn't be out yet because, when I looked at her punches in the computer, I had found that she ALWAYS punched the clock within a minute of 6:00 pm, and it was only 5:50 pm now.

I wrote my phone number on a piece of paper and folded it. I held that paper in my hand because I didn't want to lose it. I walked to the front doors, and I was surprised to see that she was already there. She broke her routine! I hoped that was a good sign.

She was a little distance from the front doors, and when she saw me, she walked up to me. "Hi!" she said. I replied, "Hi! Thanks for meeting me. I just wanted to talk you, but not while you were working because it's not about work." She said, "Ok."

My heart jumped out of my chest as I prepared to say what I would say next. I said, "I just think you seem like a great person and I was thinking maybe we could get to know each other a bit, outside of work."

I wondered if I had just made a fool out of myself. Then something incredible happened. Margaret looked up at me, gave me the most beautiful smile I had ever seen in my entire life, and blinked a couple of times, making me notice her sparkling green eyes behind her gorgeous, long, natural lashes. She said, "I would like that!"

I tried not to start giggling. I thought, "Holy shit! She would like that!" I said, "I wrote my number down so that you can call or text me. Maybe let me know when you're free and we can meet up sometime." "Ok great!" She said.

I floated to my car and drove home. I was overjoyed! I was wondering what would come next. I wondered if she would text me soon or call me. What if she didn't? She did take my number and she did say she would like to get to know me. Only time would tell.

It didn't take long. By the time I reached my house, which was a ten-minute drive, I received a text message. It read:

"Hi Allan, it's Margaret. I'm looking forward to knowing you better outside of work. I thought I would send you a message so you can have my number, too!"

I was like, "Yup, she likes me! She likes me a lot!" This was unreal to me. I still had mixed emotions about seeing someone from work. I pushed those thoughts out of my head because the excitement about dating Margaret was so intense, I really didn't care about anything else.

Margaret and I texted for a bit before we had an actual date. Looking back, it feels like we were texting for a month before our date. In reality, it was a matter of days. I asked her out on August 9th, 2012 and we had our first date on August 13th. I felt like I knew her. It sounds crazy, but I knew I was in love with her. I just had a feeling about her.

I wanted to make our first date absolutely perfect. I didn't really know Vernon that well. I drove around looking for a place to bring her that would be romantic. I found a little park with giant willow trees, and a grassy field that looked like a great place to have a picnic.

I thought, "Ok, a picnic is nice, but how do I make this special? I needed to do something more. I figured it out! I decided that I would take a picture of the willow tree, and frame it, and then hang the framed photo of the willow tree ON the willow tree! This way, she could keep a photo of the place we had our first date.

I took the photo and framed it. My plan was coming together nicely. But I needed to do more. How could I make this so special she would remember it forever? I decided to write her a love letter.

I sat down and began to pour my heart out on paper. I spoke of the deep love I already had for her. I spoke of how I just knew we were meant to be together forever. I told her she was the love of my life, and wrote many, many more things, all of which I meant with all of my heart and soul. This girl and I were made for each other and I knew it.

As I read the love letter over and over to myself, the thought occurred to me that perhaps it was too soon to say such things to her. I knew these things were all true, but how would she react?

Here's a guy that is taking her on her first date, and he is going to tell her that he is madly in love with her, and that they are destined to be together forever? Yes, I definitely needed to look at this from both sides, not just my own perspective. I would come off as a strange stalker-type weirdo.

I tried to figure out what I would do with the letter. Perhaps I would put it away for a later date? But what if I forgot about it, or even worse, what if I lost it? I thought and thought and finally came up with a plan.

I decided to fold up the letter and put it between the photo of the tree, and the back of the frame. I hid it inside the picture frame that I was going to give her! This way it would be safe, and if everything worked out between us, I would tell her about it on our one-year anniversary.

The day came for our first date. I went to the park ahead of time to set the scene. I brought the framed photo and hung it on the trunk of the tree. I laid out a blanket and set up our picnic.

I had brought a cooler with many types of fruit, all cut up, and some fruit and veggie smoothie juice that I had bought from the produce department at Walmart. I thought she would appreciate that.

We were supposed to meet at 3:00 pm. I had told her the name of the park and a brief description of where it was. 3:00 pm came and she wasn't there. She called me saying she was trying to find the place. After a short discussion she found it, and I directed her to a parking spot at the side of the park.

We walked across the grass to the willow tree. She saw the stuff all set up and she said, "Oh wow, a picnic." I showed her the photo. She said, "Oh that's a really nice picture. You put it here?'" I said, "Yes, it's actually a photo of this exact tree. It's for you." "Oh, thank you!" she said.

We sat on the blanket and ate our fruit. We talked about random stuff. The nice summer we were having, how work was going, and how happy all the dogs in the park looked. I found out later that this was, in fact, a dog park. Margaret did not tell me this on that day; we just enjoyed our picnic.

I can still remember how beautiful she looked, sitting on my blanket under the willow tree. She was wearing white jeans and a red top. She didn't wear a lot of makeup, but she had some mascara on and those amazing lashes caught my attention. Her blonde hair was flowing gently in the wind. As she spoke, her words hypnotized me. I was caught up in a very powerful spell. A spell called love.

After about an hour at the dog park, I thought perhaps I should invite her out for dinner. I asked if she would like to come with me to Earls. She happily accepted the offer. We each took our own cars and drove to Earls, which was only five minutes down the road. We got a table and menus and ordered our food.

We had great conversation over dinner. I wondered what I should do next. Was dinner the end of the date? If so, did I kiss her? Was it too fast to kiss on the first date? What if I went to kiss her and she said, "What are you doing?" I would be so embarrassed. All these thoughts were in my head during dinner.

I remembered that there was a nice park across the street. We ordered some dessert and when we finished, I asked her if she wanted to go for a little walk. She agreed. The bill came and Margaret offered to pay. Of course, I refused to allow this, and paid for our meal.

We left the restaurant and walked across the street to the park. I was so nervous. When we entered the park, we saw a couple holding hands. I wondered if I should hold her hand. I decided not to.

I saw some empty wine bottles and some garbage. This, I decided was not a good place to stop. I wanted to kiss her, but the scene had to be just right. I began walking fast. I didn't know it at the time, but later Margaret told me I was practically running, and she had a hard time keeping up with me!

Next, I saw a nice cedar awning. I thought this was perfect. But when I stopped, Margaret asked, "Is this all bird poop?" I looked down and all around us was goose poop. It was everywhere! This was not romantic at all! I said, "Yup that's gross, let's walk back."

As we neared the entrance of the park, I knew I didn't have any time to waste. If I was going to kiss this girl, I had better do it now because once we left the park, the moment would be gone. At least that's what I had in my head.

Just before the park entrance, I stopped walking. Margaret stopped, too. I turned to face her. I said, "I just stopped because I was wondering if I could give you a hug." She smiled and said, "Of course!" I gave her a big hug, then I looked into her eyes and put my lips to hers. It was magical!

I held her close as we continued to French kiss. I eventually had to come up for air. Then I held her hand and we crossed the street back to the Earls parking lot.

Before I let Margaret get into her car, I pulled her close and kissed her one more time. "Goodnight!" I said. She smiled at me and said, "Goodnight!" I drove back to my house so excited I could hardly contain myself. Margaret had my heart! She was the most incredible girl I had ever laid eyes upon. I couldn't wait to see what the future had in store for us.

CHAPTER TWENTY-FOUR

I WOKE UP THE NEXT DAY with great enthusiasm. Margaret was working mornings the rest of the week. She worked one week evenings, then one week mornings, and they alternated like that week to week. I knew I would see her that morning. It was my turn to do the morning meeting. I wore my tight grey dress pants because I knew I looked very good in those. Before I lost my weight, I couldn't wear them, but now they fit just perfectly.

As I read the morning meetings notes, I noticed Margaret standing at the back of the crowd. She was so cute. She was wearing black dress pants and a white blouse. I tried not to stare at her.

I invited her over that evening. She came to my house for dinner. I made sure that I cleaned the entire place top to bottom and paid special attention to the washroom and kitchen. Now that I think about it, the bedroom was given special attention as well. I washed the bedding and made the bed perfectly, just in case we ended up in there. I wasn't trying to rush things, but I didn't want the bedroom to be a mess, if we ended up in there.

When Margaret knocked on my door that evening, I opened it and I was greeted with that amazing smile. When I closed the door behind her, she said, "No kiss for me today?" "Of course!" I replied. I pulled her close and gave her a deep, passionate kiss. "Great way to start the evening!" I thought to myself.

That evening I had prepared a nice dinner for Margaret—Braised Swiss Chard wrapped in Sole Fillets, served on a bed of wild rice. I didn't really know what I was doing, but I remembered my brother had done this before, and when I googled "Romantic dinner recipes," it was one of the search results. It turned out well and I believe she was quite impressed.

After dinner, we sat on my couch and watched TV together. We had amazing conversation and I felt like I could talk to her forever. We told each other about our lives and the more I learned about her, the more I loved her.

I spoke to Margaret about my family, my son, my previous Walmart Stores and other things, but I got very nervous when I thought about telling her about my addictions. I knew I had to; I was just afraid of how she might react. What if it was a deal breaker? At this point, I was 10 years clean and sober, so I hoped that would show her I was a different person.

We had only been dating about a week and a half when I had that conversation with Margaret. One day when she came to my house, I sat her down and told her that I had something to tell her. She looked nervous.

I said, "I just need to be completely honest with you about my past and I'm really hoping that it doesn't change your opinion of me. "Okay…" She said, nervously. I took a deep breath and started to tell her.

I said, "So I wasn't always the same person I am today. I had some struggles in life. Basically, what I want to tell you is that I struggled with addiction issues for several years."

Margaret wanted to know a couple of things. "What kind of addiction issues?" she asked. I said, "I'm an alcoholic, and I smoked a lot of weed, and I was addicted to crack for several years as well."

Margaret looked shocked. "And how long have you not done that?" she asked. I told her, "Actually on September 3rd, I'll be celebrating 10 years clean and sober." "Oh wow!" she exclaimed. "That's a long time." I said, "It is. I just hope that my past doesn't make you respect me less or change your opinion of me."

Margaret said, "Getting clean and sober is a huge accomplishment, and if anything, I respect you MORE! Thank you for being honest with me. I would have been upset if I found out some other way. It must have been difficult for you to tell me."

I told Margaret that it was very difficult to tell her, but that I wanted her to know everything about me. She said, "I never would have guessed that you were addicted to drugs. Never in a million years!" I said, "Yeah, well I'm a totally different person now, so most people are shocked when I tell them."

Soon it was time to meet Margaret's family. They actually lived just down the street from me. Margaret lived with her entire family, which was a bit different than anything I had experienced before. Given the situation though, it made sense to me.

Her mother had met her father in Ontario. Her mother was Canadian, her father was Greek. They ended up moving to Greece. Margaret was born in Greece, then later on, her mother and father divorced and the family moved back to Canada.

Margaret lived in a house with her mother, brother, sister, brother-in-law, and her niece and nephew, her sister's kids. It was a full house, for sure. It was very obvious to me that this family was very close, and there was nothing they wouldn't do for each other. That in itself, was very attractive to me.

When I went to Margaret's house, I met her whole family. I already knew her mom, brother, and sister from work. I walked in and her mom greeted me with a big hug. We laughed about how it was a bit strange to see them all in a different setting.

I was dealing with some fairly major personal issues when I began dating Margaret. I was still paying the bankruptcy fees, and had no credit whatsoever. I was also fighting a huge battle in court, as Nicky was attempting to get me to pay Spousal Support as well as Child Support, and the amount she was asking was ridiculous.

My monthly income at the time after taxes was $3,000. The Child Support Guidelines for my income said, $500/month. Nicky had a free lawyer, courtesy of the Ministry of Children and Family Development. I could not afford a lawyer and made too much to qualify for legal Aid.

Nicky's lawyer was fighting for me to pay $1,500 in Spousal Support Payments, in addition to the $500 Child Support. When presented with this in court, I of course, was strongly opposed to the idea. After Nicky's lawyer made her arguments, I had nothing to say because I didn't know what I could say in my defence.

The judge said, "Ok then. We will be making an order today that orders Mr. Strain to pay a total of two thousand dollars monthly. This will be five hundred Child Support as per the Child Support Guidelines on an income of fifty-eight thousand, seven hundred and thirty two dollars and forty nine cents. Then we have Spousal Support as agreed here today, in the amount of one thousand, five hundred dollars."

I immediately jumped up and said, "Excuse me your honour, but that is not a possibility." The judge said, "Excuse me? I did not hear any evidence from you or even an argument about why the amount was not acceptable."

I explained to the judge that I only take home $3,000/month and my rent alone was $825/month. Clearly, I would not be able to give $2,000 of $3,000 and survive on $1,000/month total. I said, "If this is your ruling I'm going to go back to Vernon and buy a tent! That will be my home! A fucking tent!"

"MR. STRAIN!" The judge yelled, "This is a court of law! Please be mindful of your language. You need to tell the court what legal argument you are using here. You can't simply say that you don't have enough money. What is the legal argument?"

I said, "Your honour, I apologize. I am not a lawyer, nor do I have any education on family law whatsoever. I cannot be expected to walk in here and adequately defend myself against someone who IS a lawyer."

I took a breath and continued. "I'm sure there are numerous arguments to be made in my defence, but I don't know what they are. I need time. Time to seek legal counsel, your honour. Otherwise this would be an extremely unfair judgement. Please, your Honour."

The judge sat back in his chair. He looked at me closely. He said, "I agree. You need to seek counsel. We will adjourn this matter. Go outside to the JCM and ask for a court date. And when you return, Mr. Strain, do not tell me you can't afford the amount. Come back and explain before the court why the law says you are not legally responsible to pay that amount. That is the only thing I can hear. The court is only interested in facts. Saying you cannot afford it is an opinion, not a fact. I may agree with you. I may even know what your defence is. But unless you make the correct arguments, you will not be successful here."

I told the judge I completely understood, and I thanked him very much. We went out to the JCM to get a court date. I had no idea what a JCM even was. Apparently, it stands for Judicial Case Manager. I didn't really care what it stood for. I was happy that I would have a chance.

I went to the JCM with Nicky and her lawyer. She whispered, "All you care about is money! You're a fucking loser!" I replied, "I need to be left with enough to survive." Nicky's lawyer gave me a smirk and shook her head. I asked, "What? You don't even care about the people in this case. I was going to go to Vernon and sleep under a bridge!"

The lawyer kept smirking at me and said, "Just doing my job, Mr. Strain." I responded with, "I sure hope you can sleep at night when you finish doing your job."

I went back to Vernon and googled "Family Law" and "Legal help for those who don't qualify for legal aid." Through my searching, I found out that I could go to the courthouse on Wednesday mornings and get free legal advice. I had to wait in line, but it was free.

I took this opportunity and went for it. I ended up speaking with a female lawyer who helped me very, very much. She did ask what my income was. When I told her, she said, "Well, this is supposed to be for low income, but you seem like you're really needing to talk, so I'll let it slide."

I thanked her very much. She asked about the divorce and all of the details. I told her everything. She was shocked to hear that Nicky was discharged from the bankruptcy right away.

She asked about how much of the debt in the bankruptcy was Nicky's personal debt. I told her about all of Nicky's debt and the line of credit for $13,000 and about the fact that we both owned the house, so half of that debt was Nicky's as well.

The lawyer had a lot to say about this and asked me to take notes. She told me that because my bankruptcy payments increased when Nicky left, from $225/month to $450/month I should go to court and claim something called an "Undue Hardship." An undue hardship is a special circumstance that either partially or completely makes a person exempt from payments in a given situation.

I wrote down everything the lawyer told me. She strongly suggested that I try as best I could to get a lawyer to help me in court, especially because Nicky would be arriving with one. I knew that wasn't a possibility. I was so broke at the time. I was paying Child Support of $500/month and driving back and forth to Chilliwack and I just didn't have any spare cash at all.

I decided I would give it a shot anyway. I called around to lawyers in Chilliwack. I found one that was only $225/hr. They said that they would need to do a conflict check to see if they were already representing the other party. The next day they called back and said they couldn't represent me because they were already representing Nicky.

I said, "No that's impossible. She has a lawyer that is appointed by the Ministry." The lady said, "Oh, no sir. We are representing her in her other case. The car accident." I was silent as I processed this and then I said, "Great, thank you."

I called Nicky and asked her about the car accident. She played dumb. "What do you mean?" she asked. I said, "I called the lawyers office to get a lawyer. They said they represent you in your case for your car accident. Were they lying to me?"

Nicky knew she was caught. She said, "Oh right, that. It was no big deal. I'm still dealing with it." I said, "Ok thanks." I knew that we both were required to disclose all of our income from all sources when we went back to court.

When the court date came, I was as prepared as I could be. I was extremely nervous. My life was on the line here. There was no way I could live on $1000/month. If I lost here today, I would most likely quit my job and tell the court I had no money, which would be true. I would live a life of poverty after working so hard to have a better life.

Margaret wished me the best of luck. She gave me an angel pin that she attached to my tie. She said, "For good luck!" I was so grateful to have her in my life through all of this. I think the stress and drama of an ex would have been too much for a lot of women. She stood by my side and supported me through everything.

I arrived at court dressed in grey dress pants, a very nice dress shirt, a tie, and my lucky angel from Margaret. I got the same judge as before. Nicky's lawyer began first and took most of the morning.

While the lawyer was talking, I was fiercely writing down notes so I would remember what points I wanted to comment on. Eventually I had the chance to call witnesses, and I put Nicky on the stand.

Now I finally had the chance to show my evidence, and tell the story from my point of view. The first question I asked was, "Is it true that you and I both declared bankruptcy together?" She replied, "Yes." I asked, "And how much of the debt that was included in the bankruptcy was yours?" Nicky said, "I'm not sure."

I continued and asked from my notes, "Did you have a MasterCard with a credit limit of five thousand dollars?" "Yes," she answered. "And a Visa with a credit limit of three thousand?" I asked. "Yes," she replied. "Ok." I said.

Next, I asked "And were those two credit cards maxed out?" "Yes," answered Nicky. I asked, "And do you recall that we had a thirteen thousand dollar line of credit?" "Yes," she answered. "And is it true that you yourself used the thirteen thousand for your debt and your school?" "Yes, it is," Nicky answered.

Next, I asked "And those debts, were they solely your responsibility to pay? The credit cards were in your name, and you spent the money, right?" Nicky said, "Yes." Moving on, I asked, "And how much money did you have to pay back to those creditors?" Nicky said, "Nothing. They were all included in the bankruptcy."

Next, I asked "And how much money did you need to pay towards the bankruptcy?" Nicky said, "Well I didn't make any payments, but that's because I was discharged right away." Then I asked, "And why was that?" She said, "Because when I left you, I had no money and I couldn't afford to make the payments, so they discharged me."

I turned my attention to the judge. I said, "Your Honour, I would like to inform the court that while Nicky was discharged from the bankruptcy immediately and never made a payment, my payments actually increased from two hundred and twenty five dollars a month to four hundred and fifty dollars each month."

The judge asked "And what is the point you are trying to make Mr. Strain?" I said, "Your Honour, I would like to claim undue hardship, and I have brought with me all of my receipts for each payment to the bankruptcy agent. I have entered them into evidence as Exhibit A." The judge took some notes and said, "Thank you Mr. Strain. The court will take this into consideration."

I turned back to Nicky. I said, "While I was calling around looking for a lawyer, I discovered that there was a lawyer representing you in another case. It was for a car accident. How much money did you receive for that, and have you brought receipts to show this income?"

Nicky simply said, "I don't understand." I asked, "Were you in a car accident?" She replied "Umm, well yes." I asked, "How much money did you receive?" She said, "Well, it's not over yet." I asked, "Have they paid out anything yet? Were you not working at a Casino? I assume you had lost wages as part of your claim, didn't you?"

Nicky looked at the judge and said, "Your Honour…" He said, "Answer the question, please." Nicky looked back at me, and asked, "Sorry what was the question?" I said, "Let me make it simple. Other than your disability cheque, and your child tax credit, and the Child Support I send you, how much additional money have you received from the car accident?"

Nicky squirmed a bit in her seat. "Since when?" she asked. "I don't know…" I said. "… how about we say from the last time we were in court?" She said, "Well for that car accident I've been receiving nine hundred dollars a month for lost wages for the last five months."

I quickly wrote a note in my notebook. I wrote, "That accident? More than one?" I asked Nicky, "Ok, so four thousand five hundred dollars? Does that sound right?" "Yeah I guess," she answered. I turned to the judge and said, "Your Honour, I just want to say that Nicky and I were asked to come here with full financial disclosure. I have done that. I would like the court to be aware of the fact that there is forty-five hundred dollars here that was not disclosed to the court."

Nicky asked, "Is that all then?" "No, it is not," I said. I turned to my notes. I said, "Your answer to one of my questions, leads me to another question. When I asked about your settlement you said, 'That accident.' Was there another car accident for which you received money?"

Nicky said, "You're not making any sense. I don't know what you're asking me." I said, "Was there another car accident for which you received money?" Again, she turned to the judge and said, "Your honour…" and again the judge said, "It's a pretty straightforward question. Answer the question, please."

Nicky said, "Ok, what do you wanna know?" I said, very slowly "Was there... any other car accident... that you filed a claim for that you have been awarded money?"

Nicky said, "Well there was one. I was in the drive-through getting coffee and the person behind me bumped me. The insurance refused to pay because there were no marks on my car, but I had injuries."

I asked what happened next. Nicky said, "I never signed off. When I got side-swiped, they had to close the other claim so they just settled with me so we could proceed with the next claim. Does that answer your questions?"

I was a bit shocked. I responded with, "NO!!!" She said, "What do you wanna know then?" I said, "How much??? How much did you get?" She said, "Well, ummm, they had to settle... so they gave me... umm... five thousand."

"Five thousand dollars?" I asked. "Yes," she said. I asked, "When did you get that cash?" "Three months ago, in March," she said. I could not believe this. This was huge and I knew it.

I turned to the judge. I said, "Once again, your Honour, I would like the court to be made aware of the fact that both myself and Nicky have been asked to come here with full financial disclosure. Now we have shown that there is another five thousand dollars NOT DISCLOSED that I have had to drag out of her."

My adrenaline pumped as I continued. "This changes her income for last year and should be considered, along with the undue hardship I am claiming when deciding on the amount that I am responsible to pay for Spousal Support!"

That was not the end of court. It went back and forth all day, and I fought my ass off! Every time I got nervous or didn't know how to proceed, I rubbed the angel on my tie and thought about Margaret.

In the end, I was able to get the Spousal Support portion down to $600/month. Combined with the Child Support portion, I was ordered to pay a total of $1,100/month. A lot of money, but I could work with that. Much better than the original $2,000/month.

Out of all of this, I want to make two important points. First, I have never, not once, ever missed a payment or been late on a payment. Not for Child Support and not for Spousal Support. I'm very proud of that because there were months when money was so tight, I ran out of gas and had only hotdogs to eat for dinner.

The other point I want to make is the most important one. Margaret has been my rock through this, as well as through the hardest times I have ever had to face in my entire life. She has been by my side through everything, and thanks to her, I have overcome some of life's biggest challenges.

There is nobody else on this planet I would rather share my life with. Which is why I proposed to her. That proposal was the beginning of a whole new chapter of my life.

CHAPTER TWENTY-FIVE

BEFORE I COULD KNOW FOR SURE if Margaret was wife material, I would need her to accept my son and for that, they would need to meet and spend a bit of time together. I introduced my son to Margaret after we had been together only a few months.

When I told my brother that I planned for Margaret to meet Eli, he didn't completely agree with my decision. He said, "I know that you love her, and that's great—I'm very happy for you—but it's still new, and introducing a child to a partner is a huge step." He felt I should wait a bit.

I thanked him for his opinion and then I just went ahead as planned. I brought Margaret with me on one of my visits. Eli was three years old at this point. I introduced the two of them and they really hit it off.

From the very beginning Margaret loved Eli like he was her own son. This was one of the things I loved about her the most. She loved him because he was my son; she knew he was part of me, and she loved me.

Eli always enjoyed the company of Margaret as well, and he was immediately accepted by the entire family. Whenever Eli came to Vernon, I brought him to Margaret's house and he would hang out and play with Margaret's niece and nephew. I really began to feel like we were all family, even in the early stages of our relationship, and I was grateful to be so fully accepted by all of Margaret's family.

February was our very first Valentine's Day. I knew I had to do it up right. Margaret had expressed to me that she really wasn't into Valentine's Day because she felt it was a bit fake.

Margaret felt that if you love someone then you don't need a day to tell you that you need to treat them nicely, it should just be something you do naturally. Nevertheless, I wanted to do something special.

I decided I would make a special dinner and also make a fancy dessert at my house. I also bought her some chocolates, a dozen yellow roses (her favourite colour), and a really nice card, in which I wrote some beautiful kind words.

After we finished dessert and our evening came to an end, Margaret and I made love very passionately, and then she went home to her family. I sent her a text a while after she left. I wanted to tell her I had one more gift for her.

She replied to my message saying, "You already spoiled me so much. What else could you possibly have for me?" I wrote "Do you still have the picture I gave you on our first date?" "Of course!" She replied. I wrote "Ok, take the back off, like you were going to remove the picture from the frame."

After a minute or so, I sent her a message and said, "Are you still there? Did you understand what I meant?" She sent me a message back. "I am lost for words. I cannot even express how I feel right now! You are the most amazing, incredible man in the universe! Thank you so much!"

I replied with "If I'm amazing it's because YOU make me amazing. I love you so much. Happy Valentine's Day, my love!" She replied, "I love you so much, and I always will! You're incredible!"

Margaret and I had a conversation the next day. She said, "You did all this crazy romantic stuff in the beginning. Maybe you should have saved some stuff because you're going to be all out of romance, and everything will seem not as exciting."

In a way she was right. It's very difficult, in fact nearly impossible to maintain this level of romance. I didn't care about that. I decided I was going all out. Around this time, I began looking around at engagement rings.

I window-shopped for quite some time. I found a ring I loved, and more importantly, one I thought Margaret would love. A beautiful diamond that caught the light so well, and would look absolutely amazing on my love's finger. I bought it and put it away for the special day.

My next task, of course, was to figure out the how. How exactly was I going to propose? I couldn't be all out of romance yet. I remembered that Margaret and I had discussed our bucket list items. One of her biggest bucket list items was skydiving. I decided I would propose to Margaret, while helping her to cross something off her bucket list.

The plan was to have a giant sign that said, "Margaret, will you marry me?" I would somehow have it set up in a way that she would see it as she was descending. I decided I would write my question onto a giant tarp with duct tape.

While I was at work one day, I bought a blue tarp that was 20 feet long by 10 feet wide. I decided I wanted to use yellow duct tape, since it was Margaret's favourite colour, and it showed up well against the blue tarp so it would be visible from a distance.

I bought the last two rolls of yellow duct tape and went home, spread the tarp out on the living room floor and began to put the words together. I quickly realized that I would require more duct tape. I wrote "Margaret will" and I was out of tape.

I went back to work to try to find more. I thought maybe we had some in the back. Turned out, we were out of stock. I went to every other store in Vernon, every hardware store, every dollar store, everywhere I could think of. They all had duct tape. None of them had yellow duct tape.

I called the Kelowna Walmart. They had one roll. I asked them to hold it for me. I called the Westbank Walmart and they had four rolls. I asked them to hold it until closing that evening. I got in my car and drove towards Kelowna.

Margaret called me when I was on my way to Kelowna. I told her I was on the way to Kelowna Walmart to get some stuff that I needed. She asked what I needed. I said, "Duct tape." She asked "You had to go all the way to Kelowna to buy duct tape?" I said, "Well, it's special duct tape and we are sold out in Vernon." She asked "Why is it special?" I said, "Because it's yellow."

Margaret was more than a bit confused. She asked "Why do you need yellow duct tape?" I said, "For a little project I'm working on." Margaret asked, "And you couldn't find a single roll of yellow duct tape in all of Vernon?" I said, "I found two rolls but I need like five more rolls."

Margaret wanted to know why I would need seven rolls of yellow duct tape. I said, "I have told you already. I'm working on a little project." Margaret asked "What project?" I told her I would show her when I was done. She said, "Man, you're weird."

I eventually finished my sign. It looked amazing. Now I had to figure out when I would take Margaret skydiving. I decided I would work it into our upcoming vacation. I really wanted to show Margaret the beauty of B.C and I had some things already planned.

We booked our vacation from work at the same time. We travelled together to Vancouver and we stayed with my best friend Mike. I had planned a huge hike, in which we would camp on the mountaintop overnight, and then a couples massage the next day, and I planned to end with the skydiving proposal.

We went to my friend Mike's house and woke up the next morning to start our long drive to Pemberton, B.C. I had planned to do the Black Tusk hike to Garibaldi Lake. The hike is intense, switchbacks all the way up to the top, about a six-hour hike one way.

We were about 30 minutes into our hike when Margaret said, "You didn't tell me it was like this! This is so stupid! I don't think I can do this!" I'm not sure how I described the hike to her, but there's a chance I may have used the word "moderate." Margaret apparently did not feel this was moderate at all.

I told Margaret that we could turn back, but reminded her that we had just travelled all this way to be here, and I also told her that the scenery at the top was totally worth it. She reluctantly kept walking.

I had with me a giant backpack that weighed about 70 pounds. I had our tent, camp stove, bottles of propane, lots of bottles of water, and blankets and food. I was also getting really tired, but we pushed on, all the way to the lake.

When we eventually did arrive at the lake, Margaret was completely overwhelmed by the beauty of it. We set up our tent together, put our food in the cabin they had for food storage, and went for a walk around the lake.

We took many pictures and spent the rest of the evening relaxing. Later, we ate some food and rested more. That evening we went for another little walk and looked at the stars, which are absolutely amazing up there, away from the light of the city.

The next morning, we took down our tent, packed up everything, and started the trip back down. Going down is much more enjoyable than going up, even though I still had everything on my back. Admittedly, the backpack weighed less now, because we were almost out of water, and we ate most of the food as well.

At one point we passed a Chinese lady who was on her way up the mountain. She looked at us and laughed, saying "Hahaha! I like your style!" I wondered what she was talking about. After a few more steps she turned around, looked at us, laughed again and said, "Haha! I like your style! Man carry everything! Haha!"

We came away from that trip with lots of amazing memories and photos, and also sore legs. We went for our couples massage the next day which was absolutely amazing! Margaret said it was one of the best massages she's ever had! I would have to agree, it was fantastic!

After our couples' massage, we stayed another night at Mike's house and the next morning I told Margaret that I had a surprise date. She really wanted to know what we were doing. I told her she would have to wait and see.

I went to the washroom at Mike's house and snuck in a quick call to the skydiving centre. I told them to expect us, and that I would give them the ring and the tarp when I arrived, as planned.

Margaret wanted to stop for coffee. I told her that was fine, but that she should not eat, or at least not eat too much. I was worried about her throwing up when she jumped out of the plane.

The skydiving place was in Abbotsford, B.C which is a 45-minute drive from Mike's house in North Vancouver. She wanted to know where we were going and why it was taking so long. I told her to be patient.

We ended up driving down several dirt roads, past farms, and fields and Margaret was getting more and more curious the whole time. She kept asking, "Where the heck are you taking me?" and I kept telling her, "If I told you it wouldn't be a surprise."

We eventually got to our destination. I parked in front of the building. Directly in front of our car, on the building was a huge sign that read, "Skydive Vancouver." Margaret looked at me and said, "We're not falling off a plane right?" "No of course not! We are jumping out of a plane!" I said, subtly correcting her incorrect wording.

She said, "Nope! No way! That's the stupidest idea I've ever heard of! I'm not doing that!" I was shocked. I did not expect that reaction at all. It was on her bucket list. I truly thought she would be excited.

I said, "Ok… well that sucks." Margaret got very upset. She asked "Are you kidding me right now? ARE YOU KIDDING ME???" I said, "No, I'm not. I was going to take you skydiving." She said, "Let's go in and get your money back!"

I informed Margaret that I could not get a refund. I could use the money for a jump on a different day, but I could not get the money back. She said, "This is so ridiculous! How did you think this was a good idea?" Then she asked how much I paid. I said, "Well, it doesn't matter." She said, "HOW MUCH???" I said, "Well, about fifteen hundred all together."

This angered Margaret even more. "Fifteen hundred dollars?" I said, "Well yeah." She said. "Get out of the car! Let's go!" I asked where we were going. She said, "I'm not going to let you lose your money! Come on! We are going to fall off of a stupid plane!"

I cleared my throat a bit and said, "Umm, again, jumping out of a plane, not falling off." "Whatever!" she said "You're so good at speaking the only language you've ever spoken! Good for you!"

I stopped Margaret for a moment. I said, "Wait! One more thing!" "What?" She asked. I said, "Thank you for doing this. I just want to ask if you could look a bit happier." "Happy?" She asked. "YOU should be happy because I'm doing this! I will be angry, and scared, and terrified and upset, and I will be whatever the hell I will be, but at least I'm going!"

I said, "Ok, that's fine. I just didn't want you looking pissed off in the video." "VIDEO?!" She screamed. "They're going to record this? What the hell! This is so stupid!" I said, "I just thought you would want to remember it." "Oh, I'll remember!" She replied.

Margaret started marching towards the entrance of the building. I ran to catch up with her. We walked in and a lady said, "Good morning! You must be Allan!" "Yes indeed!" I said. Margaret stood there with her arms crossed, displaying the biggest frown I have ever seen.

The lady asked, "Is everything ok?" Margaret said, "Yes, except for the fact that he didn't tell me we were doing this and I'm pretty scared and frustrated right now. I need to use the washroom."

The lady pointed Margaret towards the washroom and when she was out of earshot, the lady looked at me and said, "You know… this could go either way!" "I know!" I replied. "I've never seen her this mad before."

I quickly ran back to the car and grabbed the tarp and the ring. I put the tarp outside by the back stairs and entered the building again. I gave the ring to the lady and told them where the tarp was. They told me they would take care of the rest.

When Margaret returned from the washroom, she came and hugged me. She said, "Ok look. What you planned is actually very sweet. I'm just super scared and I did not expect this at all."

I said, "Well you said, it was on your bucket list so I wanted to do it for you." Margaret said, "Yes, on my bucket list means I want to do it before I die. I don't want it to be the way that I die! I haven't even said goodbye to my family!"

I assured Margaret she wasn't going to die. I told her that these guys are from the Russian air force and between the two of them they have 20,000 jumps. Margaret told me that she just needed some time for it to sink in. She did want to do it; she was just caught off guard.

After I was in my jumpsuit, the guy that was jumping with me began to take a video. The guy that would jump with Margaret began to film her. Next we all walked out to the field. It was time to board the plane. We all got on, Margaret first, and they had me go on last, because that would put me at the front, and I could jump out first.

The plane took off down the runway and began to ascend. I couldn't tell if Margaret was nervous or what was going on with her because she was behind me, and we were all facing forward. There were a few others that were jumping with us. The plane was small, and I could feel the vibration of the roaring engine through my whole body.

We reached 14,000 feet, and it was time. My instructor had me scoot towards the door and kneel. He came behind me, wrapped some straps around me and clipped them onto my harness. He pulled the straps tight and double-checked everything before opening the door.

"Put your feet out!" He yelled in his thick Russian accent. I put my feet out and I felt the wind blowing in my face. The cameraman exited through the door to the wing, where he stood and waited until it was time.

My feet dangled in the sky while I sat on the floor at the door of the plane. I could see everything from Chilliwack to Vancouver and beyond our borders to America. What a feeling!

The excitement of today's jump was unmeasurable, because I knew I would be asking the love of my life to spend the rest of her life by my side. I just hoped she would accept my proposal. I was in fact, more nervous about that, than I was about falling from 14,000 feet.

As we approached the safety of land once again, I lifted my feet in preparation for landing. They tell you not to put your feet straight down, because people have broken their ankles that way.

We landed, my instructor removed the straps and I stood up. He looked at me and smiled. "Good jump, man! Now for the hard part!" He said. The lady I had given the ring to ran up to me with it. "Congratulations!" she said. "We'll see!" I replied.

I saw my love coming in for the landing and I prepared myself. Once she had landed, and was on her feet, I took a deep breath and walked over to her. I apologize because the next part is horribly cheesy, but it's just what came out of my mouth.

"Thank you for falling for me!" is what I said. Then I got down on one knee, looked up at her and said, "I love you and I want to spend the rest of my life with you. Margaret, will you marry me?"

She smiled and giggled and said, "Of course I will!" I kissed her and placed the ring on her finger. We were officially engaged. Everyone clapped for us. Margaret turned to me and said, "That jump was incredible! I want to do that again!"

Right away, Margaret said, "I need to call my family!" She called her mom, who was having lunch with her family at Earls with a gift card I had given her for Christmas.

Margaret's family had no idea what I had planned. Margaret's mom said that it was a good thing that she told her after the fact, because she would have completely freaked out if she had told her that she was going skydiving.

So I pulled it off! I convinced the love of my life to "fall off of a plane" with me AND she agreed to marry me! I felt like the luckiest man alive! We set a date for a year down the road. In the meantime, though, I got to work on some family stuff, which would change my life again.

CHAPTER TWENTY-SIX

WHEN I FOUND OUT SARA WAS not my birth mom, and that my birth mom was native, I was always interested in who the rest of my family was. Lillian told me that she had lost contact with her siblings years ago. Apparently, she was raised in a foster home with her brother, but they were separated at some point and she didn't know where he was.

Aside from wanting to know about my family, it was very important to me to get my Status. Somehow getting a Status card meant that I was a "real" native. It really meant a lot to me. I was always very interested in that part of my culture.

When I was about fourteen years old, a social worker did some research and told me that she felt my family was from Hope B.C. She brought me to the reserve in Hope and we tried to meet some family members.

Everyone was very accepting of me. We visited a couple of homes of people who were loosely related to me, but I never found any first or second cousins or aunts or uncles, like I had hoped for.

I was in contact with Indian Affairs at this time, and they told me that my birth mom was eligible for Status, but that she had never applied. They said if she applied for Status, she would get it, and then I could get Status as well. I decided to approach her with this at that time.

Lillian told me that she had no interest in getting her Status and she was angry that I had even brought it up. She said, "I don't even want to acknowledge that I'm native! It has always been a bad thing. In my foster homes, I was always made to feel like I was less than everyone else because I was native." She asked me never to speak to her about it again. Clearly it was a sore subject.

At that point, I kind of gave up any hope of getting my Status. It always bothered me, but I tried to let it go. Shortly after I got engaged to Margaret, I decided I would look into it again. I remembered that my grandmother's name was Mary Joe, and I knew that she was from the reservation in Hope B.C. One day while I was at work in the Vernon Walmart, I decided to google "Band Office Hope B.C." I got a result for Chawathil Indian Band. I called the number.

A lady answered and said, "Good morning, Chawathil!" I said, "Oh hi there. I'm calling because I'm trying to get my Status card, but first I need to find my family. I was adopted out, and my mom was adopted out, so I don't know a lot, but I think my grandmother was from Chawathil."

She said, "Ok then. Who's your grandma?" I said, "Mary Joe." She said, "Hoooleee! Who's your mom then?" I said, "Lillian Bruce." She said again, "Hoooleee!" I said, "So you know who I'm talking about then?" She said, "One of your blood relatives just walked in the door. Wanna talk to him?" I said that I did.

He said, "Hello! Who's your grandma?" I said, "Mary Joe." He said, "That's my Auntie! Your grandma is my dad's sister! You're my cousin!" I was completely shocked. This I had not expected at all. The man told me that his sister would very much like to know about me. He gave me her number. I called later that day.

When I called the lady answered in a soft voice, "Hello?" I told her who I was. She started to cry. She said, "I just can't believe this. Auntie Mary and I were so close. I loved her so much. She talked about your mom all the time. Now, decades later I'm talking to her grandson! This is unreal. It's overwhelming!"

The lady who was first cousin to my mom was named Sadie. She asked if I would call her Auntie Sadie. She explained that in our culture, first cousins are so close, they're like siblings, so when your cousin has a child, that child refers to you as Auntie or Uncle.

I agreed to call her Auntie. Auntie Sadie wanted to meet. She told me that she had a son who lived in Vernon and that she was driving up to see him the following weekend. We arranged a time to meet.

I met Auntie Sadie and her son that weekend. During that meeting she asked, "Did you know that you have an uncle who lives in Chilliwack?" I thought for a moment it was going to be another first cousin of my mom's. It wasn't. Auntie Sadie told me that my mom's brother lived in Chilliwack and she had his number.

This all seemed crazy to me. Auntie Sadie called up my uncle, Uncle Chuck, and we arranged a time for me to meet him. Apparently, he was very excited to meet with me. Uncle Chuck also had a wife named Doreen.

Auntie Sadie and I arranged to meet Uncle Chuck and Auntie Doreen on one of my trips down to see my son. Before I went to see Eli, I stopped and picked up Auntie Sadie, then we went to Chilliwack and met Uncle Chuck and his wife.

Uncle Chuck is a different character, for sure. When I met him, he said, "Hi Nephew! I'm Uncle Chuck! 'Round here they call me Chilliwack Chuck!" I said, "Hi Uncle. It's very nice to meet you."

Next, Uncle Chuck introduced his wife, Auntie Doreen. Doreen was also a different character. She immediately began to tell me stories about fights she and my uncle had. She told me one story that stuck with me.

She said, "You know, your uncle and I love to drink. Sometimes we both get a little wild, ok? And this last time, your uncle went to jail for a bit." Of course, I had to ask her what happened, and she was more than happy to explain.

She continued. "Well, we got drinkin' perty good, then I started to get lippy ya see?" "Ok…" I replied. She said, "Yup, well everyone knows I can be a bitch. I provoked your uncle and I guess I pushed him too far and he stabbed me a little."

I was pretty shocked. I had just met this lady and she was telling me some pretty intense stuff. Then she said, "You know what? Your uncle is a great man. It's just that sometimes when he drinks too much… well he gets a little stabby!"

It was pretty clear that they were in a dysfunctional marriage. I laughed and said, "A little stabby eh?" "Yup," she answered. She said, "I told the cops that I deserved it but they still charged him. I tried to tell them it was just a quick in and out, it's not like he twisted the knife around in there or nothin' like that."

I was actually very shocked to hear that my Uncle Chuck had stabbed his wife. It didn't match his demeanour. He came across as someone who was very soft spoken, gentle, kind. That's the thing about alcohol. It affects everyone differently.

I had some revealing conversations with my Uncle Chuck. He had immediately asked about my mom. He said, "The last time I saw my big sister was in the spring of nineteen seventy-eight! She was gettin' FAT! She was so fat she waddled! She was waddling like a penguin!"

I told Uncle Chuck, "Um, Uncle that may have been me. I was born in April of seventy-eight. I don't think she was fat; I think she was pregnant with me!" He started laughing. "Hahaha! Really eh? Well that would make sense. She sure waddled around a lot!"

Uncle Chuck told me he never lost contact with his foster mom. He told me that he still went for dinner with her every Sunday. This was strangely similar to my relationship with Sara.

I was a bit confused because my mother, who was raised in the same home, had told me that the foster home was extremely abusive. It appeared that they had different opinions on the matter.

Uncle Chuck asked if I would come to visit his foster mom. I agreed. I parked out front, and my Uncle led me around to the back door. He knocked and then opened the door. I looked in and saw an elderly lady. She greeted us warmly.

I removed my shoes, and walked into the living room, which I couldn't help but notice was decorated in a very old-fashioned style. Similar to Sara's living room, there was a China cabinet and the walls were decorated with family photos. Lace curtains hung in front of the windows and fell behind the velvet chesterfield.

"Come in, come in!" The lady said, in a thick German accent. "Who's the friend you have brought?" she asked. This lady was about to get the shock of a lifetime. Uncle Chuck said, "This is my nephew! This is Lillian's son, Mom!"

The lady stopped talking right then and there. Her smile fell from her face. I noticed her right hand began to tremble. She walked towards me and said, "You are Lillian's son?" "Yes, I am." I replied. As she got close to me, she placed her cold, wrinkled, frail hands on my face, one hand on each cheek.

Her eyesight was beginning to fail. She looked closely at me. Her lips began to tremble, and it looked as though she was trying to speak, although no words came out. Tears began to pour down her face. She said, "I'm so sorry!"

Confused, I asked, "Sorry for what?" She said, "I'm so sorry! Your mother lived here in our home for many years. When she was older, she began to get into trouble. She was sneaking out and seeing boys. We had rules and we needed to stick to those rules."

I asked, "So what happened?" She told me, "Your mother disappeared for a bit when she was older, around eighteen. She came to us later, she was twenty years old now. She told me she was pregnant and needed help. She had nobody and she wanted us to help her. We turned her away. I'm so sorry, dear."

I said, "Well, I think I can understand the situation you were in. It must have been a tough decision. It's ok." She said, "I cannot believe this. It feels like my foster daughter was pregnant just yesterday, and here before me is her son, a grown man! How overwhelming! This is very emotional for me!"

She hugged me and apologized again. I told her it was ok. She wiped away her tears. She said, "I wonder if things would be different if I had accepted her back. Did you have a hard life, dear?"

I told her that I actually ended up in a foster home with a couple who loved me very, very much. I told her that I was raised well and had a great life. I also told her that I had met my mother and that she was doing well, too. She was very happy to hear this. She told me she often wondered about her.

All of this was so overwhelming and, in fact, unbelievable. All of this happened because I decided one day to make a phone call to the Band Office in Hope. Now I wanted to work on getting my Status card.

I found out that the rules had changed. I no longer needed my mother to apply for Status. I was eligible, but I needed some information. Indian

Affairs wanted my long-form birth certificate, my mother's long-form birth certificate, my grandmother's birth certificate, and also any and all of my grandmother's marriage certificates. This would be a challenge.

Auntie Sadie told me that my grandmother had passed years ago. I needed written consent from her to get her birth certificate. I called Vital Statistics and explained that I could not get written consent from her as she was deceased. They told me that if I provide them the death certificate and proof that I was related to her then they would send me the birth certificate.

I asked, "How do I get her death certificate?" The lady on the phone said, "We have it. You need to provide us with the date of death and the city of death in a letter, along with your long-form birth certificate and your mother's long-form birth certificate. Those documents show that you are your mom's son, and that your mom is your grandmother's daughter, proving that you are related and that you are entitled to receive the documents.

I had a couple of obstacles. First, my mother wanted nothing to do with any of this. She would not write to Vital Statistics for her long-form birth certificate. Second, I did not know when or where my grandmother died. Auntie Sadie and a bit of luck helped a lot.

Auntie Sadie went to the Band Office and found out what funeral home buried my grandmother. Then she went to the funeral home and asked if they had the date. They did, and even had a copy of her obituary.

Turns out that my grandmother passed away on December 25th. As strange as this is, being Christmas Day, it is even stranger because December 25th happens to be my mother's birthday as well. I was shocked again when I spoke with Uncle Chuck.

When I told him about all of this, I said, "It's so strange because my mom was born on Christmas Day. He said, "I know! Me too!" I said, "You guys are twins?" He said, "No! Your mom is a year and 16 minutes older than me… and she probably looks it too!"

I found this all so crazy. What a crazy coincidence! My mom and her brother, both born on Christmas Day, and their mom then dies, also on Christmas Day! It was strange, to say the least.

I now had the date my grandma passed away as well as the city. I needed my mom's long-form birth certificate. For this, I would need to get a little creative. I turned to Margaret for help.

I knew that my grandmother was born in Hope, B.C. I had heard from my mom that my grandfather was born in Norway. I needed this information to get my mom's long-form birth certificate, but because my mom wouldn't call, I asked Margaret to pretend to be my mom.

Of course, she agreed. While we were at work together one day, we went into a private office and I dialled the number. The lady asked Margaret for details to confirm her identity. As the questions were asked, I wrote down the answers for her.

They asked about her birthday, and where she was born. We nailed that one. Then she asked what her mother's full name was and where she was born. Nailed that one as well. Then she asked about her father's name and where he was born. Apparently, my mom was misinformed. He was not born in Norway.

The lady said, "I'm sorry, I need you to tell me the country of birth." Margaret asked, "Birth country of the father?" I whispered, "Your father!" She said hastily, "Your father! No sorry, her father! I mean my father, my father!"

The lady on the phone said, "Yes YOUR father's country of birth." Margaret said, "I didn't know my father, but I was told he was born in Norway." The lady was super nice. She said, "I'll give you a hint. You're close. It's a Scandinavian country."

I whispered, "Sweden." Margaret said, "Sweden?" The lady said, "Ok one more chance." Knowing that there are only three Scandinavian countries, I whispered to Margaret, "It's Finland." Margaret guessed Finland, and of course, it was correct. The lady asked for an address to send the birth certificate to and we provided my address. I had it three weeks later.

Once I received the birth certificate, I sent both my long-form birth certificate and my mom's, along with a letter to Vital Statistics, requesting my grandmother's death certificate.

They sent me the death certificate. Next, I sent that death certificate back to Vital Statistics with a letter, requesting my grandmother's birth certificate. I received my grandmother's birth certificate a few weeks later.

I was so close now, but the next part seemed impossible. I needed to provide Indian Affairs with all the documents I had, PLUS any and all of my grandmother's marriage certificates. I called back to Vital Statistics and asked how I could get these documents.

I was told that I would need to provide the city and the date of marriage, as well as the first, middle, and last name of my grandmother's husband or husbands. There were two husbands, my grandfather and her other husband. Auntie Sadie did not know this information and had no idea where to find it. I was at a dead end.

A few weeks later I saw a commercial for an online company where you could build a family tree. If other people from the same family had uploaded a family tree that matched your information, then it would inform you of the match.

I thought, perhaps if someone from my family had uploaded a family tree, maybe, just maybe, my grandmother would be there, and if they had included my grandmother, maybe, just maybe, it would have some information on her marriages. I knew it was a long shot, but I signed up anyway.

I got to work right away, building my family tree with the little information I had. I did not receive any notifications on matches. Oh well, it was worth a shot. I decided to keep my online account open, just in case.

One day, about five weeks after I built my family tree, I decided I would log on just for fun. To my surprise, I had notifications. I clicked on it and it said, that there was a family tree in their system that was a match. I clicked a few more things, and I was absolutely amazed at what I found.

There, right in front of me, was my grandmother's name. When I took a closer look, it showed that she was married… twice! One of the names was my grandfather. The other was my grandmother's other husband.

I clicked again and I was completely overwhelmed. Not one but BOTH marriage certificates had been uploaded. I opened them and they both showed the city, the date of marriage, and the full legal names of her husbands. This is exactly what I needed!

I wrote to Vital Statistics. I included my long-form birth certificate, my mom's long-form birth certificate, my grandmother's death certificate, and my grandmother's birth certificate, and I requested both marriage certificates.

I provided the dates and cities of both marriages, along with the names of my grandmother's husbands. Five weeks passed and I got both marriage certificates in the mail.

Now I had everything. I sent a letter, along with a passport photo of myself, and all the documents I had in my possession. I mailed everything and then I waited… and waited.

I made a couple of phone calls to Indian Affairs. I was told not to worry. They were dealing with a huge number of applicants, but once they reached my file they would take a look.

Eleven months later, I checked my mail and there was a brown envelope from Indian Affairs. They had returned all of my original documents and sent me a letter.

The letter said that I was now a registered Indian under the Indian Act of Canada, and I should expect my card in a few weeks. As promised, three weeks almost to the day, I finally received my Government issued Status card! It was a long, difficult road, but I had done it! I was a "Real Indian" at long last.

I was so excited that all my hard work had paid off. This gave me hope and fuelled another desire. One that would lead me on another journey. And again, change my life.

CHAPTER TWENTY-SEVEN

WHEN I TURNED NINETEEN, the Ministry had given me a letter that was sent to me from my father. It said that he always loved me and that in his younger years he was a bit "wild," but nowadays he was much calmer and more relaxed, and taking life a day at a time.

The letter was well-written and indicated to me that my father was educated and well spoken. The letter was dated October 13th, 1994. I was sixteen years old when he wrote it. Exactly the time that I was told he was to be released from prison.

I never did write back. I had a lot of anger towards him for what he had done to my mother. Also, I heard that he had been charged with murder, but before this happened, he had actually killed a man with a hammer. My mother had told me this. She said, that he had somehow gotten off on those charges. All I knew was that he was a very bad man.

After I found my family from my mother's side, I began to wonder about that old letter from my dad. Although I never replied to it, I also never threw it away. I had kept it all these years.

I pulled it out and read it over a few times. He seemed very mature and sincere. I decided to go ahead and write back. I honestly didn't expect to hear back. Perhaps I needed closure around this. It was 2013, and nineteen years had passed since I received that letter. It was sent from a Post Office Box in Ontario. I really didn't think there was any chance that he would still have that Post Office Box.

I wrote to him and left my phone number just in case he wanted to contact me. Again, I really thought it was impossible, but wrote anyway. Imagine my surprise, when I got a call a week later from Ontario!

It wasn't my father. It was a lady. She asked, "Is this Allan Strain?" "Yes, it is," I replied. She said, "I'm calling you from a Federal institution. I've been asked to contact you. Is there anybody you know that is in a Federal Institution?"

I said, "Well I know someone who could be, but he should have been out a long time ago." She asked, "And who is that?" I said, "George Strain." She said, "Yes and what is his relation to you?" I said, "Well, he would be my father." She said, "That's correct. Can he contact you?" I said, "Yes, sure."

The very next evening my phone rang. The call display said, "Ontario." I answered it. "Hello?" I said. The male voice on the other end of the phone said, "Allan?" "Yes, it is Allan." I replied. He said, "This is George Strain… your father!"

It was surreal to me that my biological father was on the phone. I said, "Umm, well hello there." He said, "Allan, I know this must be strange for you. It's strange for me, too. I'm not sure what to say. I wish I was more prepared for this moment, but it's a tough thing to prepare for."

I agreed, and told him I understood because I felt the same way. He said, "I'm sure you have a lot of questions. I'm an open book. You can ask me anything—I'm here to answer any questions you may have. There isn't anything that you cannot ask me." I did have questions. One was particularly pressing.

I said, "Ok, well there is one thing I'm really wondering about." "Go ahead," he urged. I said, "I was told that you went to prison in nineteen eighty one, and you were apparently scheduled to get out of prison approximately 1994. Is that correct?" "Yes. Yes, that's right," he said.

I said, "Well I can't help but notice that it is now 2013. Did you go back? Or are you still there from eighty-one?" He said, "I haven't left since I came here in eighty-one."

I said, "So just to confirm then, you've been in prison thirty-two years?" "That's correct." He said. "Sounds kinda long when you say it like that doesn't it?" I said, "It does, because that's a very long time."

I continued with my questions. "My question is, if you were supposed to get out in ninety-four after thirteen years, why are you still there after thirty-two years?"

"That's a great question!" He said. "Do you know why I'm in prison?" I said, "I assume it's for murder." He said, "Yes. I was downtown Vancouver getting drunk, having a great time, and I hired a prostitute. I got angry and I beat her in the face. I beat her over and over and over until she was dead."

Wow. This was a very violent crime. I still wasn't convinced though. I wanted to know more. I asked, "But if they gave you a sentence of thirteen years, it doesn't explain why you're still there after all this time."

He said, "They say I'm not rehabilitated; they say that because I refuse to enter a sex offender rehabilitation program. I'm not a sex offender and I didn't survive thirty-two fucking years in a max security prison by saying I'm a sex offender. They don't survive long around here."

He went on. "I'm a violent criminal yes. Did I hire a prostitute? Yes, I did. Did I beat her in her face with my bare hands until she died? Yes, I did! So, I'm a fucking loser, sure, but I am NOT a sex offender. I didn't rape her. I paid for sex, then she pissed me off and I killed her. Cold blooded killer, NOT a sex offender. Big difference!"

I said, "Wow. It's crazy they've kept you there so long. I do have one other question, though, if you don't mind." "I don't mind at all," he said. I wanted to ask my father about the guy he killed with a hammer. I didn't want him to know it was my mom who told me, because my mom was terrified of him. She always said he could get out of prison and come after her, so I told him it was a social worker who told me.

I said, "Ok, so I heard from a social worker that you killed a man with a hammer before the other crime occurred. What happened there?" Apparently, I hit a nerve. He lost his composure and got extremely angry. He started screaming.

"This is why I HATE social workers! They spread fucking lies! That's such bullshit!" I said, "Ok, so that's not true?" He said, "Absolutely not! Lies! All lies!"

I said, "I wonder why he told me that." He yelled, "Ok, listen, LISTEN! I did get mad and cave in the right side of a guy's skull with a hammer… but he didn't fucking die!"

I was lost for words. What do you even say to that? I was beginning to understand why the prison had said he was not yet rehabilitated. He was never rehabilitated in my opinion.

We did write back and forth a few times. I was honest and told him that I wasn't sure what type of relationship if any I wanted from him. He seemed understanding, however, he made a move that told me that he wasn't understanding at all.

He called me one day and said, "Allan, I have made a request to be transferred to a prison in B.C. It's in Ferndale, just outside of Chilliwack." I thought, "Oh shit! He's going to be close to my son."

I decided to tell Nicky. She freaked out. She told me that she was going to be in danger now. I told her that he didn't know about her or have any idea that she was in Chilliwack. She was still furious and claimed that I had put her life in danger.

A few weeks later I got a call from my father. He said, "Hey, I have a friend who gets day parole. He went to a 12 Step meeting in Chilliwack. Do you have an ex-wife there?"

I tried not to discuss it much with him and when I got off the phone, I called Nicky. I asked her how my father knew about her being in Chilliwack. She proceeded to tell the story.

She said that she was at a meeting. There were a few people from the prison who were on a day pass to attend the meeting. This guy Ron shared his story. She wondered if he knew my father.

After the meeting, Nicky approached Ron. She said, "Hey, just wondering do you know a guy named George Strain?" Apparently, he started laughing. He asked "How do you know old Georgie?" She said, "I married his son!" Ron said, "George is my cellmate!"

I was furious. I asked Nicky how she could possibly approach this guy. She said I put her life in danger. Now she went and introduced herself to my dad's cellmate and told him she was my ex?

Nicky said, "He was taking a 20-year cake! He's been clean and sober for 20 years! Plus, he seemed nice." I said, "Yeah he's been clean and sober 20 years… he's been in prison!" I was so mad at her for this.

I eventually wrote my father and told him that I just couldn't have any relationship with him. He got very upset and wrote back. His calm demeanour and nice elegant handwriting all changed. He was quite rude. He wrote, "Get your head out of the clouds, boy! Give your head a shake! Think about this and figure it out IF YOU CAN!"

The pen had been pushed against the paper so hard that there were spots where it tore through. He was extremely angry. I decided at that point that he was definitely not someone I wanted in my life. If I had any doubts about the previous letter, I sent him, they were gone now. I couldn't be more sure.

I had removed one person from my life, but I was about to commit my entire life to another, the one I loved, the one who was made for me. Our wedding day was quickly approaching, and I was super excited!

CHAPTER TWENTY-EIGHT

MARGARET AND I HAD A DATE in mind for the wedding. It was August 1st, 2015. I had a friend who I had met in a 12 Step meeting back in North Vancouver, and I was still in touch with him. He had moved to Alberta to work in the Oil and Gas industry, specifically pipeline work, and he strongly suggested I do the same.

My friend Mark said that he got on with the union and was dispatched to a pipeline job in Northern Alberta. He was a labourer and was making a net income of $2,800 weekly. This was about what I made monthly at Walmart.

I had pushed hard at Walmart. I was continuously promised that I would have my own store soon, and I kept working harder and harder every time I heard this; however, I was never promoted. I had now been with Walmart for 15 years.

I spoke with Margaret and her mother about this idea of leaving the province in search of more money. It would mean being further away from my son, which was the biggest concern I had.

We decided that the increased income would allow me to fly to see my son, and I figured I could see him as much, if not more, than I did currently. When we asked Margaret's mom how she felt, she said, "There's no question you guys would be better off doing that." We went for it.

I gave my two weeks' notice. I had already done some courses that I knew were required in most oil field jobs. I had my First Aid certificate, Confined Space, Fall Protection, Pipeline Construction Safety Training (PCST), Construction Safety Training System (CSTS), and Ground Disturbance.

I had already sent dozens of resumes to companies and had applied for many job openings for pipeline jobs, labourer jobs, scaffolding positions and many others, to no avail. I realized that these companies probably had hundreds of online applicants and decided I would just need to go there in person.

I had no idea where in Alberta to go. I pulled up a map on my computer. I saw that Edmonton was central and thought that since it was the capital city, it must be pretty good. The morning after my last shift at Walmart, I kissed Margaret goodbye and started the long drive from Vernon to Edmonton.

I arrived in Edmonton that evening and checked into the most affordable hotel I could find. I had a car full of belongings. My job now was to find employment, and a place to live for Margaret and I and our two dogs.

I woke up early the next morning and started looking up addresses of pipeline companies and any company that was involved in the oil and gas Industry. I drove to each one of them and gave them my resume.

Before I left for Alberta, I had responded to an ad online for a swamper job on a hydrovac. The gentlemen had told me that if I came into his office when I arrived, he would give me an interview. I called him the second day I was in Edmonton and went down to see him.

The interview went well. The guy who interviewed me was impressed that I had taken the time to get all my tickets on my own. Usually the companies paid for employees to obtain whatever tickets they required. He said, "You wanna work!" I agreed that I did. He hired me that day. He said, I would need to go and buy boots and come back the following day.

It wasn't the crazy Alberta money I was expecting. They gave me $20/hr. Still, my first month there, I took home $4,000, which was $1,000 more than I made at Walmart as a Manager, after 15 years. I wondered why I had not done this years ago.

I had absolutely no idea what a hydrovac was at that time. I learned that they are trucks that have a water pump and a blower, which produces vacuum through the boom. Basically, we used high pressure water combined with vacuum to dig holes in the ground.

The part of the boom that is placed where you want to suck is called the dig tube. We use a metal wand with various types of heads on the end to cut the ground with water. The wand cuts the dirt, the dig tube sucks it up.

We would hydrovac for a variety of reasons. Typical hydrovac work is digging to locate underground utilities. Hydrovacs are the safe option for excavation. We located the utilities before the heavy equipment begins to dig.

We located utilities such as water lines, gas lines, power, sewer, communication lines, and anything else that may be in the ground. Other hydrovac work includes digging trenches, vacuum only jobs such as drill support, when we suck up drilling mud and many more.

I hated the job at first. I wasn't used to the manual labour. There was a lot of walking, lifting, pulling, crouching, climbing, etc. By the end of a 14-hour day I was exhausted. I thought I worked hard at Walmart, and I did, but it didn't compare to working in the sun all day in 30-degree weather, or standing in a field spraying water, when it was minus 40.

I searched and searched for a place for Margaret and I to live. Rent prices were extremely expensive at the time, thanks to the booming economy. I had a very hard time finding a place that was affordable and would allow two dogs.

Eventually, I did meet one couple who said they would take me and Margaret and our two dogs. It started as a temporary place for me, while I continued to look for more suitable housing. While I was staying there, looking for a home, they approached me and said they had a suggestion.

The male, Doug told me to come downstairs with him. We went to the basement. It was a fairly large space, unfinished with a cement floor and no drywall so the insulation and pipes were visible.

Doug said that Margaret and I could live down there with the two dogs and we could have one washroom upstairs to ourselves. He would charge us $700 plus 1/3 utilities. The price was right, but I would need to speak with Margaret.

Margaret wasn't thrilled about it, but she understood it was difficult to find a place and this was only temporary until we could find a more suitable situation. She was about to give her notice at Walmart. Around that time, I saw one of my old managers in the Walmart, near the place I was staying in. She was surprised to see me.

I told Margaret I had seen my old manager Michelle. Margaret mentioned it to our matchmaker Brenda in Personnel at the Vernon Store, who then called Michelle. Michelle said, that she had a position for Backup Personnel. Margaret got a job as Backup Personnel Manager.

We made the basement as nice as we could. We had a queen size mattress and a box spring, no bed. There were plugs, so we set up our TV in the corner, and the computer was set up with the TV as the monitor. We had a dining room table and four chairs, and a bookcase where we stored our dry food. I was quite content. Margaret, not so much.

Margaret was good about the situation at first. She understood it was a transition period. After a few months though, she started to become frustrated, and I was also frustrated by the situation.

We had a picture in our heads of what Alberta would be. I imagined abundant wealth, a bank account that would grow steadily, a nice home, a truck, and perhaps a nice boat later. Neither of us expected for me to be making $20/hr and for us to live in someone's unfinished basement.

I felt like I had failed us both. Margaret trusted me. I was sure that I would make at least double what I made in B.C. My income was ok when I worked a lot, but there were a lot of slow times.

I couldn't stop thinking about how Margaret had left her whole family to be with me. Now it was just the two of us living in an unfinished basement. It was not the fairy tale we imagined.

Margaret and I began to argue almost daily. Our relationship was facing challenges for sure. I think we were both just so tense due to our current situation and we took it out on each other.

We made the most of the situation. We took our dogs for walks; I cooked some nice meals and once I baked a cheesecake from scratch. We went places together, but I knew something had to change, and soon.

Eventually the decision was made for us. Doug approached us one day and said, that his wife's mother in Ontario was ill and they needed to move there. The actual owner of the house did not know we were living there. We would need to move by February 28th. It was February 21st.

I got on it right away. I posted an online ad for an urgent need of a house or apartment and at the same time I looked at classified ads. Margaret and I looked at a few places. That same week we found a two-bedroom apartment that would take both dogs. The price was $1400/month and it didn't include utilities.

In addition to the first month's rent, we would need to give half a month's rent for damage deposit as well as a $500 pet deposit. I also needed to rent a moving truck and hire a couple of guys to help me.

This would not be cheap, and I was pretty nervous about the cost of it all. Through all of this, I still had to pay $1100/month to Nicky, and make sure I flew down to see Eli as often as possible.

We managed to come up with some of the cash we needed, and we had some help from family as well. We moved into our new place. It was a lot nicer than the basement that's for sure. We made one room into a room for Eli. We wanted him to always feel like this was his home, too.

We were at this apartment a few months when Sara started to have some serious health issues. One time when I called her, she sounded drunk. I knew this was a problem, because she didn't drink.

Sara told me that the night before, she had spent all night trying to find her bedroom. This was particularly concerning as she lived in a very small apartment, approximately 600 square feet. You can't miss the only bedroom.

Suddenly Sara stopped speaking to me. I told her I was calling an ambulance. She said, "You can't! I haven't had a bath today." I was happy that she was actually responding to me now. I told her to stay on the phone with me.

I used Margaret's phone to dial 9-1-1. I explained that I was in Alberta, but I was calling for my mom who was in B.C. I gave the dispatcher Sara's address. I stayed on the phone with both Sara and the dispatcher until the ambulance arrived.

I called my brother and told him what happened. I immediately booked a flight to Vancouver where I rented a car and drove to the hospital. I met my brother at the hospital.

At the hospital, we met with a doctor. He told us that Sara's heart was in an abnormal rhythm. He said, that the top two chambers of her heart were fluttering rather than pumping so her brain wasn't getting enough blood.

The doctor said I should go in and speak with Sara because they needed to shock her heart, but there was a potential for a clot to have developed and if that was the case, it would go into her artery and she could die instantly.

I went and spoke with Sara. She was quite confused. I told her I loved her. She said, "Right then, that's nice of you." I guess some things don't change, even in a completely delusional state.

My brother was there as well. We sat and waited to hear from the doctor. After a while the doctor came out. He told us that they had succeeded in shocking her heart back into a normal rhythm and we could go and see her soon.

Sara was extremely grateful to me for recognizing that she wasn't well and getting help for her. She went and got some new medication and did well for a while.

Every now and then Sara would tell me about how she was gardening and woke up on the grass. She was, from time to time, randomly losing consciousness.

A short while later my brother called me. This was after Sara had been having ongoing health concerns for some time. He said, "I have something to tell you." I kind of knew what he was going to say. He said, "Mom died last night."

The news was very sad, although not a surprise. I had been expecting this for some time now. Sara was such an important person in my life. She supported me in my most difficult times, not only financially, but emotionally as well.

At times she made me so angry I just wanted to scream at her. We had a lot of times that we were frustrated with each other. But she was always there for me no matter what.

Sara played such a huge part in my overall success in life. Sara helped shape me into the person I am today and my life would have been completely different had it not been for her selfless dedication and commitment to me. She would be sorely missed, no doubt.

After six months at the hydrovac job, I was promoted to driver. I had heard that drivers of bigger hydrovacs made a lot more. I was currently driving just single axle hydrovacs. I wanted to make as much money as I could. I went and got my Class 3 licence and began looking for better work.

August 1st, 2015 was approaching quickly. I was getting very excited for our big day. Margaret's mother and sister planned most of our wedding. They helped us find the venue, organized the decorations, the timeline, the wedding commissioner—pretty much the whole thing.

We decided that we would have the wedding in Vernon. We booked a hall, almost beside the home of Margaret's family. In the back was a beautiful grassy area with trees to shade us from the hot sun. It would be an outdoor wedding.

Margaret and I found a photographer in Vernon and met with him. We gave him a deposit and booked him for our special day. I looked online and found a catering service. We paid a deposit for that as well. We made a couple of trips back to Vernon to look at the venue, and to make plans. It was all coming together nicely.

I asked my brother if he would be my Best Man and he happily accepted. Margaret asked my sisters to be her bridesmaids, along with her friend and her own sister. Mike and Graham and another friend were my groomsmen. I'm so happy to say that after all these years my two closest friends in the world are still in my life and we keep in touch regularly. Mike and Graham are lifelong friends and I truly value their friendship.

Margaret had another idea, which I truly loved. She said to me one day, "Why don't we see if we can have a traditional native wedding?" I was shocked that she wanted to do this, but also very honoured. We asked my Auntie Sadie if she would help with this.

Auntie Sadie was thrilled. It was such an honour that we asked this of her. She told me that we would need two eagle feathers. She explained that they needed to be given to us, we couldn't just go buy them. Auntie Sadie said that she would give us one, but the other would need to come from somewhere else.

In the years I had been clean and sober, an amazing thing happened. My friend Rudy, the one who lived with his dad at the crack house, had also become clean and sober. He was five years clean at this point. I had added him as a friend on Facebook a while back.

I sent Rudy a message on Facebook. I explained the situation and asked if he knew anyone that could give me an eagle feather. He wrote back immediately, and said, "I have one!" I had my best friend Mike, who still lived in North Vancouver, meet up with him to receive it.

At the wedding, Auntie Sadie smudged those who wanted it and laid cedar bows at the arbor. It was beautiful. I was dressed in my tuxedo, and I waited in position.

I heard music playing. I watched with pride as my son walked down the aisle, carrying our rings on a pillow. I saw Margaret's niece come out and drop flower petals. Next, I saw Margaret's nephew come out with a sign that said, "Uncle Allan, here comes your bride!"

I waited patiently on the grass, in my tuxedo in front of all my family and friends. I couldn't wait to see her. Finally, she emerged from the building.

The moment I laid eyes upon my bride the tears began to flow. I tried to contain it, but it was hopeless. She was by far, the most beautiful woman I had ever seen.

Auntie Sadie wrapped Margaret and I in a blanket, symbolizing that we are now connected. She then told us that to make the marriage official, we needed to stay wrapped up together for four days. Margaret gasped. Auntie Sadie burst out laughing and said, "Haha, just kiddin'!"

We also had a wedding commissioner, so that we could be legally married. We had chosen our own vows. When the vows were read, I got emotional again. I didn't think I would cry at my own wedding, but it was extremely overwhelming. It was actually happening. I was marrying the love of my life!

My mother Lillian also attended. I was extremely happy about this. My relationship with Lillian has been up and down. I had a hard time feeling a part of that family because I wasn't raised with my sisters, and there were all kinds of emotions that went along with that. After taking years to get to know her though, really know her, I've discovered she is a very special lady, and I love her very much.

Lillian has always been apprehensive about meeting her biological family. I think she was longing for a relationship with them, but feared rejection. It was very nice to see her there. Uncle Chuck was there as well. I'm so happy the two of them met again and had a chance to reconnect after 37 years.

The wedding was absolutely amazing. Everything went as planned. I don't think there's anything I would have changed about it at all. We have continued to build a life together as I will explain in the following chapter.

CHAPTER TWENTY-NINE

MARGARET AND I HAVE HAD A pretty good life in Alberta, but it didn't just happen overnight. Both of us have worked extremely hard to achieve the most out of life. Margaret is an extremely dedicated person in all areas of her life and her managers at work have always noticed this.

Not too long after we moved, Margaret was approached by her store manager. She wanted to know if Margaret would be willing to take on more responsibility. Specifically, she wanted to make her an Assistant Manager.

Margaret accepted this offer and her income increased a significant amount. I was so proud of her when she told me they wanted to promote her. If anyone deserved it, she did.

Margaret's strong work ethic and commitment to her responsibilities are things I admire deeply about her. It was nice to see that others saw this, too, and rewarded her for it.

As for myself, I now had a class 3 licence. The problem was that nobody wanted to hire me without driving experience. I eventually found employment, driving a water truck. I went from $23/hr at the time to $25/hr.

My job was to deliver potable water to the refineries in Edmonton. I also delivered water to homes that did not have city water, and I filled tanks at pipe yards and other industrial sites as well.

One of my tasks while delivering water to the refineries in Edmonton was to fill the hydrovacs on site with water. These were much larger than the hydrovacs I had driven when I first came to Edmonton. I got to know these guys very well. I told them I used to operate a hydrovac as well, and that I missed it.

The hours at the water hauling company weren't that great to begin with, but I knew I was in trouble when they lost the contract with the refinery. Another company got the contract to fill the wash cars, but they still had me filling the hydrovacs.

One day when I was filling hydrovacs at the refinery, I spoke with one of the drivers, Seth. Seth actually worked for a guy named Bobby who was an Owner Operator for this hydrovac company. Bobby owned two of his own trucks.

Seth asked me what I would do now that we lost the contract. He mentioned that my hours must have dropped. I told him that indeed, I was only getting about 20 hours a week and I was in fact quite worried about it.

He said, "Why don't you apply with us? You already know how to hydrovac, and you obviously have your class 3 if you're driving a water truck right?" I said, "Perhaps I will. Do you have a contact number I can call?" He gave me a phone number and said he would put in a good word for me.

I called the number the next day. The manager on the phone said he would be happy to interview me. We made an appointment for the following day. I found my way to his shop and he asked me to have a seat in the office.

The first thing he wanted to know was whether I had any hydrovac experience. I told him I had done hydrovac work for a year and a bit, and that I was a driver for the last seven months of my employment there. He seemed pleased about this.

He asked me to follow him into the shop where all the trucks were parked. I looked up at these huge hydrovac trucks wondering if I could really be the driver of one of these. It was intimidating, for sure.

The Manager said, "Well here they are! You have your class 3 right?" I said, "Yes, I have my class 3 and I have been hauling water for 3 months now, but I have been in an automatic. I just got my class 3 a few months ago, so I really don't have a lot of experience driving the manual trucks. I'm still practicing my shifting."

He looked at the truck to our right, then looked at me and said, "Yeah, but you can drive it right?" I said, "Well... I mean, I can *DRIVE* it yes." "Good enough!" He said. "Let's go back to the office and talk money."

We went back to the office and sat down. He said, "I can hire you as a driver, but I'll put you shotgun for the first while with an experienced operator. You can drive back from the job sites once in a while until you're all trained up."

I said, "Wow, ok, thank you very much!" He said, "No problem. How much money do you want?" I had to spit out a number. I had heard that some operators made about $30/hr, but I wasn't really sure. I didn't want to sound greedy and I didn't want to sell myself short.

I said, "Well, I think what's fair is about thirty bucks an hour, like twenty-eight to thirty range." He said, "Yup, I can do twenty-eight." I said, "Can you do thirty, though?"

He said, "Listen, twenty-eight is just to get you in the door. Once you're signed off as a driver, I'll bump you up to thirty. How's that?" "Great!" I said. And just like that, I was hired at three dollars more per hour than I was making hauling water.

I rode with a guy named John for a while. Once in a while he would let me drive home. I was grinding every gear in the beginning. It didn't help that the size of these trucks overwhelmed me a bit. We were also coming into winter and I was pretty uncomfortable driving these huge trucks around the city. Mostly, I sat as a passenger and tried to watch and learn. After about a month I was assigned my own truck.

We did all kinds of jobs. We got on a huge project at one of the refineries in Edmonton. We were working 13 hours a day, six days a week. Although I only made $3/hr more than my last job, I did well. Now I was taking home $1500/week. I was pretty happy with this.

I worked regularly and got experience doing all types of jobs. We worked on construction sites, we did pipeline work, we cleaned tanks, we did road construction, and many other jobs.

In 2015, Margaret got pregnant. We were so excited! We had been trying for some time without any luck. At the time, I think the only thing Margaret wanted was to become a mother. We were both thrilled about this.

The pregnancy wasn't perfect. From fairly early on, there were concerns about the baby's growth. We were told that they would keep a close eye on the baby and see how it went. We were both quite concerned, but I tried to pretend that I wasn't. I wanted to reassure Margaret and put her mind at ease.

We were told that Margaret had a unicornuate uterus. This is a type of congenital uterine abnormality. Generally, the uterus is about half the regular size, and this was the case with Margaret. Margaret also had a rudimentary horn. In some cases, this horn is not connected to the uterus and in some cases it is. In Margaret's case it was connected.

The effects of this are growth restriction for the baby, as the uterus is smaller. We were very concerned when we learned about this, but I continued to assure Margaret that everything would be fine, even though I had no way of knowing if we would be ok or not.

I got onto a big project at one of the refineries in Edmonton. One of the tanks that held diesel had been leaking into the ground. Our job was to go into the tank and hydrovac out the entire floor of the tank, one foot down. The tank was 150 feet in diameter.

The company had asked Bobby, the Owner Operator if he would help supervise the job. Bobby was supervising, but also worked with us in the tank. Seth was also there with one of Bobby's trucks, with his swamper Rick.

One day, Margaret had another appointment with her doctor. I was at work on this tank project. We took turns going into the tank, each person going in for about an hour or so. When I finished one of my turns and returned to my truck, I checked my phone. There were some missed calls from Margaret and a voicemail.

I checked the voicemail and Margaret had left me a message. I could barely understand what she was saying because she was crying a lot. I made out that the baby was too small. I immediately called her.

When Margaret answered the phone, she was in tears. She explained that our baby was not growing at the rate she needed to, and they needed to discuss some options. She said, "I just wish I didn't have to do this alone." I told her she didn't have to and I would meet her at the doctor's office. I told Bobby that I needed to leave. He was really good about it and said it was no problem at all.

I got to the doctor's office an hour later. The doctor went through some options with us. She said, "Baby is very small. We can give steroids and hope she grows in the womb, or we can just take her out now."

We asked about the risk factors of both options. She said, "If we take her now, she will be a preemie. There will be no long-term health effects. She will just be small and may need to be in the NICU for a while. If we try to get her to grow in the womb, she may grow, but we risk a stillbirth."

We both knew that we were going to take this baby out early. We were not about to risk a stillbirth. The doctor said, "Ok then, we will do it tomorrow!" I think we were both shocked that this was happening so soon. We were 35.5 weeks pregnant.

We went into the hospital the next day. Margaret's mother had come to stay with us to help out a bit. Margaret was assigned a room. We waited there until it was time. We placed bets on what the time of birth would be.

It seemed like forever, but they finally came and got us. They took Margaret to prepare her for surgery. I went and got dressed in scrubs and they gave me a mask as well.

After a short while, the doctor came and got me from the hallway. They had given Margaret freezing and they were ready to begin surgery. They put up a sheet to block my view from the neck down. I held Margaret's hand as they began.

As the doctor started the incision, Margaret yelled out, "Oww, Ouch!" She squeezed my hand super tight. The doctor looked up. He asked, "Are you feeling actual pain, or just pressure?" She said, "Pain, pain, like you're cutting me!"

The anesthesiologist said, "Ok, I'm sorry. I'll give you some more anesthesia and we will just wait a few minutes and then we will be good. After a few minutes the doctor started touching Margaret's skin and asking if she could feel anything. Margaret said, "No I don't think so."

They said, they would begin again. Once again, I held Margaret's hand and once again, she squeezed super tight and this time let out a cry. I looked at her and saw tears coming down her face. The doctor asked, "Are you feeling pain?" Margaret replied, "Yes, I feel pain, a lot."

They apologized and said, they would try once more. They gave more anesthesia and waited. I was so scared for Margaret. Again they did the touch test. She didn't feel anything. They began their incision. This time Margaret did not feel any pain at all.

I heard the doctor with his tools. Then I heard that beautiful sound. The sound of my daughter's first cry. It makes me emotional just thinking of it. The doctor called out, "Dad, you're up!"

I went and saw my daughter for the very first time. We had named her Willow, after the willow tree we sat under for our very first date. I cut the cord and then they weighed her and took her to NICU. She weighed just 3 pounds, 12 ounces.

Willow stayed just 13 days in the NICU. She did so well. She began breast feeding after just a few days and we were able to remove her feeding tube. When Willow was two weeks old, we were finally able to bring her home.

Eli came and stayed with us from just before Willow was born, and stayed about three weeks. He was such a great big brother. He would sing to her and gently stroke her head when she cried, and to our surprise, he was often the only one that could calm Willow.

Both Margaret and I really wanted one more child. We asked the doctor about risk factors due to Margaret's unicornuate uterus. The doctor reassured us and said we should be fine.

The horn was attached to the uterus, and was basically a second, non-functioning uterus. We were told this wouldn't be an issue because a baby would never be implanted in the horn.

We were having some issues getting pregnant and Margaret started to take fertility treatments. It was just a prescription that she took daily. Very shortly after Margaret started taking the prescription, she announced to me that she had taken a pregnancy test and it was positive!

We were thrilled to be having one more child. It really didn't matter to us whether it was a boy or a girl. We just really wanted one more baby to make our family complete. I couldn't wait to see our new baby.

There were issues with growth again from early on in the pregnancy, but we expected this. Again, Margaret was concerned throughout the pregnancy, and again, I tried hard to convince her that everything would be fine.

Work was quite slow. Margaret was about five months pregnant now, and I was getting pretty stressed about money, especially since we had a new baby on the way. I spoke with my manager and explained that I really needed to work.

About a week after I had the conversation with my manager, he told me that there was a project, but it was out of town. I would need orientation and I would need to be willing to stay at camp in Wabasca, which is about four hours north of Edmonton. At this point, I was willing to take anything. I needed the money.

I packed my bags and said goodbye to my family. It sounded like I would be gone about 3-4 weeks. I grabbed a hydrovac from the shop and began my long drive up north. It was February and very cold.

The following day I went to orientation. I produced all of my tickets and I was ready to go to work. I did a walk through with the foreman and the other operators who had arrived before me.

The first few days went well. We worked 12-hour days and went back to camp around 6:00 pm. The food at camp was excellent. I would need to make sure I watched what I ate here, because I knew it would be easy to gain weight.

On my third day there I received a call from Margaret . She was very upset. She said that she had been to another appointment. She had been referred to another hospital and she was now waiting to be seen.

The doctors were very concerned about the pregnancy. They felt there was a possibility that our baby had been growing in her second, non-functioning uterus. If this was the case, they would need to terminate the pregnancy.

I was very worried at this point. I tried to stay positive. I told myself that everything would be ok. I was in my truck at the end of the day when Margaret called back. She was in tears. She said, that indeed, our baby was growing in the horn, not in her uterus.

Although I knew, I asked what this meant. She said, through her tears, "They need to terminate the pregnancy." My heart sank. This could not be happening. Margaret had asked if there was any option, other than terminating the pregnancy. The doctors informed her that her uterus wall was so thin that it would soon rupture, and when that occurred Margaret would bleed out and likely die, even if she was in the hospital at the time. Also, they added that even if they did not terminate the pregnancy now, the possibility for our baby to survive was zero. Unfortunately, the only option was to terminate the pregnancy.

The emotions I felt at this time are nearly impossible to explain. Margaret was 26 weeks pregnant. We knew we were having a girl. I had felt my daughter's kicks on my wife's belly. For us to lose her now seemed unreal. I didn't have many words for Margaret. What could I say? I told her I would call her shortly.

I returned to camp and called Margaret back. I told her that I would drive back to Edmonton right away. She said that wasn't necessary. Margaret told me that she was going to tell them to just knock her out.

She explained that she didn't want to know anything. She would be put to sleep and wake up not pregnant. She said, that this was the only way she could do it, because the whole situation was just way too hard to deal with. I told her that was fine, but I would still leave camp to be with her. "Whatever you want," she said.

I called my manager. I told him the situation and I told him I needed to leave immediately so that I could be with my wife. He told me that he would make some calls and get back to me right away.

My manager called back about 20 minutes later. He said that he had found a swamper who could come and switch me out. He said that Mike was leaving now and would reach me in about four hours. Once he arrived, I could get in the pickup that he came in and drive it home to Edmonton.

Our camp was deep in the forest. We had to take an old logging road off the main highway and then follow directions on a map. We had to drive through the forest and turn at the indicated roads, watching for the markers that identified each road.

Because Mike had never been here, and because it would also make my trip home faster, I was asked to drive a hydrovac to the entrance of the forest at the side of the highway and meet Mike there. I needed to bring an operator with me as he would need to drive the hydrovac back to camp.

I packed up all my stuff and brought it to the hydrovac. It was about a 45-minute drive through the forest to the highway. I was told that Mike would arrive around midnight, so I got the other operator at 10:30 pm, and we started the drive through the forest just before 11:00 pm.

Mike arrived on schedule, just after midnight. I quickly transferred all my stuff from the hydrovac to the pickup, said, goodbye, and started the drive home to Edmonton.

This was the longest drive of my life. Yes, of course I had driven more kilometres and for longer hours at a time, but because of the current situation it was, by far, the longest drive of my entire life.

I drove the pickup back to our shop and switched everything over to my personal vehicle. I left the shop and started the drive to the hospital. Margaret called and asked where I was. I told her that I was about 30 minutes away. It was now about 5:00 am.

I finally got to the hospital, found parking, and ran in. After asking a few nurses, I figured out where to find Margaret. I ran down the hallway, and found my way to the room she was in. I walked in and saw Margaret lying on the bed.

We made eye contact and Margaret burst into tears. I walked up to her and just held her. She started crying uncontrollably, screaming "My baby! My baby! Oh God! My baby!"

I also began crying uncontrollably. Once we were able to stop crying enough to have a conversation, Margaret told me that what made it worse was that our daughter was kicking and moving all night long. She was just talking to her, telling her "It's ok baby. Just sleep now."

Margaret also told me that while she was waiting for me, she had changed her mind about being put to sleep. She had asked the doctor to explain how the procedure would go. She said, "Do you know what they're going to do with her? They're going to put her in a tray until she dies."

Crying, Margaret said, "I can't do that. She will die alone and cold and afraid and I just can't do that to her. I don't want her to die alone in a tray. I just need her to feel loved and comforted."

A while after this, a doctor came in. He said, "Ok there's been a change of plans. We will deliver your baby by C-section, but we will keep you awake. Your baby will be born alive, but she won't live long. You can have her with you, and Dad can be there if he chooses."

I felt myself getting shaky. I said, "This makes everything so real." The doctor excused himself and Margaret told me that being there or not being there is a super personal decision. She told me it was totally up to me and that she wouldn't be upset if I couldn't do it.

I said, "No, no I need to be there. As much as I know it will be way too hard to be there, I need to because I don't want to have regrets. I don't want to wake up a year from now or two years from now, wishing I had seen her or held her. I just need to be there, too."

We found out that they weren't able to get us in until that evening. What a long wait that was. We spent most of the time crying. We passed the time talking, and I went out a couple of times to get us coffee. We did whatever we could to pass the time.

That evening, the doctor came and said they were getting ready for us. He said we would be heading down in about 20 minutes. He came back and started to wheel Margaret's bed down the hall, with me walking alongside her. Margaret looked up at me and said, "Here we go."

When we got to where we were going, the doctor told me to wait while they prepped Margaret for surgery. I was super nervous. I called my brother, but it went to voicemail. He was on a trip and out of cell phone range. I was actually quite happy about that because at the time I was crying so hard I could not actually form words.

I left a lengthy text message with my brother. It was almost time now. I was crying and shaking and had no idea how I was going to actually go through with this. I took some deep breaths and prayed and tried to prepare myself. Soon the doctor came and got me.

I went into the room and sat at Margaret's head. She was shaking and crying. I held her hand. They administered anesthesia and waited a bit. They began the surgery. Before long we had our daughter. We had named her Isabella.

The doctor asked Margaret if she would like to have skin to skin time with Isabella. She said that she did. They put Isabella on Margaret's chest. Strangely, I did not feel that overwhelming sadness anymore. There was a sense of peace.

Margaret held Isabella on her chest for a while. She was able to have that skin to skin contact and I know that our daughter felt so loved at this time. This was extremely important to both Margaret and I.

After Margaret had her time with Isabella, she said to the doctor, "I'm ok now, her Dad can hold her if he wants. The doctor asked if I would like to hold my daughter, and I said that I would very much like to hold her.

I held Isabella in my arms. She was swaddled and she was wearing a cute little hat. I told her I loved her. I gave a little kiss on her head. I touched her hand and she held onto my finger for a brief moment.

Margaret was smiling at me. I said, "She knows that she is loved." Margaret said, "That's all I wanted." The doctors came once in a while to check Isabella's breathing and heartbeat.

I held our daughter for some time. I'm not sure how long; perhaps it was about 30 minutes. At some point while I was holding her, she passed. I think I already knew it, but the doctors confirmed it when they came to check on her.

The doctor looked at me and said, "There's absolutely no rush whatsoever, but she's gone now. You can have as much time as you need with her." We didn't need any more time. I placed her in the little crib and I wheeled her over to where Margaret was going for her recovery.

After a short while, I went back to the room. I prepared to leave, as Willow was at home with Margaret's mother, and I needed to go and take care of her. The next day, we all went to visit Margaret.

They had Isabella in what they called a grieving room. It looked like a little nursery. She was lying in a little bassinet that was temperature controlled, to keep her cool.

We had another chance to be with her for a bit. Margaret and I went separately and we each had our own personal time with our daughter as part of our grieving process.

The next day or two was all up and down emotionally. I thought I was ok, and then suddenly something would trigger a wave of emotion. At one point a nurse came in and gave us a pamphlet, and when I read the cover, I just lost it. It read, "When hello is goodbye."

The next day or two, I just tried to figure out how to get through it. The very first day after losing Isabella, I made a trip to Starbucks. I asked Margaret if she wanted anything and she said she didn't. I walked in and tried to decide what to get.

I always enjoy the Reserve coffee, which is very high quality, and somewhat rare. These coffees change every few weeks. I looked up at the board to see what Reserve coffees they had. Written in chalk, I saw the words, "Guatemala Santa Isabella." I told the girl, "I want that one. Isabella."

I found out later that whoever wrote it, made a slight mistake. It's actually Isabel, not Isabella. Either way, I took this as a sign that my daughter was somehow letting me know she was ok. As a matter of fact, the fact that it was misspelled to the exact spelling of our daughter's name made it even stranger.

Losing our daughter was by far the hardest thing I have ever endured in my life. I thought it would be way too difficult to be there for the birth of my daughter, who I knew we would have only a short while. As it turns out, I'm extremely grateful that it happened the way it did. We had our time with her, and most of all, she had her parents comforting her and loving her.

Margaret and I got through this and continued to live our life. I don't think it is something either of us will ever "get over." We need to carry on, as there are two more kids counting on us, and they deserve for us to be at our very best. Life's challenges weren't over yet, though. We were about to get surprised by another big event.

CHAPTER THIRTY

I CONTINUED TO FLY TO SEE ELI regularly and continued to pay my Child Support. In October of 2018, I had Eli for a visit. We stayed at my brother's house, as usual. When I attempted to return him to his mother, I had the shock of a lifetime.

Eli had asked me if he could be dropped off a bit early because he wanted to go to his friend's birthday party. I told him I would need to ask his mother. I called Nicky and told her the situation. As I was speaking with her, it seemed that something was abnormal. She started to cry.

I asked what was wrong. She said, that a man was going to propose to her in the rain, at a lake. I asked who, and she said, that it was a guy she had been on a couple of dates with.

I asked her if she was ok. She pulled it together a bit. She apologized and said, that she was just emotional. I thought this was strange, but continued with my original question. She said that I could bring Eli back for 1:00 pm.

I was still a bit apprehensive so when we got close, I asked Eli to call his mom on my phone and tell her we were close. He put her on speaker phone so I could hear.

Nicky asked, "What do you want Eli?" He said, "We are getting close to the house so we just wanted to let you know." She said, "Where are you going? Tell me the address right now! Tell me the address!"

Eli said, "Our house, Mom! It's our house!" Nicky said, "Yeah well, there is a problem. I ain't there and I ain't gonna be there!" Eli asked "Why not?" She said, "Cause I'm in a field." Eli asked "Why are you in a field?" She said, "Because I'm looking for a kid!" Eli asked, "What kid are you looking for mom?" Nicky replied, "Jay! Kay! Thirty-six! Fifty-seven! Bee! Tee!"

I knew we were in trouble. Eli started to cry. I asked him to give me the phone. I spoke to Nicky and said, "What is going on with you?" Nicky said, "Ok, ok you need to help me. Hold on. Swipe right! Swipe right! No! Go that way! I see him!"

I asked Nicky where she was. She told me she had no idea. She said, that she was lost in a field and had no idea how to get out. I told her that I had to go but I would call her back.

I stopped at a gas station and asked Eli to wait in the car for me. I didn't want him to hear me talking on the phone. I called my brother and asked him if I would be overreacting if I called the police. Carl strongly suggested that I call the police.

I followed my brother's advice and called the non-emergency line. I told them my situation. The dispatcher asked me what Nicky's phone number was. I told him and he said, he would be in touch.

I got back in the car. Nicky started calling on Eli's phone. Eli was crying a lot and tried to ask his mom what had happened, and why she was acting so strange. She was talking gibberish. Eli said, "It's ok, Mom, Dad is sending the police to find you, it's ok, they will help you!"

Nicky said, "Yeah send the fucking police! I haven't done anything wrong other than making a few bad choices." Eli said, "Ok Mom, it's ok. I really have to let you go now. I love you so much!" When he got off the phone, Eli started to cry a lot.

He said, "She's probably been kidnapped and they drugged her and the police are going to find her dead corpse in a field."

I assured him that this would not happen and tried to comfort him as much as I could.

I was heartbroken for my son and furious at his mother at the same time. I wasn't sure what was going on, but I knew it could not be good. I waited for the call from the police and at the same time I tried to comfort my son.

About an hour later the police called me back. They said they had located Nicky from her cell phone location. She had indeed driven into a field and was lost there. The officer told me she had been arrested for her own safety and the safety of the public and that she would be hospitalized soon. He couldn't tell me anything else due to confidentiality.

I told Eli that we were going back to his uncle's house. I called my brother and explained that I needed to come back and stay there and that I would explain when I arrived.

I got to my brother's and filled him in. He already knew a bit about it since I had called him earlier. Carl was as shocked as I was. Like me, Carl was definitely not a fan of Nicky, but I don't think either of us expected this.

My next call was to Margaret. I waited because I didn't want to speak in front of Eli. I told her that I didn't know what was going on, but explained that I would not be on my flight that evening. Margaret was as shocked as I was, probably more.

I waited the rest of that evening to hear from Nicky. I did not hear from her. When I called her phone, it went straight to voicemail. I had to call my work and explain the situation and let them know that I actually had no idea when I would be able to return. They were extremely understanding and supportive.

Two days passed before I heard from Nicky. When she finally did call, she said, "Hey! Sup?" "What's up?" I said. "Really? What's up with you? I've missed my flight home and I have our son and we have no idea what is going on with you!" She said, "I've been through a lot! I really don't need your shit right now!"

I asked Nicky the main question that was on my mind. I asked "Did you relapse?" She started to cry a bit, and she said, "Yeah I did." I said, "Ok. Well I'm an addict and I know drugs. I don't think you were smoking weed or drinking. I'm pretty sure it was something that causes psychosis, right?"

Nicky admitted to me that she had been using methamphetamines on and off for a while. I actually felt extremely stupid. I asked myself how

I missed this. It is true that I was not in contact with her daily or even weekly. Also, she could choose when to take my calls and when not to. She did a great job of hiding it.

I told Nicky that I wouldn't be able to bring Eli back. I explained that even though the court order said he lived with her, and I had visitation rights, I absolutely would not return him to her at this time.

Much to my surprise, Nicky agreed. She said, "I broke that kid, Allan! You take him and you fix him ok?" "Ok," I said. Next I would need to get some of Eli's belongings and I also wanted to go to the courthouse and submit a request to obtain custody of Eli. I had a lot to do and I needed to hustle.

I spoke with my brother's wife, Elizabeth. I asked if she would mind watching Eli for the day while I went out and took care of things, as I did not feel comfortable bringing him. Elizabeth was so helpful that day. She told me to take as long as I needed.

I knew that I could not serve Nicky papers to change an order myself. I needed a third person to do that, as per the legal requirements. I called my Auntie Sadie and she agreed to help. It was pretty stressful because the courthouse would close soon, and I had to fill out a ton of paperwork, then find somewhere to make four copies, and then return to the courthouse and have all four copies stamped.

I got to Nicky's house with Auntie Sadie and I started by getting a suitcase full of Eli's clothes. At the end, before I left, I explained to Nicky that we had some paperwork for her to sign. I asked Auntie Sadie if she would kindly serve the papers. Nicky quickly read and signed them.

The courthouse had now closed. I had to stay another day so that I could return and submit the signed copies to show that Nicky had been served. I had booked a new flight for Eli and I in the evening, and planned to catch the flight in the evening after finishing at the courthouse.

Nicky asked if I could just meet with her once, before I got on my flight back. She wanted a chance to give Eli a hug and say goodbye. I let sympathy get the better of me and agreed to meet with her.

Eli wanted his game consoles and games. Nicky agreed to meet us at Starbucks and said, she would bring Eli's belongings. When I got to Starbucks, I got a bad feeling. I called the non-emergency police number and explained the situation. They said, they could attend but it would be a while. Just then, Nicky pulled up outside.

I told the police she was there. They told me to keep the phone open so they could hear. Nicky asked me to sit with her at the table outside. As I sat with her, she started to try to explain to me what happened.

She told me that she used to "run dope" for some very big players in Chilliwack. Recently, she had been reacquainted with some of them and had gotten involved with them. Now she said, she was just in too deep. She had been using and selling drugs for a major gang.

As I sat there, Nicky got edgy. Suddenly, she grabbed Eli and yelled to him, "Run!" Nicky and Eli started to run across the parking lot. She opened her passenger door and started to shove Eli into the car.

I grabbed my phone and I told the police on the other end what was happening. The officer said, "Get in the driver's seat of her car so she can't drive away." I got into the driver's seat as instructed.

Nicky pulled Eli out of the car and ran with him. I chased her and told her I had the police on the phone. She stopped, turned around, and punched me in the side of my head, knocking my phone to the ground.

I picked up my phone and just then, a police car pulled up. I was holding my phone and my other phone started ringing. I had one phone that was given to me from my work, a company phone, and I also had my personal phone.

Nicky yelled at the cops, "He has two cell phones! Drug dealer, drug dealer! Check his phones!" The police separated Nicky and I. I explained to the officer that I had a plane to catch and I had to take my son to Edmonton. He said, "Well she has custody, you're not taking him anywhere."

I was so mad! I said, "She's on drugs! You guys arrested her two days ago!" He said, "Well she's not on drugs right now and she has custody of that kid." He eventually agreed to call Child Protective Services. We arranged an emergency meeting that would take place within the hour.

We met with a social worker. The social worker said that I should take Eli with me to Edmonton. We agreed that I would return him for another meeting in three weeks, on or before October 30th.

One thing that angered me more than anything was what the social worker told me about the process. He said to me that when I returned in a few weeks Eli would most likely go back to his mom.

I could not believe he would say this, and I wanted to know how on earth they could decide such a thing. I said, "So you're ok with my son living with his mom if she's been clean for only three weeks?"

He said, "It's not realistic for us to ask an addict not to use drugs. Addicts use drugs and its unlikely that they will stop. Nicky said, "Allan is an addict!" I replied with "I've been clean for sixteen years!"

The social worker said, "Well you are both addicts, so what is the difference if Eli is with you or with his mom?" I said, "Excuse me, but the difference is sixteen years versus one day clean! That's significant don't you think?" He said, "We will ask Nicky to have a safety plan, in writing, and if we see she has that, then we will suggest that Eli goes back with her."

I was furious. I asked, "What does a safety plan look like?" He said, "We would ask that she have a babysitter that she can call on when she feels the urge to use meth. We would ask her to commit to not using while in the company of your son."

Of course, I had something to say about this. I said, "We *could* do that… OR, get this… this is going to sound crazy to you…. we could put my son with my wife and myself, two people who are DEFINITELY NOT ON METH!"

The social worker said that we could discuss all of this when I returned with Eli. He mentioned that their role is not to determine custody, but rather to ensure the safety of the child. He added that custody would need to be determined through a court of law, and we would attend court once a date was set to review my request to change the order.

Child Protective Services set up a meeting at my home. They wanted to check and see if our home was suitable for a child. After meeting with Child Protective Services in Edmonton, the decision was made to keep Eli in our home until we got a court date. They suggested this and were supportive of this decision.

I got to work looking for a lawyer. Once again, Nicky went and got a free lawyer because she was low income. The next year was full of court dates that got adjourned, and more court dates. The whole time, Nicky was driving us absolutely mental.

It was a very long year. Nicky was actually fine with the situation until I told her that I was not paying Child Support unless a court ruled that Eli would go back to her. When she found out that I wasn't going to pay she absolutely lost it! She believed, with all her heart, that I should continue paying $1,000/month child support, even though Eli wasn't living with her. When I asked her how she could possibly think this was logical, her response was, "I got bills ya dumb fuck!"

Nicky was still using and drinking. There were many nights when she would call and tell Eli that I had kidnapped him and that I was going to be in "big trouble." Nicky threatened to kill me on several occasions and also told Margaret that she better "watch her back." Later she told me I would regret going for custody because she was going to blow her brains all over her room and that the suicide note would have my name all through it.

Nicky said and did a lot of hurtful things throughout that year, but there was one thing she said, that has always stuck with me. In the middle of one of her screaming fits, she said, "Eli has always lived with me! You are a kidnapper." She went on to say, "Eli is not a pawn in this game and he is NOT a replacement for your fucking dead baby!"

I'm still working on total and complete forgiveness, for my own well-being, however that comment has made it difficult. I just keep reminding myself that the most hurtful comments Nicky has said to me have been fuelled by mental health issues, and the use of narcotics and alcohol. I remind myself that she was not in a good state of mind at the time. This seems to help me a lot.

Nicky's lawyer was free and because she was extremely angry with me for "kidnapping" Eli, she did everything she could to make me spend more money on my lawyer. She said, "You may not be paying me Child Support, but you will pay in the form of legal fees because I will bring everything possible back to court and drag this shit out as long as possible." I asked why and she screamed, "BECAUSE I'M FUCKING MAD!!!"

I had some huge challenges to face if I was to go through with this custody battle. One of the biggest obstacles was that Eli had always lived with his mom. My lawyer said, this was difficult because the courts prefer to follow the status quo.

I didn't really know what this meant. My lawyer explained that to follow the status quo, means to keep things as they've always been. Regarding custody, this meant the courts prefer to keep things as they've always been, regarding the home the child has known.

There was some good news, though. Eli was living with me now, and the courts continued to delay our hearing dates, which meant that Eli ended up living with Margaret and I for over a year. My lawyer said this meant we had created a new status quo. We had changed what Eli knew as normal. The new status quo was that Eli resided with myself and Margaret.

After a year of court dates, and $10,000 later, we were awarded custody of Eli. It was agreed that I would pay for two visits per year. We would be responsible to pay for Nicky's round trip flight to Edmonton, and her hotel and transportation while she was staying. It was also agreed that Nicky would pay $57/month in Child Support.

Not long after this major event, we were successful in our attempt to have another baby. It was really difficult for me to attempt this again. I was terrified of a risky pregnancy again. I wasn't sure if I could handle nine months of fearing the worst. Having said that, both Margaret and I really wanted another baby to complete our family.

We got pregnant, and in March of 2020, Margaret gave birth to our beautiful baby girl. We named her Zoe, which is the Greek word for life. This was Margaret's idea, and I loved the name immediately. It seemed fitting.

Of all my children, I think Zoe resembles me the most. She is now nearly two years old and she has brought us much joy. Having Zoe and my other children has been such a blessing in my life.

I could try to explain the extent of my love for them all, but unless you are a parent, you will not understand. The love between a parent and a child is indescribable. I literally love them more than words can say.

I am extremely grateful for the life I have today. Getting to where I am today has not been easy. Perhaps getting to where I'm going won't be easy either. One thing I know for sure is that no matter what challenges I face, they are always easier to face clean and sober.

All the promises people told me about recovery came true. They said it would be hard. That was an understatement, for sure. They said it would be worth it. That is definitely true. They said my worst day sober would be better than my best day drunk. You may be thinking that one is not true, but it is.

The thing is, we never know what life will bring us. Bad things happen sometimes. Sometimes, unimaginable things happen. The worst day of my life, the loss of my daughter Isabella, happened when I was 16 years clean and sober. I can tell you this, I'm sure happy I was clean and sober when this happened.

Living a life of sobriety has allowed me something that is priceless. I am able to have experiences, both good and bad, and today I have the ability to properly process what is happening and react accordingly. Living a life of sobriety allows me to be present, and that is truly a gift.

So that promise has come true. Saying that my worst day sober will be better than my best day drunk doesn't mean bad things won't happen. It means the outcome will be better, due to my reactions. It means that drinking makes my problems a hundred times worse. It means I have the ability to cope with whatever life throws my way, and as a result ALL of my days are better.

I am by no means perfect. I have many faults. Sometimes I get frustrated and irritable with my family during times when they need patience and understanding. I get carried away with earning money rather than taking a little extra time to be with the ones I love. I am passive-aggressive and overreact to little things. I take criticism too personally. I drink way too much coffee, and I enjoy carbs far too much. But I get up every single day and try to do a little better than the day before.

I still live my life by the same principles I told Sara all those years ago. I try to do what's right. I try to be a good person, and I still believe today that if I do that, everything will work out.

My life today is an example of this. I was bankrupt. I had to pay over one-third of my income to Nicky. Several people suggested that I quit my job, and work under the table somewhere, because then I would have no reportable income and I wouldn't be giving Nicky $1,100 each month. I thought about it, but I knew that was not the right thing to do.

So often, the thing that's right is also the thing that's most difficult. I hated sending Nicky all that money when I couldn't even afford to put gas in my car. I still did it, though. I never missed a payment, no matter how hard things were.

I was told that once you foreclose on a house, you will never be approved for a mortgage again. Two years ago, Margaret and I were approved for a mortgage and bought a house in Edmonton. I also purchased a van for which I am the sole owner, no co-signers, it was financed to me.

These things would not have happened if I had quit my job years ago. In fact, I never would have met Margaret, either. Today, I am married to my best friend, (Margaret, not Mike). We own our own home, we each own our cars, we have two beautiful daughters, we have custody of my son, and on top of a dresser in my son's room… Mr. Bear.

A very well-loved Mr. Bear

I definitely have some thoughts about how to overcome addiction. My journey of recovery hasn't been easy. This is not a book about 12 Step programs, but I do strongly believe the solution to the problem of addiction lies within the steps.

There are a few fundamental principles I got from doing the steps that I believe got me to where I am. First, to fix a problem, we need to admit there is one. Once we get past denying that a problem exists, we can begin to fix it. We also need to remember that we are never able to drink or use socially. For us, one is too many and a thousand is never enough.

I think the next most important thing I learned from doing the steps was to let go of resentment, and this happens when we are honest enough with ourselves to admit our part in our confrontations with others. This doesn't mean we will never be angry. That's impossible, because we are human beings. It just means that we will be honest with ourselves about our shortcomings and be willing to change.

Also, it is important that we make amends to people we have harmed and try not to do it again. I got so tired of making amends that I began to recognize when I was doing something that I would later need to make amends for. Eventually, I got to a place where I recognized negative *intentions*, before I acted on them. When you can do this, you can change the way you act from day to day.

If we can change our negative behaviour, treat others with kindness and respect most days, recognize where we have fallen short, and wake up each and every day with an honest and sincere effort to do a little better than the day before, I believe that our progress in life and our success has no limit.

Furthermore, the part of the fourth step where we admit our own part is really about eliminating excuses. We need to stop blaming others for our problems and start to take accountability for our own life. I really believe that people who are not able to do this one thing are destined to fail.

Once we have succeeded in all of the above, and only when we are in a good place spiritually and emotionally, we should take what we have learned and attempt to help others. I believe that by trying to carry our message to those still suffering the grip of addiction, we will avoid complacency.

We should never look at people with addiction issues in a negative light, for this would mean that we have forgotten where we came from, and that, I believe is extremely dangerous for us. The twelfth step is as important as the preceding eleven.

This book is in fact, one of the ways that I am practicing Step twelve. If my story helps even one addict find a path to a clean and sober life, I will consider it a success. Why take the time and effort to do this? Because somebody did it for me.

There are so many factors in life that we have no control over. We don't get to choose our parents, our environment, whether we are loved or neglected, born into wealth or poverty. These things are chosen for us.

We do have choices, though, and it is our responsibility to choose well. Our children don't have any more of a say in their life than we did in ours. Do you want to know what's really powerful though? We do have choices.

We get to choose how we raise those kids. We need to ask ourselves if we want to raise them the way we were raised, or if we want to do a little better, and give them the gift of a good start in life. They are counting on us to make good choices.

This is true for everyone, not just those who had a rough upbringing. Every parent can learn from their own parents' mistakes and do a little better. We don't need to have had a bad life in order to want more for our own kids. We should all strive towards doing better, regardless of where we are starting from.

If we do not have the willingness to do these things, then we have chosen to pass along our shortcomings to our next generation. If this happens, chances are when those kids are adults, they will continue this cycle. This is why you see the same issues from generation to generation.

Most will follow the status quo, and most of their children will do the same, creating an endless cycle of dysfunction. If we want the future to look bright, we must break the cycle. We need to change the status quo to something new.

Keep in mind, this is not just about substance abuse. There are endless negative cycles that need changing, from addiction issues, to abuse, to low self-esteem, to anger issues, and so on. Our examples, both good and bad, will be passed along to our kids. If we do not have children, we should make these changes for ourselves and for those around us. Our actions affect everyone we come into contact with.

Imagine if we could reverse generations and generations of negativity. If our negative examples have the power to ruin our children's lives, imagine the power of positive examples. I personally come from a biological family that has been plagued by generations of substance abuse, depression, and poverty. So imagine, for example, that my kids are raised in a clean and sober home, with parents who love and respect each other, and do their best to contribute to society while earning a decent living, as opposed to a family ruled by addiction, neglect, poverty, and abuse. How much different will those children be when they become adults?

My children have never seen me drunk or high. I hope that my example leads my children to make good choices in life. I hope that they go on to be great examples to their own children and do a little better for my grandchildren than I did for them. I am breaking the cycle in hopes that future generations will have a better life.

I truly hope that this book has been inspirational. My goal in sharing my story is to help others who are struggling in life, and it is primarily targeted to those who struggle with addiction issues. I am forever grateful to those who helped me and for everyone in my life who did not give up on me.

Today I realize that to drink or use because of something that happens in my life is nothing more than an excuse. There is no good reason for me to relapse. I have not had a drink or a drug since September 2nd, 2002, and this is the longest I have ever been sober.

CPSIA information can be obtained
at www.ICGtesting.com
Printed in the USA
BVHW022326300622
641074BV00004B/11